THE SPORTSMAN'S WORLD OF
GOLF

Arnold Palmer, elected in 1970 as American athlete of the decade was the first to personify the modern professional golf hero-aggressive and spectacularly stylish in his play.

THE SPORTSMAN'S WORLD OF
GOLF

Marshall Cavendish London & New York

Edited by Martin Tyler

Published by Marshall Cavendish
Publications Limited,
58 Old Compton Street
London W1V 5PA

© Marshall Cavendish Limited,
1969, 1970, 1971, 1976

Some of this material has previously
appeared in the partwork *The Game*

First printing 1976

ISBN 0 85685 119 1

Printed by Henri Proost,
Turnhout, Belgium

Right **Jack Nicklaus,
nicknamed 'The Golden Bear'
has achieved 'super star' status
throughout the world, and is
the natural heir to Arnold
Palmer's throne.**

Overleaf **Photographer Harold
Edgerton used multiple flash to
describe the powerful swing of
golfer Dennis Shute.**

Introduction

If you have ever queued patiently in the early hours waiting to set foot on the first tee, you will know just how popular golf has become. Millions of devotees slavishly seek out a round each weekend; businessmen have taken to clinching deals on the fairways; and package holiday operators have made enormous profits from transporting enthusiasts to play on the finest courses in the world. Though the game may not be amongst the best spectator sports, it is relayed to vast audiences world-wide through television, and a few individuals in the game make the kind of living previously reserved only for tycoons and film stars.

World of Golf takes a deep, analytical look at this unique and compelling game — a game based on such a simple principle, but which is bound by the most complicated set of rules; a game which offers complete satisfaction at one minute, and total frustration the next. It delves into the history of golf, and traces its development from primitive sources to the sophisticated, money-spinning industry of today. It tells the drama of all the major events on the golf calendar in Britain, Europe, the Far East, and of course, on the lucrative United States circuit.

Each action-packed story is backed up with a mass of comprehensive statistical information, which will help solve any questions of detail. Written by a team of experts, and superbly illustrated throughout with lots of vivid colour photographs, *World of Golf* also takes a close look at the men whose exploits have so popularized the game. Read about legendary golfing giants like Harry Vardon and Bobby Jones, and more contemporary heroes such as Jack Nicklaus, Gary Player and Lee Trevino—the inspirations behind every aspiring golfer as he waits at the tee.

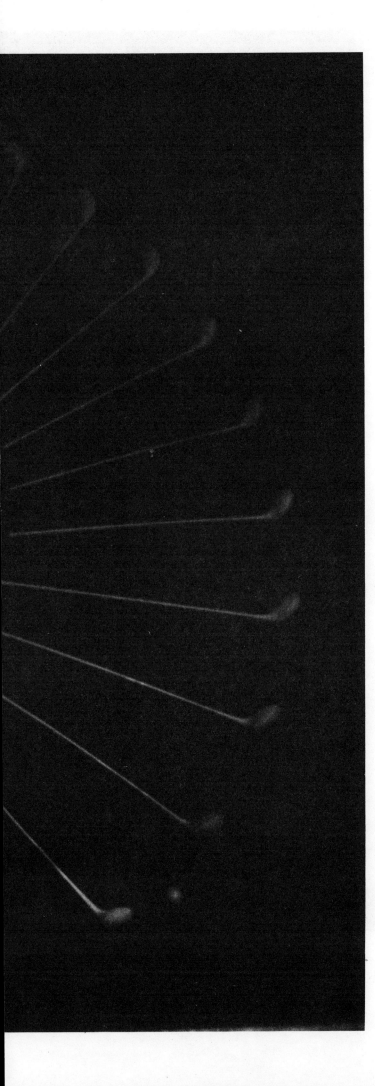

Contents

8

The Game

Politicians and statesmen play golf; comedians, golfing addicts themselves, make jokes about it; millions enjoy just watching it, and because they do, a small group of professionals make millions of dollars from it. It has been called many things, both by exasperated devotees and by their wives, yet the definition that is the first rule of the game makes it seem almost dull in comparison with some other games: 'The game of golf consists in playing a ball from the teeing ground into the hole by successive strokes in accordance with the rules'. It hardly does justice to a sport that is royal, ancient, and modern. One that goes back 600 years in British history, has, since its earliest days, appealed as much to dustmen as to dukes, and has spread throughout the world.

This sport, which satisfies what must, somewhat incredibly, be one of man's basic urges—to knock a ball in a particular direction with a stick—has developed until it has become the most commercialized outdoor activity in the world. In 1970, prize money on the American professional circuit—the world's biggest—had climbed to $6 million; the production of equipment and accessories had reached the proportions of a major industry. And even though the rules limit the number of clubs a player may carry on a round to 14, the manufacturers still produce an infinite variety of clubs within that range.

Television too plays an important part in the golfing industry. For while there is a limit to the number of spectators that can find a place on a championship course, millions can watch the great championships live on television. This mass exposure has greatly raised the prestige of the sport's leading personalities. And at the same time, golf has spread outwards and become far more international in character. Both in the professional and in the amateur game, international competitions have sprung up to supplement the old traditional contests between nations, such as the Walker and the Ryder Cup matches.

Yet the true heart of golf does not lie in these much publicized advances in the game. That heart beats as surely in the humble courses lying in the shadow of slag-heaps in the North of England or in rough areas hewn out of jungle as it does in the luxurious country-club atmosphere or on the great championship links of the world. The essence of the game can easily be found in playing a few holes on a solitary course in the quiet of evening. The holes

may even be played alone, for it is a main feature of the game—and one that is true of hardly any other sport—that it is not necessarily dependent on the performance or interplay of an opponent for its enjoyment. It is possible for any player to match his skill against either a known standard of play for the course or his own previous performances. On a smaller, but no less genuine scale, the humble player can experience all the emotions of the game—the pleasure of a well-hit stroke; the frustration of missing a short putt; the humility after a poor stroke; and the tension as a crisis approaches. They are common feelings for the game that provide a bond that overcomes every national frontier and unites the giants with the rabbits all over the world.

Many attempts have been made to establish the origins of golf, and one scholar has seen a link between it and a game called *paganica* that was introduced into Britain by Roman legionaries. A later development of this was *cambuca*, which was played in the 14th century with a bent stick and a wooden ball. The word golf itself suggests that the sport was introduced to Britain from Holland or the Low Countries, and it probably derives from the German *kolbe* meaning club, the Dutch form of which is *kolf*. Early Dutch prints show players engaged in some sport with curved sticks and a round ball directed towards a hole.

The first official evidence that golf was played in Britain, however, comes from Scotland where, in 1457, a statute prohibited the exercise of golf on the grounds that it was interfering with the practice of archery. In 1471, the Scottish Parliament decreed against football and golf, and twenty years later it was ordained 'that in na place of the realme there be usit futteballis, golfe, or other sik unprofitabele sportis for the common gude of the realme...' For such steps to be taken, the game must therefore have had a firm foothold in Scotland as early as the beginning of the 15th century.

And by the end of the century, ministers of religion were no more successful in keeping their parishioners away from the public links on Sunday than their 20th-century successors. The records of Edinburgh Town Council show many instances of the conflict between conscience and love of the game. In 1604, for example, Robert Robertson and others were convicted 'of profaning the Lord's Sabbath, by absenting themselves from hearing of the Word, and playing at the Gowf on the North

Fred Kaplan/Black Star

Through his personality and temperament, Arnold Palmer did more than any golfer to popularize the game in the 1960s.

Inch, Perth, *in time of preaching*'. Robertson, the ringleader, was fined and with others ordered 'to compear the next Sabbath into the place of public repentance, in presence of the whole congregation'. It was tough in those days to be a good Presbyterian and a keen week-end golfer.

By this time though, golf, historically speaking, was becoming reasonably established. James IV and James V of Scotland both played in East Lothian, and Mary Queen of Scots is reported to have played at St Andrews shortly after the murder of Darnley. Her son, James I of England, took the game south and it was played for a time at Blackheath. Charles I and Charles II were both partial to it, and an old print shows Charles I receiving news of the Irish rebellion while he was playing golf at Leith, with the messenger on his knees on the fairway and his horse cropping grass in the rough.

Origins of the game

For centuries after the game was first played in Scotland, it remained a classless, unorganized sport with no code of rules and no clubhouses. In England though, it quite failed to capture the imagination, Royal Blackheath remaining an outpost of the game, an appendage of the Royal court. On the one hand the game was kept alive by the nobility with their private courses. But on the other, the humblest club-maker's apprentice could go freely to the links at St Andrews or Leith without paying a green fee. And in such circumstances, it is not surprising that few names have come down to us as giants of the game. One exception, however, is William St Clair of Roselin, who was brought to life by the pen of Sir Walter Scott. A man of formidable appearance 'built for the business of war or the chase', he serves as a link with the next stage of the game, for he was one of the early captains of the first known golf club to be formed—that of the Honourable Company of Edinburgh Golfers in 1744. At this time, the Honourable Company was operating over five holes at Leith, and it later moved to Musselburgh before becoming established at Muirfield. Before that date, as Mr Robert Browning, one of the game's most distinguished historians, said: 'courses were purely natural; the only green-keepers were the rabbits'.

The formation of this and other clubs arose from the decision to offer a prize for annual competition, and as such a competition required organizing, the group developed into a club. And from this club came the first code of rules, 13 in number and wonderfully simple by modern standards.

In the early 19th century, there was a steady growth in the number of clubs, and then, slowly at first, the idea took up in England, where

Scotland's Prestwick club, original hosts of the Open championship, contributed greatly to the spread of the game.

But there were other changes and developments taking place in the game, and one of them featured the composition of the ball. It has been suggested that the earliest golf balls were made of solid boxwood, but the ball that was in use for several centuries after the game arrived in Scotland was made of leather and stuffed with feathers. Then about the middle of the 19th century, an employee in a company manufacturing cables insulated with gutta-percha applied this substance to a new golf ball and tried it out at Royal Blackheath. It had both its advantages and disadvantages. For one thing, until some form of marking of the surface of the ball was introduced —the equivalent to the modern dimpling—the ball flew badly and it made the game hard work. In addition, its unyielding solidity frequently imparted an unpleasant jar to the arm if the shot were mishit. But the ball was cheaper and indestructible, and as clubs could be adapted to its use, with an increasing emphasis on iron clubs, it was accepted. Public competitions at this time took the form mainly of challenge matches, often over 72 or even 144 holes, between the giants of the day for a modest prize. The undisputed champion was Allan Robertson, victor of many such matches. And it was after his death that the Prestwick club, perhaps intending to find his successor, decided in 1860 to hold an open championship—the first of its kind in the world. The trophy was a challenge belt in red morocco, to become the property of anyone winning it three times, and it was won in 1860 by Willie Park who headed the other seven competitors with a score of 174 for 36 holes.

A new era

Although it was some years before the entry increased noticeably—it did not reach three figures until 1901—a new era had begun. Golf, for the first time, was to have a show window as its best players came to be known more widely, and golf, in a literal sense, was on the move. In its early years, the championship was highlighted by the rivalry between the first winner and old Tom Morris of St Andrews. And then towards the end of the 1860s there arose a greater player than either of them, the latter's son, Young Tom Morris. A golfer of genius, he won the belt outright, won it a fourth time in 1872, and died at the age of 24, inconsolable after the death of his young wife in childbirth.

Golf now entered a period of stability in preparation for the great explosion of events about the turn of the century. In the 1880s and 1890s, English golf began to make up for the slow start that had

left it far behind Scotland. The year 1894 saw the first victory in an Open championship of that great figure from Westward Ho!, John Henry Taylor, who with Harry Vardon and James Braid made up the 'Great Triumvirate' that dominated British golf for the next 20 years. That year, the prize money totalled £100, with £30 to the winner. In 1946 the total had risen to £1,000, and 25 years later it had gone up to £40,000, most of that increase occurring in the last decade.

In 1902, a new ball—the Haskell, made of rubber strips wound round a rubber core—was introduced from America. Its qualities were hotly debated before the Open championship, with most of the big names, including the Triumvirate, opposed to it. But Sandy Herd was converted to its use after a round with the famous amateur John Ball, and when he won his only Open with it, the old 'guttie' ball was dead.

About this time also, the game was spreading to the United States. Traces of its being played there can be found as far back as the 18th century—in the *Georgia Gazette* of 1796 mention is made of the Savannah Golf Club. But the first sustained wave of enthusiasm begins only in the 1880s and is once again attributable to Scottish influence. In 1887, a Mr Lockhart returned to New York from his native Dunfermline with a supply of clubs and balls and was, in the same year, arrested for hitting a golf ball about on the sheep pasture in Central Park.

But other Scots rallied to the cause and helped to form the first recognized club, the St Andrews golf club of Yonkers, outside New York. Another early club was Shinnecock Hills formed in 1891. The game received a boost from the immigration around the turn of the century of experienced players and craftsmen from Carnoustie and other Scottish cities. And then in 1900 the great Vardon went over and won the American Open. Three years later, the Oxford and Cambridge Golfing Society sent over the first international team to compete in the United States, beginning a rivalry that has grown ever since.

During the first half of the 20th century, America exercised a growing influence on the game throughout the world. They were not always the first to spread the gospel, for in many countries this had been done by British colonials. Royal Calcutta, for example, was founded in 1829, Royal Hong Kong in 1889, and even the French club at Pau, the oldest in Europe outside Scotland, was started in 1854 thanks to Scottish officers who had stayed on after convalescing from the Peninsular War. But once the Americans had become fired with enthusiasm, it was inevitable that by sheer weight of numbers and with their vigour and financial backing they

should come to dominate the game, not only in the skill of their greatest players—Jones, Hogan, Palmer, Nicklaus—but in their attitude towards the game and in fashioning its equipment.

Britain stood out for a time against the centre-shafted putter with which Walter Travis won their Amateur championship in 1904, and were also slow to accept the steel-shafted club of American design, an innovation which, by giving increased length and by reducing the effects of a bad shot, revolutionized the game almost as much as the rubber-cored ball had done. But as the factory bench turning out graded sets of 14 matched clubs took over from the craftsmen, so the game became more and more of a science and British and world golfers were forced to follow American trends and developments.

Development of the game

Other directions in which American influence is felt today are in slowness of play, the watering of fairways and greens so that a high pitch shot can be played to the flag instead of the running shot needed for dry ground, and the predominance of stroke-play over match-play. Yet in spite of the difference between golf in America and Britain, the governing bodies of the two countries work together and as far as possible determine a common policy.

Whereas the Royal and Ancient Golf Club evolved naturally as the headquarters of the game after its foundation in 1754, other governing bodies were formed much later. Its counterpart in America, the United States Golf Association, was formed in 1894 at a meeting called between five clubs, and it now has a large headquarters in New York and 20 sub-committees to deal with the needs of about nine million golfers in their country alone. The R and A in Britain controls the rules of the game and of amateur status, as well as those championships entrusted to it; and the national unions of the four home countries, the Professional Golfer's Association, and the Ladies' Golf Union all look to it for guidance.

The spread of golf has been rapid in the old Commonwealth countries, such as South Africa, New Zealand, and Australia, and has been encouraged by such world-wide competitions as the world team championships for men and women, and by the Commonwealth tournament, first held to commemorate the bi-centenary of the Royal and Ancient club. Circuits are now established in South Africa, Australasia, and the Far East and these annually attract many of the world's finest golfers. But the size of the American prize list is still the most powerful magnet. Ambitious young men from every country know it is there that they must

1 An early 19th century print of golfer and caddie at Royal Blackheath, the club that was an outpost of the game in England until the latter part of the century. **2** Mary Queen of Scots played golf at St Andrews in 1563. **3** 'Old' Tom Morris, the grand old man of golf who won four of the first eight British Open championships when Prestwick, his club for many years, was the regular venue. His son succeeded him to the title in 1868, and won the championship three years in a row. **4** Bobby Jones, the great American amateur who between 1923 and 1930 won the British Open 3 times, the US Open 4 times, and the US Amateur championship 5 times. He later became the driving force behind the course in Augusta, Georgia, which is the home of the American Masters. **5** Bobby Locke of South Africa drives from the 16th tee at Royal Lytham in 1952 when he won his third British Open. **6** Walter Hagen, winner of a record five American PGA titles in the 1920s. **7** Ben Hogan won the Open, American Open, and Masters in 1963.

try themselves out, for it is there that the best golf is played. It is a tough school, though, and all but the strongest go to the wall.

The advent of television on a big scale—TV cameras standing on lorries were being tried out as early as 1939 at a golf tournament outside London—gave added impetus to the sponsors who were ready to pour money into golf tournaments. Through the medium of television, no figure has done more to popularize the game than Arnold Palmer. By the colour of his personality he has become a household name to thousands of people all over the world who have never and may never play golf. The game has made Palmer a millionaire, and it has given players such as Peter Thomson, Bill Casper, Gary Player, and Lee Trevino a way of life far beyond the imagination of the early professionals. Perhaps only one player has rivalled Palmer's popularity in the 1960s— Jack Nicklaus. While still in his twenties he won all the major tournaments in the world.

But the televising of championships is an expensive, complicated process, and TV companies have gone in for the staged match between two or three players, or more easily manageable spectacles such as 'par-three golf', 'two-shot golf', or 'target golf' to a series of greens at varying ranges with the flagstick as the bull's-eye and the green marked with concentric white circles with varying points values. But the normal tournament remains a stroke-play event in which every shot played over the four rounds counts. Both television and professionals prefer this kind of play, which is a surer test of ability and is certain to finish on the last green, to matchplay, the traditional form of settling amateur championships. In this, the result depends on the winning of a greater number of holes and not on the total number of strokes taken in a complete round. It is the form in which the traditional matches between Britain and the United States—the Walker Cup for amateurs, the Ryder Cup for professionals, and the Curtis Cup for women—are decided. But among professionals, it is kept alive only by one or two events, including the British matchplay championship and the Piccadilly world match-play.

It is possible that the years ahead may well see the co-ordination of the existing tournament circuits round the world so that a professional can always be seeking his fortune somewhere. It is a lucrative game, well worth the necessary effort.

But, as the rewards become bigger, there may well be a tendency for players to travel less. For the world professional, golf is a hard grind, far removed from the relaxing game that it was intended to be and that most amateurs find it.

Mary Evans

AMATEUR GOLF

For the most part, amateurs represent that section of the iceberg of golf that lies below the surface. They are as old as the game itself, and the most famous star of the professional game recognizes that in the last analysis he owes his livelihood to the great army of week-end golfers, most of them duffers compared with himself. But without the demand for the game, for goods, instruction, and courses, there would be no purpose in the professional game. For once the amateur loses his taste for the game, the demand for the spectacular side of it would cease to exist.

The first landmark in the organization of the amateur game was the action taken by the Prestwick club, who in 1857 invited a number of Scottish clubs and Blackheath from England to St Andrews to take part in a knock-out foursomes competition. The trophy, a silver claret jug, was won by the Blackheath pair. The next year, the idea of club foursomes was abandoned in favour of an individual contest, but this attempt to start an amateur championship came to nothing, and the championship proper dates from 1885 when the Royal Liverpool club issued an open invitation. The history of that club is closely intertwined with the history of amateur golf, for it was there that the English championship was inaugurated in 1926 and it was also the venue of the first international match between England and Scotland and later between Great Britain and the United States. It was also the home of some of the greatest amateurs of the times, notably John Ball, whose eight Amateur championship victories spanned a quarter of a century, his last one coming in 1912. Other distinguished members of the club were Harold Hilton, who, in addition to winning the Amateur four times, won the Open twice and the US Amateur once, and Jack Graham.

After World War I, three outstanding golfers, Roger Wethered, Cyril Tolley, and Ernest Holderness, bestrode the scene. As in the professional field though, the scene became increasingly dominated by the Americans who went over to play in the Walker Cup matches between the two countries. This was especially so after World War II, but British golfers, Joe Carr and Michael Bonallack, checked this tendency, Bonallack winning five championships from 1961 to 1970.

As the game became more international, so the number of world-wide fixtures increased. The United States and Britain had been contesting the Walker Cup since 1922. but after World War II, a number of international events emerged, among them the world team championship for the Eisenhower Trophy; the Commonwealth tournament, inaugurated in 1954 to mark the bicentenary of the founding of the Royal and Ancient club; the European team championship; and the match between Great Britain and the Continent of Europe for the St Andrews trophy. Competition for places in these teams is strong, but the time taken in justifying selection and then in taking part in these events is raising increasing difficulties for amateurs, who are drawn more and more from the ranks of those who find it difficult to take a lot of time off their work.

And the rules of amateur status are more strictly observed in golf than in many other sports. The prize an amateur may take is limited to £50 in value, and the expenses he may allow others to pay are clearly defined. The result is that more and more young amateurs are obliged to turn professional, and the incentive becomes all the greater when they see young men such as Bobby Cole and Peter Oosterhuis so quickly making a success of their careers. But if the question of amateur status may eventually raise difficulties, in other respects the amateur scene encourages every kind of young player. Amateur golf gives the appearance of being ordered without being regimented, and in many parts of the world the young player of promise is encouraged from the start.

1 Jack Nicklaus in a studious mood on the green. One of the game's longest drivers, he is also one of golf's leading money-winners and is, along with Gary Player, Gene Sarazen, and Ben Hogan, the only golfer to have won all four major titles—the British and American Opens, the Masters, and the American PGA. 2 Even the best miss them. Gary Player shows just how he feels after missing a vital putt in the 1968 British Open. 3 And some of them, like 'Arnie', wind up in the strangest places. 4 But when the putt goes down, every player from the pro, like Brian Barnes, to the weekend golfer is well entitled to jump for joy.
5 A fan finds two periscopes better than one. But many golf fans never even see their heroes live. Extensive television coverage brings all the major tournaments into their sitting room. 6 John Ball, the leading amateur golfer before World War I, won the British amateur championship eight times. 7 Peter Townsend, one of many amateurs to turn professional and seek fame in America. 8 Michael Bonallack—five times British amateur champion.

Transworld

H. W. Neale

Peter Dazely

1 Sandra Palmer (US), 2 Carol Mann (US), 3 Michelle Walker (US), 4 Kathy Whitworth (GB), 5 Donna Young (US).

H. W. Neale

H. W. Neale

Peter Dazely

Peter Dazely

WOMEN'S GOLF

Apart from the general belief that Mary Queen of Scots knocked a golf ball about in the grounds of Seton Castle shortly after Lord Darnley's death, evidence is almost non-existent about the early days of women's golf. The fishergirls of Musselburgh used to compete for prizes at golf, but otherwise little seems to have happened before 1880 beyond a little gentle putting.

But for all the awkwardness of their clothing the women were not to be denied. The St Andrews Ladies Club, the largest and probably the oldest in Britain, had 500 members on its lists in 1888, and even in the respectable seaside resort of Eastbourne the ladies' club numbered 100. In view of this, it is not so surprising to find the formation of the Ladies Golf Union and of their championship, in 1893. This event grew steadily in popularity among the higher levels of society between then and 1914, though it remains a wonder that women's clothing, which hardly moved with the times, allowed them to play at all. Miss Enid Wilson, herself three times winner of the Ladies' Championship in the 1930s, has written of this earlier era; 'The tempo of those days was leisurely, and those ladies who took their golf seriously enough to enter for competitions conducted their championships on a country-house party basis. Everyone knew everyone else and after a day in the open air, they indulged in musical evenings together.

In the 1920s, two great golfers, Miss Joyce Wethered, as she then was, and Miss Cecil Leitch, brought a new atmosphere to women's golf and set new standards of play. Women's golf naturally lacks the power of men's, for they are generally much weaker in hand and wrist, but these two brought a power that had not been seen before. Miss Wethered in particular was a supreme stylist, who won the Ladies Open Championships on four occasions and the English Ladies Championship five times.

In the early 1930s two international matches were inaugurated —the Vagliano Trophy, an annual encounter between Britain and France, which was later turned into a Continental team, and the Curtis Cup match between Britain and the United States. This followed the pattern set by the men, but in all other respects the women went their own way, devising their own handicap system and perpetuating the principle already adopted in such women's clubs as Formby and the Wirral of having their own clubhouse and course.

In the years before World War II, a young girl, Pam Barton, came to the fore and became the first woman to hold the British and American championships simultaneously. It was not until 1974 that this feat was to be emulated by the American, Carol Semple. Pam Barton was a great believer in practice, and might have had an important influence on the game had she not been killed on active service during the war.

The outstanding figure immediately after the war was the American, Babe Zaharias. A world-class athlete, she could hit the ball great distances, and in her free swing and uninhibited manner the emancipation of women's golf was fully expressed. After winning the 1947 British Ladies' Open, she returned to the United States where she established a reputation as the first woman professional of great merit.

Women's professional golf was slow to come to life, and it was not until the late 1960s that it began to receive recognition. But as ladies' tennis before it had, women's golf caught the eye of the commercial sponsors. Aided by the determination and complete professionalism of players such as America's Kathy Whitworth, the most successful woman golfer ever in terms of winnings, and Carole Mann, the perceptive president of the PGA, a rich tour was established.

By 1970, more than one million dollars could be won in prize money on the American women's circuit. For the first time, leading young amateurs were swiftly turning professional to reap the rich pickings available, and the top women golfers were no longer to be found in the amateur ranks. Additionally, attractive young golfers like Laura Baugh of America and Australia's Jan Stephenson brought a commercial feminine image to the game.

In 1974, Colgate-Palmolive introduced the European Ladies Open, with prize money totalling £22,700. Rapturously welcomed by British television, the event won higher audience rating than the British open, held a month earlier.

1 19th-century ladies' golf was restricted to gentle putting. Leading personalities of the 20th century: **2** Pam Barton (GB) and **3** 'Babe' Zaharias (US), both champions, and **4** Laura Baugh, of the US.

Associated Press

The tension of big-time golf is paradoxically built up to a backdrop of great natural beauty on golf courses all over the world. **1** Looking down on the 16th green on the Augusta National Golf Course, Georgia, where spectators enjoy the shade from stately pines as they watch the Masters in progress. **2** The Royal Dar re Salam Golf Club: players in the Moroccan Open cross the bridge leading from the 9th green to the 10th fairway oblivious of the scenic beauty. **3** If Bob Charles were not concentrating on his iron shot to the 11th green, he might be reminded of his native New Zealand by the peaks of the Bernese Alps at Crans-Sur-Sierre during the 1974 Swiss Open, which he won. **4** The 9th green at La Manga, home of the Spanish Open, with the first nine holes stretching away to the mountains.

H. W. Neale

3

4

H. W. Neale

Heather & Pine International

Ed Lacey

5

1 Spectators on 'Maidens', a high hill on the Royal St George's course at Sandwich, Kent, have a bird's-eye view of the 7th green. 2 The spectacular 11th at Turnberry in Scotland, where players have to hit their tee shots over the crags to the green. 3 A well bunkered 11th green at Worthing Hill Barn Golf Club in Sussex illustrates the problems golfers face on courses all over the world. 4 Water hazards, such as this one at Augusta, Georgia, home of the US Masters, are a feature of American courses. 5 A guide to Royal Birkdale during the 1968 Alcan. It is the 'rough' which is the challenging feature on British courses.

COURSES

Although it was not always so, most golf courses usually consist of one circuit of 18 holes; there are, however, still a number of 9-hole courses and even some with anything from 8 to 16. Not that this is in any way odd. For when golf began, there was no set number of holes. The players gathered together at the start and played to as many holes as the land seemed to offer naturally. This varied from place to place, and it was not until much later that 18 holes became the standard the world over.

Because of the primitive equipment used in the early days, courses were quite short, but today, with more sophisticated clubs featuring steel or aluminium shafts and balls that are complicated products of the rubber industry, courses have to be around the 6,000-yard mark for the 18 holes. In fact, many are much longer, and for championships the standard is over 7,000 yards—a figure that is by no means a maximum.

One of the unique pleasures of golf is that, although a course may have been prepared for a championship and its stars, it is possible for a club member to go out immediately afterwards and tread where the great have trodden. This pleasure, however, is denied to followers of many other sports. Only in his dreams does the football fan play at Wembley or the cricketer at Lord's.

Some of the finest courses in the world are found in Great Britain, where the climate results in the growth of the finest golfing grass and nature has provided seaside linksland that is the envy of the world. The Lancashire coast and parts of Scotland boast splendid courses that have tested, and often beaten, some of the world's greatest players. Australia has also produced a number of first-class courses, but these have been modelled on American, rather than British, lines.

America, without Britain's advantages in types of grass, has done away with the sort of punitive rough that is a feature of British courses and has concentrated largely on sand and water hazards. The tee shot has to be carefully placed, not to avoid the rough, but to set up the second shot to the green. The Americans have also tried to eliminate entirely the luck of the bounce, which can play a large part in the British game, and in this they have largely succeeded.

The American pattern is being followed in those countries that are not blessed with a British climate. In the hotter parts of Europe, such as Spain and Portugal, and in Malaysia and the Far East, courses, including the fairways, are kept alive by constant watering. It is in these newer golfing countries that the newer aspects of golf course design can be seen. Many clubs have three or four nine-hole loops that start and finish by the clubhouse, and even these loops have more than one starting point to ease the pressure at weekends. The fairways are wide and the rough sparse so that time is not wasted in looking for balls. The whole emphasis is on getting people round the course without undue delay.

Golf course architecture. One of the tests of good golf architecture is that the result should give the appearance of being entirely natural, of having grown that way without the benefit of man. Of the earlier generation of architects, Willie Park (Sunningdale Old) was an outstanding artist and Sunningdale also provides an example in the New Course of the work of another master, H. S. Colt. In the United States many fine courses were built by expatriate Scots, notably Donald Ross (Pinehurst) and Dr Alister Mackenzie (Augusta National, in collaboration with Bobby Jones).

One exception to the generalization that great architects are notable for the unobtrusiveness of their work is the American Robert Trent Jones, one of the busiest and most successful practitioners. He stamps his signature unmistakably on his work, with raised and extravagantly sculptured greens, eccentrically shaped bunkers, and the liberal use of artificial water hazards.

He sculpts the landscape, making full use of earth-moving machinery to build mountains if he feels them to be necessary. At Baltusrol, New Jersey, the members complained that the short fourth hole, involving a long carry over an artificial pond, was excessively difficult after he had redesigned it for the 1954 US Open. Trent Jones returned to the club, placed a ball onto the tee and struck it over the pond, onto the green, and right into the cup for a hole in one. Pausing only to remark, 'I think that answers your criticism, gentlemen', he strode from the scene.

EQUIPMENT

The basic items of golf equipment are clubs and balls. Both vary enormously in price, but most are efficient enough for the golfer who plays for pleasure. The rules of golf prohibit the introduction of gimmicks such as variably angled club faces and the croquet-style putter, so all clubs are basically variations on a well-defined theme. There are few differences in the quality of clubs of various prices that will substantially affect their playability. The main difference is in the quality of the shaft.

The rules of golf limit the number of clubs a player may carry on any round to 14, but a set sufficient for normal play will include only 8—numbers·2 and 4 woods, 3, 5, 7, and 9 irons, a wedge, and a putter. Such a set enables the golfer to play the ball in almost any predicament. The tournament professional no doubt, requires the full range, but his technique has been refined to an enormous extent.

The length of the club shaft may vary with the player's physique, and also with the club used. The longest shaft is found on the No. 1 wood, and the length decreases progressively through the low irons (2, 3, and 4), the medium irons (5, 6, and 7), the short irons (8 and 9), the wedge, and the putter. The degree of loft of the club face also varies progressively from about 11° on the driver to 59° on the sand wedge. The weight of the club, like the length of the shaft, is a matter for individual preference. The 'feel' of a club is more important than its weight, although most men use heavier clubs than women do.

Two types of golf ball are in general use. The traditional British ball with a minimum diameter of 1.62 inches and maximum weight of 1.52 ounces, and the bigger American ball (minimum diameter of 1.68 inches) coexist uneasily in the golf world. It is generally considered that the American ball induces a higher standard of play, although many British professionals have had difficulty in adapting to its behaviour in flight. For the everyday golfer, however, there will be little substantial diference, as the aerodynamic idiosyncrasies of the ball are more likely to originate in the way the ball is hit than in its actual construction. Modern golf balls are hard and elastic, and this quality is a result of their composition: the core is a small sac filled with liquid silicone or a similar substance, and this is surrounded with tightly wound rubber threads, and the whole is covered with a thin rubber or plastic case. Balls are normally white, though the game's fanatics use dark balls when they are playing in snow!

A third practical item of equipment is the tee, a small plastic or wooden support on which the ball is placed prior to playing it from the teeing ground (also known as the tee). It is brightly coloured so that it can be easily recovered after the ball is played.

All these items are carried round the course in a large, waterproof bag, but as a round may take some time to play, many golfers carry the bags on a two-wheeled trolley, known as a caddie-cart. On some courses small electrically powered cars are available for the less energetic player.

Almost every player wears spiked shoes to give him better purchase during the swing and the right-hander will wear a glove on his left hand to give him a better grip. The weight of the bag is increased by markers, which indicate the position of the ball on the green when it is lifted for cleaning, and by a miscellaneous assortment of towels, rags, rule books, and bad weather equipment.

TECHNIQUES

The techniques of golf are at once basic and elusively subtle. They are basic in that all one has to do is to stand still and hit a stationary ball in a chosen direction. An apparently simple task, yet as soon as you attempt it you realise how incredibly difficult it really is. There are in fact so many variables involved that some people play the game all their adult life and never even approach perfection, which, in golfing terms, can be defined as the ability to play a course in par figures. To make things easier the different clubs have been designed to fit particular situations in which a golfer may find himself, but essentially the flight of the ball in the air or its path along the ground depends directly on the manner in which it is struck.

There are three main types of shot in golf, just as there are three main types of club. There are the strokes used with the woods and long irons, the short irons and wedge, and putting. The angle of the club face and the length of its shaft determine the distance and path of the ball, but the success of any shot depends directly on the correct actions of the player himself.

The drive is the basic golf shot, and its execution can be dramatic in the case of Jack Nicklaus or traumatic in the case of the nervous weekender who fluffs it on the first tee outside the clubhouse bar. The first essential of any successful shot is the grip. There is no one correct way to grip a golf club, but certain elements apply to all golfers. The illustrations show the placings of the hands on the shaft which have, in general produced the best results for the greatest number of people.

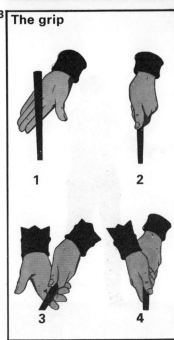

The grip

Opposite page, **Equipment proves an irresistible fascination for most golfers and they read every golf book out and endlessly debate the pros and cons of various items. One of the current controversies centres on the merits of the British ball, foreground, left, and larger American one, right. 1 The four woods and 2 some of the many putters available. Putting is a matter of touch and confidence and the search for consistency brings out some curiously shaped clubs. 3 In order to play any shot correctly, the golfer needs the correct grip. Simply, this is the one that allows him to hit the ball where he wants it to go and most golfers use the 'V' grip. The drawings show the various stages used in taking up the grip which was originated by the great Harry Vardon and is usually known as the Vardon Grip.**

The hands should be in such a position that if the fingers are opened the palms of the hands are directly opposed to each other. Basically, the 'V' formed between the forefinger and thumb of each hand should (in the case of a righthanded player) point to a spot somewhere between the chin and the right shoulder.

Two basic faults—the slice and the hook—often arise through an incorrect grip. For the right-hander, if the ball swings from left to right in the air it has been sliced. In other words it has been hit with the club face 'open'. If it is the grip that is at fault both hands should be moved to the right on the shaft, as a unit. If the ball is hooked—from right to left in the air for the right-hander—then the reverse remedy applies. If the ball flies straight—in any direction—through the air, then the grip is satisfactory. By intelligent experiment, every golfer can quickly find his own perfect grip. If the ball is flying straight but not in the intended direction then the player must look for some other fault in his technique.

The angle of the club face at the moment of impact determines the character of the ball's flight. The actual direction of flight is dependent on the direction of the swing, while the distance the ball travels depends on the speed of the club head at the moment of impact. The easiest way to achieve the 'perfect' swing path is for the golfer to stand with the feet, hips, and shoulders all parallel to the intended path of the ball. If the body is placed in this position and the club is correctly gripped and swung the ball should travel in the intended direction. In taking his stance, the golfer places the clubhead behind the ball, aiming at the target, and then adjusts his grip and feet position so that he can reach the ball comfortably. For the long-shafted woods, he will stand farthest away, and get progressively nearer the ball when playing with the higher irons. When, at last, he reaches the green and plays with the putter, he will stand with his head directly over the ball. If he stands too far from the ball, the chances are he will 'top' it, and the ball will be hit into the ground. If he stands too near, he will get underneath it and the club will probably dig deep into the earth, and the ball will fly into the air much higher than intended and land short.

The purpose of the swing is to return the clubhead to the ball at point of impact in exactly the same position that it was in at time of address. The backswing is the source of power in the golf shot. It is the coiling of the body spring, that governs the position from which the club can be swung into the back of the ball to project it straight to the target. In order to achieve a square hit into the back of the ball it is necessary to maintain the direction of the swing and the angle of the club's approach to the ball.

Above all, the backswing is one smooth movement of shoulders, arms, and club into the preparatory position. Then comes the moment of truth—the downswing. The purpose of the downswing is to release the power that has been built up in the backswing but at the same time the golfer must maintain the plane and direction of the swing. At all times during the downswing the golfer must keep his eyes on the ball, and as the spring of the body is uncoiled the rotational effect of the swing forces the body round. Thus, in the case of a right-handed golfer, the body is twisted to the right, and the whole combination of torso, arms, and legs, untwists to the left. This action will force the head to turn after the ball has been struck, and the right foot to rotate on its toes. The left foot is kept firmly on the ground. A combination of hand, body, and eye makes for a successful shot.

As the length of the shaft decreases, so less body movement is used and more wristiness comes into the stroke. The legs will also be bent more, especially on difficult lies in the rough or in bunkers. Approach shots are normally played with the higher numbered irons, so that the ball descends almost vertically onto the green and does not run beyond it. With these shorter shots better players are able to put extra 'back-spin' on the ball so that it stops almost dead on the green or even runs backwards.

More words have been written on the art and problems of putting than on any other feature of the golf game. Equally, there are probably as many theories on successful putting as there are golfers, so it is impossible to generalize. To see equally proficient golfers using quite disparate techniques on the green, and for all their practice missing the most simple of putts, is one of the everlasting mysteries of golf. Some grip the top of the putter, others grip it halfway down the shaft. Some even place one hand at the top of the club and the other near the bottom, or putt with their hands the wrong way round—that is a right-hander putting with his right hand at the top of the shaft, a sort of 'backhand'. But in putting the composition of the green plays a larger part than the course otherwise plays in the approach shots. Course architects introduce subtle slopes and runs into the green that can add many shots to the careless or luckless player's score. The well-holed long putt in excess of 25 yards is a sight more dramatic than the longest drive.

Golfers must, therefore, master a considerable number of skills if they are to reach the top. As well as the physical art of hitting the ball true, they must be able to judge distances accurately and master the quite considerable physical and mental demands of playing two full 18-hole rounds a day in tournaments.

Equipment Lillywhites/Photo Alan Duns

1 The irons from 3 to 9 and two wedges (far right). The angle of the face, or 'loft', of irons determines the length of the shot. As is illustrated in 2, the length the ball is hit decreases as the higher-numbered irons are used. Clubs with more loft are used for approach shots and the wedges are used for high, short pitches and for getting out of bunkers. The distances given in 2 are approximately those that the average golfer should reach. 3 The short chip to the green. 4 Blasting out of a bunker. The wrists are kept firm throughout the shot. 5 Bob Charles lives up to the axiom that good golfers take turf with their irons. 6 Gary Player plays a delicate chip to the green, allowing the ball to land short and run up to the hole. 7 The basic swing is applicable to most shots.

Colour Sport

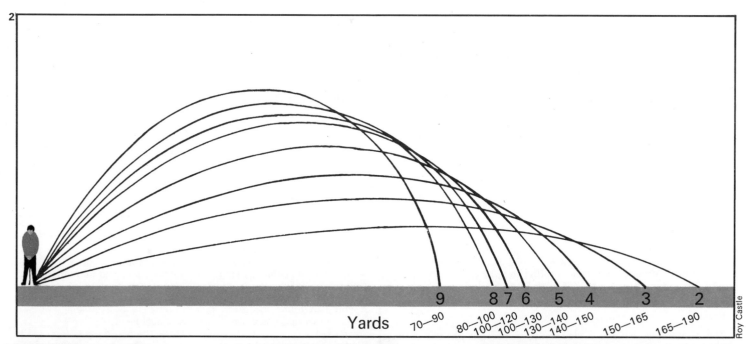

Yards   70—90   80—100   100—120   100—130   130—140   140—150   150—165   165—190

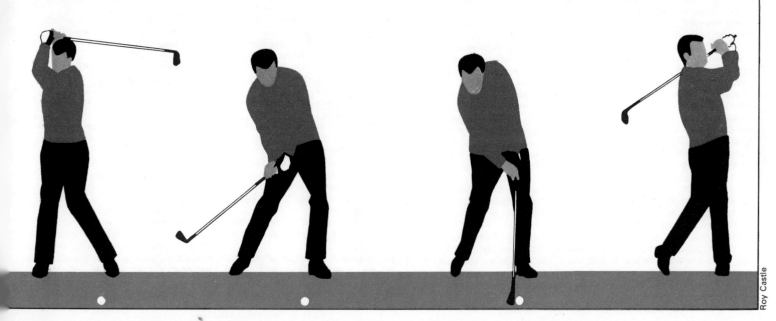

OFFICIAL SCORE CARD

SUNDAY APR 1 4 1968

Hole	1	2	3	4	5	6	7	8	9	Out	10	11	12	13	14	15	16	17	18	In	Totals
Yardage	400	555	355	220	450	190	365	530	420	3485	470	445	155	475	420	520	190	400	420	3495	6980
Par	4	5	4	3	4	3	4	5	4	36	4	4	3	5	4	5	3	4	4	36	72
Player	2	4	3	3	4	3	4	4	4	31	4	4	2	5	4	4	3	4	5	35	66

I HAVE CHECKED MY SCORE HOLE BY HOLE.

PLAYER SIGNATURE _____
ROBERTO DE VICENZO

ATTEST _____

Neil Leifer for Sports Illustrated

Roberto de Vicenzo's card for the final round of the 1968 US Masters. His marker scored a 4 instead of a 3 for the 17th and both Vicenzo and Aaron failed to spot it. The 65 would have given him a play-off with Bob Goalby.

RULES

Though it is basically one of the simplest games, golf has one of the most complicated sets of rules of any sport. And yet, ironically, every single one of them can be rendered useless by a dishonest player. Everything in golf depends on the integrity of the player, and the only real answer to the habitual, knowing cheat is not to play with him. It is impossible, although the rulemakers—the Royal and Ancient Golf Club—have tried to legislate against all the tricks.

'The Game of Golf', says Rule 1 (Section 3) 'consists of playing a ball from the teeing ground into the hole by successive strokes in accordance with the Rules'. This has to be done with clubs and balls that conform to the specification of 'not substantially different from the traditional and customary form and make'. There is a maximum of 14 clubs to a set (there is a stiff penalty for carrying more), and each of these 14 have to be 'composed of a shaft and a head, and all of the various parts shall be fixed so that the club is one unit; the club shall not be designed to be adjustable'.

There are, of course, as many ways of swinging at the ball as there are players, but the Rules are emphatic that the ball 'shall be fairly struck at with the head of the club and must not be pushed, scraped or spooned'. From the teeing ground, the ball has to be struck, in as few blows as possible, into a hole 4¼ inches in diameter and at least 4 inches deep. This would be a fairly simple operation were it not for the hazards, sometimes natural, sometimes cultivated, that are placed in the golfer's path. Most courses have a number of bunkers —sand-filled obstructions—that the average player finds difficulty in getting out of, and there is a growing tendency to use water in the same manner. There are penalties for not playing out of these obstructions in the correct manner, the penalty varying in match and stroke play. The most feared obstruction of all is *out of bounds*. The bounds of the course are defined by the club committee, and to stray from them means 'the player shall play his next stroke as nearly as possible at the spot from which the original ball was played, adding a penalty shot to his score for the hole'.

But even if a player negotiates the course successfully in a competition, he has still to avoid disqualification for failing to complete his scorecard correctly. Rule 38 (1) says: 'The competitor shall check his score for each hole, settle any doubtful points with the committee, ensure that the marker has signed the card, countersign the card himself, and return it to the committee as soon as possible.' World renowned players, such as Roberto de Vicenzo, Dai Rees, and Bernard Hunt, have all suffered at some time or other for not observing these rules. De Vicenzo failed to notice that a four had been recorded by his marker instead of a three at the 17th hole during the 1968 United States Masters, and he signed for the incorrect total. Had he noticed the mistake and corrected the total, he would have tied with Bob Goalby for the chance of a play-off. Instead he had to be content with second place.

Rees and Hunt both failed to sign their card at all and were disqualified from tournaments. And in 1969, Eric Brown, the British Ryder Cup captain, disqualified himself because he thought his caddy had cheated by 'finding' a lost ball.

To the beginner, the Rules are a web, a maze out of which he finds it impossible to escape. Many, however, are more concerned with the result and never bother to find out all the intricacies. They play to a simple self-made set of rules that enables them to get around the course in a friendly fashion and without delay. Which should, perhaps, be the object anyway.

GLOSSARY OF TERMS

Address To take up a stance and ground the club before striking.
Albatross Taking three strokes under par for the hole.
Apron Part round the green that is not mown quite as close as the green itself.
Birdie Taking one stroke under par for the hole.
Bisque Stroke conceded in form of a handicap. It may be taken at any point in a match.
Bogey Now taken to mean, especially in America, one stroke over par.
Borrow Allowance needed on a putt that is not going to run straight towards the hole, usually because of the gradient of the green.
Bunker A deliberate hazard, either an area of bare ground, or more usually a depression that is filled with sand.
Caddie One who carries or handles a player's clubs and otherwise assists him.
Carry The distance between the point of hitting of ball and its first bounce on landing.
Casual water Temporary accumulation of water.
Chip A low approach to the flag-stick made from close to the green.
Cut-up High shot played with spin.
Divot Small strip of turf taken out of ground in playing iron shots.
Dog-leg Shape of a hole turning from left to right or right to left.
Dormie Term used in match-play when a player is as many holes up as there are holes left to play.
Draw A shot, made intentionally, that, for a right-hander, bends slightly to the left.
Eagle Taking two strokes under par for the hole.
Fade A shot that when hit by a right-hander is intentionally bent slightly to the right.
Fairway The area of turf specially prepared between tee and green.
Forward press A slight movement forward of the hands before beginning the swing.
Fourball A match in which four players compete, each playing his own ball.
Foursome A match in which four players compete in pairs, each playing alternate shots with the same ball. Sometimes used to describe four players playing together.

Green The part of a golf hole specially prepared for putting.
Handicaps System of awarding bonus strokes which enable golfers of differing levels of ability to meet on equal terms.
Hole The playing area from tee to green.
Honour A player entitled to play first from the tee through having last won a hole is said to have the honour.
Hook A shot which when hit by a right-hander curves to the left, more pronounced than a draw and unintentional.
Irons Clubs, the head or striking part of which are made of metal.
Match-play The method of deciding a match by the number of holes won as distinct from the number of strokes taken in a round.
Medal-play (also **stroke-play**) A match or competition decided by the total number of strokes taken in a round and not by number of holes won.
Par The number of strokes required by a first-class player at each hole.
Pitch A lofted approach shot to the green.
Pitch and Run A shot pitched short and allowed to run up to the flag.
Pull A straight-flying shot which when hit by a right-hander, goes to the left of the line to the flag-stick.
Push A straight-flying shot which, when hit by a right-hander, goes to the right of the line to the flag-stick.
Rough The area within the course not specially prepared for play.
Rub-of-the-green When ball in motion is stopped or deflected by an outside agency.
Scratch A handicap of nought. The player neither gives or receives strokes in a match.
Slice A shot which, when hit by a right-hander, curves to the right, more pronounced than a fade and unintentional.
Stroke-play See *Medal-play*.
Wedge A broad-soled niblick, having maximum loft for playing from a bunker and for hitting short, high shots, usually to the green.
Woods Clubs, usually of four different kinds, whose heads are made with wood. Used for the longer shots.

Popperfoto

PROFESSIONAL GOLFERS' ASSOCIATIONS

The interests of professional golfers in all the major golfing nations are served by associations which perform in two broad ways: as a trade protection society for club professionals, and as the authority that regulates and promotes tournament golf.

Historically the golf professional has evolved through a succession of duties. Originally professionals were no more than caddies who were willing, at a price, to make up a match. The more superior members of this motley breed could aspire to become keeper of the green, responsible for the upkeep of the links and privileged to sell clubs and equipment. As golf developed, greenkeeping became a job for the full-time specialist, and the professional concentrated on his shop, teaching, club-repairs, and, as and when the opportunity arose, tournament play. He still retained the status of a servant, though a respected one, and was

largely content with his station in life.

At the beginning of the 20th century a number of clubs made it known that they were prepared to let the sales of the shop to the highest bidder. J. H. Taylor, then professional at Royal Mid-Surrey and the reigning Open Champion, saw this move as a threat to the livelihood of professionals. A meeting was convened, and the London and Counties Professional Golfers' Association was formed, with Taylor as chairman and James Braid as captain. This association quickly grew from its modest beginnings in 1901 to become the Professional Golfers' Association and include all British pros. In the intervening years it has established a benevolent fund, instituted training schemes for young professionals, and set proficiency standards for its members. It also regulates all official tournaments and is the governing body of professional golf.

The American professionals followed suit, and in the inter-war years tournament golf grew to such proportions that certain professionals began to devote themselves full-time to competi-

tive play. From that time golf offered a choice of two careers: golf professional and the professional golfer. Many pros continued to combine the two activities, but from this time the Professional Golfers' Associations had to cater for the needs of two distinct activities. Often, however, the interests of the two categories did not coincide and, indeed, were in direct conflict. During the 1960s the United States Professional Golfers' Association was torn by internal disputes to such an extent that the tournament players broke away and formed their own organization, the Association of Professional Golfers. A compromise was quickly reached, however, and the new body was incorporated in the PGA as an autonomous Players Tournament Division.

Sport & General

1 James Braid, five times winner of the British Open championship, was a founder member and the first captain of the British PGA in 1901.
2 David Snell—winner of the PGA match-play title in 1959, the tournament to find the best professional golfer in the British ranks.

The PGA is also responsible for controlling the influx of new players to the American circuit.

The United States Professional Golfers' Association instituted its championship in 1916 as a match-play tournament. The championship was later changed to a 72-holes stroke play affair and established itself as one of golf's four major classics. The British PGA championship ran from 1955 until 1968, when it was suspended through lack of a sponsor, but it never attained anything like the status of its American counterpart.

The British and American PGAs jointly sponsor the biennial Ryder Cup matches, instituted in 1927, between teams of American and British professionals.

Although there are many associations of professionals in all parts of the world, formed to promote and protect their local interests—there are, for instance, separate Irish and Scottish PGAs —the major and generally recognized PGAs, apart from those of Britain and the United States, are in Australia, Canada, New Zealand, South Africa, and Scandinavia.

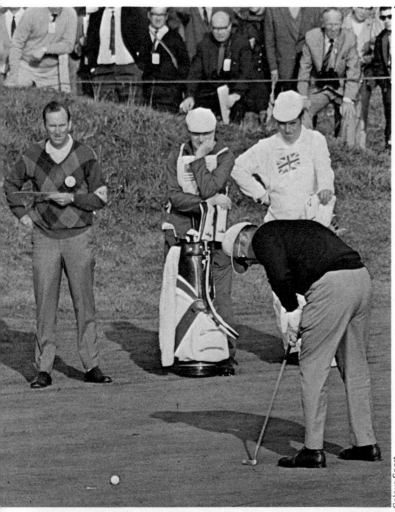

The staff of Wandsworth Prison gauge the end of the British professional golf season by the reappearance of a regular customer—a golf caddie. He lives rough in summer, then breaks the law to carry him through a centrally heated winter at Her Majesty's expense. This story compounds the legend of golf caddies as delightful rogues who opt for the vagabond life, hide under nicknames, and consider their life's work to be the acquisition of money to gamble and buy a pint.

For all that, the caddie is a true professional, and an essential item of equipment for any successful golfer. He knows the major golf courses and their subleties, and his advice can mean the difference between success and failure. American Gay Brewer acknowledged this truth with two £1,000 tips to Southport caddie Alfie Fyles when winning the Alcan Golfer of the Year title in successive years.

Max Faulkner, the 1951 Open champion, employed a regular caddie called 'Mad Mac' who wore a raincoat, but no shirt, and always studied the greens through binoculars from which the lenses had been removed. He once told Faulkner: 'Hit this putt slightly straight sir!'

The wealth of professional golf has produced a more business-like caddie who displays none of his predecessor's eccentricities. Jackie Leigh, for example, an ex-wrestler from Southport, worked with Peter Thomson in Britain throughout the 1960s. Southport, or rather Royal Birkdale, has become the unofficial 'caddie capital' of Britain, because most of the top men live there. John Allen worked in a casino until he met American champion Billy Casper, a Mormon. Allen adopted the faith and became part of the Casper entourage, staying in the same hotels as his employer, and not reduced to the old legend of sleeping in bunkers or barns. Jimmy Dickinson, who caddied regularly for Jack Nicklaus when he visited Britain, is another caddy whose importance was recognized and he is now a valuable and permanent member of Nicklaus's staff.

Most top caddies are regularly employed by home professionals for a weekly wage and a percentage of winnings. But the brotherhood of caddies is divided into these 'travellers' and the

Colour Sport

2

28

'bag carriers' or home-based caddies. Here, the more apocryphal work of the caddie flourishes, such as the hole in the trouser pocket through which a replacement ball can be dropped. In a few clubs it is understood that a caddie's client never gets a bad lie, and he must arrange it. Such trickery is spotted in major competitions, especially among professional golfers to whom cheating is a ruinous allegation.

The term *caddie* is thought to derive from the French word *cadet* meaning *attendant*. But even the advent of fuller employment, the two-wheeled trolley, the motorized trolley, and the passenger-carrying golf cart has not lessened the demand for the attendant who knows his golf course and his employer's game. The weekend hacker could save five shots a round by a good caddie's advice, claims Alfie Fyles, simply by playing sensible shots instead of thinking in terms of the perfect one. To the top professional, the caddie offers a valued second opinion, and in a way shares the burdens of this solitary game. Good caddies know their clients' habits. Their oldest custom is to use the term 'we' when talking about golf, but revert to 'he' when blame is involved.

Their duties start at dawn when they chart the position of every flagstick on the course, so that their employer knows the exact distance. Jimmy Dickinson, when he first caddied for Nicklaus in Britain, summed up this part of the job with the sentence 'My boss wants to know the distance to the precise yard and I've charted every major golf course in the country'.

Caddies are caustic critics. To the man who remarked that golf was a funny game, one replied: 'True, the way you play it.' Another asked a vicar: 'Shall I replace this divot or keep it for the Harvest Festival?' After Ben Hogan played Carnoustie, one duffer tried to copy the American's club selection. When his ball landed short on one hole and he chided the caddie, he was told: 'You wanted to know what Hogan used. He was short on this hole as well.'

1 Caddies in boiler-suit overalls watch 1969 US Ryder Cup golfer Miller Barber putt. The caddies nearly went on strike because they considered the overalls were unsuitable.
2 Gary Player brought his American-circuit caddie, a giant Negro called 'Rabbit' Dwyer, over to England to help him win the 1974 British Open at Royal Lytham and St Annes.
3 Tony Jacklin gives Jack Nicklaus a lift at Royal Birkdale. Such carts are a familiar sight on American golf courses, but have removed the need for caddies at club level.
4 A contrast in appearance. Bearded Archie Turner watches the immaculate Max Faulkner drive up the fairway.
5 A jubilant Alfie Fyles gives Gary Player a congratulatory hug after Player had holed his putt to win the 1968 Open.

Fox Photos

Syndication International

Associated Press

British Open winners at St Andrews in 1970: *Standing*, A. Havers, G. Sarazen, R. Burton, F. Daly, R. de Vicenzo, A. Palmer, K. Nagle, A. D. Locke, T. H. Cotton, P. Thomson: *kneeling*, D. Shute, R. Charles, M. Faulkner, J. Nicklaus, T. Jacklin, G. Player.

The Major Tournaments

British Open Golf Championship

Universally known as 'the British Open', the Open Golf Championship is a remarkable synthesis of old and new. Though the oldest of its kind in the world—it celebrated its centenary in 1960—it has managed to move with the times and is regarded as one of the four most important events in the world, alongside the US Open, US Masters, and US PGA. Most of the great names in the history of golf have at some time won it.

A prize list that climbed from a first prize of £30 in 1893 to a £50,000 total in 1974 cannot alone account for the Open Championship's continued buoyancy. The greatest golfers have consistently felt the need to accept the challenges beyond their own environment, and the Open has provided the stimulus. The championship, like Wimbledon, has drawn the best names. There have been times when that urge has seemed stifled, but it has always revived and in the 1960s the entry was as internationally strong as ever.

A variety of motives draws the big names to the Open. But the biggest single factor remains the belief that without victory in the British Open no golfer's achievements are complete. A minority do not take to the course and grumble at the hotel accommodation. But the rest accept the unfamiliar conditions, with a different kind of turf, uneven fairways, variable winds, and the added hazards of cold or wet weather. It is in overcoming these difficulties that much of their satisfaction lies.

So down the years, from the United States, Hagen, Jones, Sarazen, and Armour have been followed by Snead, Hogan, Palmer, Nicklaus, Lema, and Trevino to mix with the great names from the Commonwealth and South Africa—Bobby Locke, Kel Nagle, Peter Thomson, Gary Player, and Bob Charles.

Though no attempt could be made to raise the prize money to the level of the biggest American tournaments, modern business methods and the fees obtained from television have made possible substantial rewards, including four-figure prizes down to tenth place.

The Open is an expensive, intricate undertaking. Many variations have been tried within the framework of the championship, and the list of exemptions from qualifying may continue to vary each year, but a lasting formula has now been achieved. A field of 130 is determined by exemptions, based on previous achievements in orders of merit and the results of a qualifying tournament, in almost equal proportions.

For years the championship was confined to three days, the final two rounds on the last day being considered a test of stamina which was an integral part of the championship. Economic considerations, in particular the need for increased television fees and gate money, led to a fourth day being added in 1966. Every year the facilities and the side-shows surrounding the championship have increased. The amount of ground needed to house the huge spread of canvas involved, and to provide parking space for the thousands of cars that converge on the course, has led to a restriction in the number of courses that can house the event. As the organization grows—work on the next Open begins shortly after the end of the previous one—the need for a few semi-permanent headquarters for the championship to be established becomes greater.

Opposite page, **Tony Jacklin playing his way to victory in the 1969 British Open, the first home winner for 18 years.**

1 Harry Vardon, the only golfer ever to win the Open six times, tees off in 1913. The jackets of the period were loose-fitting and did not hamper a smooth swing. 2 John H. Taylor, who was champion five times and runner-up six times over a period of 20 years. 3 James Braid on the 138-yard 10th hole at Troon in 1923. 'The Great Triumvirate' – Braid, Taylor, and Vardon – captured the championship 16 times. 4 One of the spearheads of the post-war American invasion, Bobby Jones, in action at St Andrews in 1927, when he won the Open for the second year running. 5 The dapper Walter Hagen, prototype of the true professional, at Sandwich in 1928, the third of the four British Open championships he won in the 1920s.

Six or seven possible venues remain: St Andrews, Muirfield, Carnoustie, and Troon in Scotland, alternating with Royal Birkdale, Hoylake, and Royal Lytham in northern England. These have shared the event since 1951. The best British courses lie by the sea and are the traditional sites of the Open. Of these possible venues, St Andrews is at once the shortest but also the most traditional. Carnoustie is probably the most severe, and Muirfield the nearest to perfection.

The first scene of the Open in 1860, and the one on which it was played for the following decade, was Prestwick, now an anachronism in terms of championship golf, but still a pleasure to play. The trophy was not the oft-photographed jug of today, but a belt of red morocco richly ornamented with silver plating. The original entry numbered eight, against the 300-odd of the 1960s. The championship was over 36 holes instead of 72.

This was the age of the Morris's —father and son—first of all 'Old Tom' whose chief rival was Willie Park, whom he outshone by four victories to three in that first decade. Then 'Young Tom' Morris came onto the scene, a genius of a player who won the Belt four years in succession, but who died, some say, of a broken heart at the age of 24 after the death of his wife. Four victories in succession has never since been equalled, but it is important to remember the conditions. In Prestwick golf club to this day is preserved the original entry for 1870, the third of 'Young Tom' Morris's, victories; 17 entered, and their scores were kept on the back of an old envelope.

From a sluggish start the championship spread to other courses, initially to St Andrews and Musselburgh. The first contest at St Andrews had a field of 26. So long as the championship was confined to Scotland it was dominated by Scottish champions. But in 1890 John Ball, from the Royal Liverpool club at Hoylake, became the first Englishman—as well as the first amateur—to win. When a fellow member of Royal Liverpool, Harold Hilton, won the championship two years later, it was clear that the event would not much longer be confined to Scottish courses. In 1894 J. H. Taylor won the first championship to be held south of the border, at Sandwich, and with Harry Vardon and James Braid, ushered in the long reign of the Big Three of those days. Between that year and the outbreak of the war in 1914, the 'Great Triumvirate', as they were known, accounted for 16 of the 21 Opens.

In the history of the championship it is the personality of the winners that stands out rather than the means by which they won their titles. The greatest of them often won by several strokes, as Hagen did in 1929, or as

1 South Africa's Bobby Locke in 1957. He and Peter Thomson of Australia, with four wins apiece, dominated the Open in the 1950s. 2 Gary Player, also of South Africa, at Carnoustie in 1968, when he took the title after a gap of 9 years. 3 Arnold Palmer's wins in 1961 and 1962 rekindled American interest in the Open and helped to re-establish it among the big four tournaments of world golf. 4 The bunker on the left of the dog-leg 17th at Royal Lytham and St Annes, into which Bobby Jones put his drive in the final round of the 1926 Open. Jones carried the intervening rough and low hills to the green, and sank his putt to win the hole and the championship. The plaque honours the event. 5 A map to aid the crowds for the 1968 Open at Carnoustie in Scotland. *Opposite page:* **Five-time winner Peter Thomson was still attacking the British Open in the mid-1970s.**

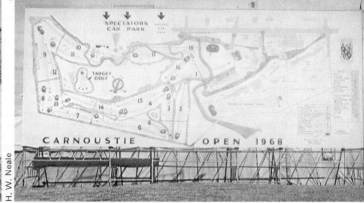

H. W. Neale

Colour Sport

Sarazen, Armour, Hogan, and more recently Palmer did after him. But it is a feature of this event that after something not far short of 300 shots have been hit the winner emerges frequently by the margin of one or two strokes. Yet the difference—and it is a big one—is more often between those who have a champion's nerve and those who under the final pressure just fail to stay the course.

George Duncan made up a lot of ground in winning the first Open after the war, at Deal, overtaking his friend Abe Mitchell who had led by nine strokes at the halfway stage. The following year at St Andrews came the first hint of the American invasion that was to come during the next decade, when Jock Hutchinson, who had migrated to the United States from Scotland, became the first of many transatlantic winners. His score of 296 included a hole in one. His partner was a young American, Bobby Jones. Playing his first British Open, Jones took 46 for the first nine holes of his third round, and retired in a fury; later he came to love the St Andrews course above all the many he played. Between them, he and Walter Hagen won seven British Opens, the latter endearing himself to the British public by his colourful personality and his contempt for the social barriers

4

Colour Sport

that faced British professionals at the time. He used to practise by driving balls from the roof of the Savoy Hotel into the Thames.

That decade of American victories from 1924 to 1933, was crucial in the history of the championship. Entries had increased from the early days of a dozen or so to about 200, but prize money was modest, even for that period. Yet the best players in America, and therefore in the world, came back repeatedly to take part, backing its great tradition with an

international flavour that established it as an event of world-wide stature.

Although nobody knew that Bobby Jones, in winning the Open at St Andrews in 1930, was on his way to a unique record as holder of the amateur and Open championships of both Britain and the United States at the same time, he was carried shoulder high from the green out of sheer popularity. Yet the public grew tired of American dominance, and when Henry Cotton broke the spell in

1934 his victory brought a much needed boost to British golf. Before the final round he was ill, but the lead he had built up was enough to give him a comfortable victory in spite of finishing with a 79. It was an indication of the strain of golf at the top; even Bobby Jones experienced it—he used to lose a stone in weight at a championship. Cotton had won his way to the top by sheer hard work rather than natural ability, but showed it was no fluke by winning again three years later in a field that included America's best.

When the championship was restarted after the war, Sam Snead slipped across the Atlantic and stole the title in 1946. But American interest waned, and it became the turn of Commonwealth players.

In 1949, the year after Cotton had won his third, a new name came to the fore that was to become very familiar during the next decade. Bobby Locke had made a brief appearance as an amateur before the war, and he now returned with his deliberate manner and uncanny putting to share the Open with Australian Peter Thomson in all but two years until 1959. In a way it was a barren period for the Open; the great American players found so much wealth in their own country that

1 Left-handed New Zealander Bob Charles, who won the Open at Royal Lytham in 1963 and came second at the same venue in 1969. 2 Leading American Jack Nicklaus won in 1966 at Muirfield and has finished in the top four on four other occasions. 3 Roberto de Vincenzo of Argentina, a player always up with the leaders in the Open and winner by two strokes from Nicklaus at Hoylake in 1967. 4 Peter Thomson, who in 1956 became the first man to win three successive Open titles since 1882. He won again in 1958 and 1965 to take his total to five—a unique performance in the 20th century. 5 The scene around the 18th green at Royal Lytham during the 1969 championship. The fact that the five winners to 1969—Thomson, Nicklaus, de Vincenzo, Player, and Jacklin—are all of different nationalities, illustrates the cosmopolitan nature of the modern British Open.

3 they lost the desire to venture abroad, and the best British players, most of whose careers had been interrupted by the war, lost the art of winning. The only British exception was Max Faulkner, a model of physical fitness and a colourful personality who broke Locke's run at Portrush in 1951—the only year the event visited Ireland.

In 1953 one more exception prevailed—the American Ben Hogan. His victory by four strokes, with a lower score each round and a final 68 over the vast Carnoustie links, had an air of inevitability, and was an important landmark. He was undisputed master in his own country, with four US Open wins, and his decision to enter for the British Open was a sign that it still held prestige among the best Americans. But it needed the example of another great American, Arnold Palmer, to restore the event to its former place in the eyes of his countrymen in 1961. Before that the championship had been reduced almost to monotony by the brilliance of Locke and Thomson.

Palmer had first come over to try to win the Centenary Open in 1960, and in a star-studded field finished one stroke behind Kel Nagle, then a little-known Australian. Palmer's turn came in 1961, when he won at Royal Birkdale in atrocious weather. His 37 for the first nine holes in a full gale is regarded by many as one of the finest pieces of golf ever played. In retaining the title the following year, he again gave an 5 unforgettable performance. Troon, not often used as a venue, was burned up and hard that year. Yet Palmer, in conditions entirely foreign to him, set a new record for the championship with 276, finishing six strokes ahead of Nagle.

Behind Palmer, and indeed behind South African Gary Player, who had remained as faithful to the old championship as any, and won it in 1959, the invaders began once again to arrive in force. Not only did the Big Three of the second half of the century—Palmer, Nicklaus, and Player—take part, but other leading players from America—Lema, Casper, Brewer, Boros—raised the event higher than it had ever stood before. 'Champagne' Tony Lema, one of the first of the new generation of flamboyant young American golfers, followed Palmer by winning at St Andrews in 1964, in what was only the second Open he had entered.

The Open has lived up to its reputation as one of the great four events in the world, and the Americans, despite dominating the top placings year after year, have never been able to re-establish their monopoly of the championship itself. Commonwealth golfers, especially, continued to offer strong competition to the Americans throughout the

1960s, and Palmer's two victories were proceeded by one of the major upsets of all. In 1963, a slight, unemotional New Zealander won a play-off by eight strokes from America's Phil Rogers, a persistent though unsuccessful Transatlantic visitor. Bob Charles was not only the first New Zealander to win the Open, he was also the first left-hander. The value of the Open was again clearly demonstrated, for this win made Charles a famous name and opened the golfing door of every country to him.

Then, in 1965, Peter Thomson scored his fifth victory at windswept Royal Birkdale, the longest of the Open venues, thus equalling Bobby Locke's post-war feat. Gary Player was another to stave off an American victory when he scored the second of his three successes in 1968, this time over the tough Carnoustie course.

In 1966 it was Jack Nicklaus's year, although his win came four years after his first major championship victory, the 1962 US Open. An even more popular winner was Roberto de Vicenzo of Argentina. De Vicenzo, then 44 and the grand old man of South American golf, was the first winner of one of golf's four big prizes to hail from beyond the golfing strongholds of America, South Africa, and the British Commonwealth.

But the highpoint of the British Open for the public during this period was 1969. After the halfway stage had been reached, the headlines in the national *Daily Express* screamed: 'Glory be, it's our Tony!' It was indeed to be glory for Tony Jacklin, as, hardened by experience over two years on the American circuit, he coolly held on to the lead at Royal Lytham to become the first Englihman to win his native championship for 18 years.

The 1971 and 1972 Opens produced a double winner who was one of the most colourful and personable characters the British public had ever encountered on their golf courses—the Mexican-American Lee Trevino. Trevino's challenger for the title at Royal Birkdale in 1971 was the equally popular Lu Liang Huan of Taiwan, who gave a firm indication of the rising quality of Asian golf as he just failed, by a single stroke, to catch 'Super-Mex'. Trevino's win at Muirfield in 1972 was his more remarkable performance, for on the 17th in the final round, he seemed to have conceded victory to Jacklin. On the monster par five, Jacklin was 40 yards short of the green in two, while Trevino, in desperate trouble, pitched just beyond the green, having played two strokes more than his opponent. Jacklin chipped on to the green and, although some 20 feet short of the pin, seemed certain to go into at least a one-

The story of a rabbit and a hare: *Opposite page*, **Gary Player's caddie 'Rabbit' helps him line up a putt at Royal Lytham in 1974.** *Above*, **Lee Trevino, distracted by a hare, misses a putt at Muirfield.**

stroke lead. Yet Trevino, with deceptive nonchalance, ran his pitch straight into the cup, and the stunned Jacklin sadly three-putted to allow the position to be completely reversed.

If the 1973 and 1974 Opens lacked the tension that had enlivened the previous three events, it was not because the quality of the golf ebbed in any way but because of the rare double occurrence of the winner leading from the very first round. In 1973, Tom Weiskopf made it four successive wins for America, a sequence that was broken the following year as Gary Player completed his

personal hat-trick of victories.

Much of the reputation of the British Open rests on the standard of golfers who have won it. Over the past 20 years, this criterion has been generously satisfied, for, without exception, the victor has already established himself among the world's leading golfers or, in other cases, has then gone on to consolidate his Open performance. But equally important is the number of great golfers who have unsuccessfully contested the Open. Contemporary golfers from overseas of the ability of Julius Boros, Tommy Aaron, Doug Sanders, and, above all, Billy Casper have challenged repeatedly for the Open—and in vain. It is the fact that the British Open remains so difficult for even the most eminent of golfers to conquer that confirms the belief that its importance will not wane for many years.

THE OPEN GOLF CHAMPIONSHIP

Year	Winner	Score	Venue
1860	Willie Park	174	Prestwick
1861	Tom Morris, Sn	163	Prestwick
1862	Tom Morris, Sn	163	Prestwick
1863	Willie Park	168	Prestwick
1864	Tom Morris, Sn	160	Prestwick
1865	Andrew Strath	162	Prestwick
1866	Willie Park	169	Prestwick
1867	Tom Morris, Sn	170	Prestwick
1868	Tom Morris, Jn	154	Prestwick
1869	Tom Morris, Jn	157	Prestwick
1870	Tom Morris, Jn	149	Prestwick
1871	*not held*		
1872	Tom Morris, Jn	166	Prestwick
1873	Tom Kidd	179	St Andrews
1974	Mungo Park	159	Musselburgh
1875	Willie Park	166	Prestwick
1876[1]	Bob Martin	176	St Andrews
1877	Jamie Anderson	160	Musselburgh
1878	Jamie Anderson	157	Prestwick
1879	Jamie Anderson	169	St Andrews
1880	Bob Ferguson	162	Musselburgh
1881	Bob Ferguson	170	Prestwick
1882	Bob Ferguson	171	St Andrews
1883[2]	Willie Fernie	159	Musselburgh
1884	Jack Simpson	160	Prestwick
1885	Bob Martin	171	St Andrews
1886	David Brown	157	Musselburgh
1887	Willie Park, Jn	161	Prestwick
1888	Jack Burns	171	St Andrews
1889[3]	Willie Park, Jn	155	Musselburgh
1890	John Ball*	164	Prestwick
1891	Hugh Kirkaldy	166	St Andrews
1892	Harold H. Hilton*	305†	Muirfield
1893	William Auchterlonie	322	Prestwick
1894	John H. Taylor	326	Sandwich
1895	John H. Taylor	322	St Andrews
1896[4]	Harry Vardon	316	Muirfield
1897	Harold H. Hilton*	314	Hoylake
1898	Harry Vardon	307	Prestwick
1899	Harry Vardon	310	Sandwich
1900	John H. Taylor	309	St Andrews
1901	James Braid	309	Muirfield
1902	Alexander Herd	307	Hoylake
1903	Harry Vardon	300	Prestwick
1904	Jack White	296	Sandwich
1905	James Braid	318	St Andrews
1906	James Braid	300	Muirfield
1907	Arnaud Massey	312	Hoylake
1908	James Braid	291	Prestwick
1909	John H. Taylor	295	Deal
1910	James Braid	299	St Andrews
1911[5]	Harry Vardon	303	Sandwich
1912	Edward 'Ted' Ray	295	Muirfield
1913	John H. Taylor	304	Hoylake
1914	Harry Vardon	306	Prestwick
1915-19	*not held*		
1920	George Duncan	303	Deal
1921[6]	Jock Hutchinson	296	St Andrews
1922	Walter Hagen (USA)	300	Sandwich
1923	Arthur G. Havers	295	Troon
1924	Walter Hagen (USA)	301	Hoylake
1925	James M. Barnes (USA)	300	Prestwick
1926	Robert T. Jones (USA)*	291	Royal Lytham
1927	Robert T. Jones (USA)*	285	St Andrews
1928	Walter Hagen (USA)	292	Sandwich
1929	Walter Hagen (USA)	292	Muirfield
1930	Robert T. Jones (USA)*	291	Hoylake
1931	Tommy Armour (USA)	296	Carnoustie
1932	Gene Sarazen (USA)	283	Prince's, Sandwich
1933[7]	Denny Shute (USA)	292	St Andrews
1934	Henry Cotton	283	Sandwich
1935	Alf Perry	283	Muirfield
1936	Alfred Padgham	287	Hoylake
1937	Henry Cotton	290	Carnoustie
1938	Reginald Whitcombe	295	Sandwich
1939	Richard Burton	290	St Andrews
1940-45	*not held*		
1946	Sam Snead (USA)	290	St Andrews
1947	Fred Daly	293	Hoylake
1948	Henry Cotton	284	Muirfield
1949[8]	Bobby Locke (South Africa)	283	Sandwich
1950	Bobby Locke (South Africa)	279	Troon
1951	Max Faulkner	285	Portrush
1952	Bobby Locke (South Africa)	287	Royal Lytham
1953	Ben Hogan (USA)	282	Carnoustie
1954	Peter Thomson (Australia)	283	Royal Birkdale
1955	Peter Thomson (Australia)	281	St Andrews
1956	Peter Thomson (Australia)	286	Hoylake
1957	Bobby Locke (South Africa)	279	St Andrews
1958[9]	Peter Thomson (Australia)	278	Royal Lytham
1959	Gary Player (South Africa)	284	Muirfield
1960	Kel Nagle (Australia)	276	St Andrews
1961	Arnold Palmer (USA)	284	Royal Birkdale
1962	Arnold Palmer (USA)	276	Troon
1963[10]	Bob Charles (New Zealand)	277	Royal Lytham
1964	Tony Lema (USA)	279	St Andrews
1965	Peter Thomson (Australia)	285	Royal Birkdale
1966	Jack Nicklaus (USA)	282	Muirfield
1967	Roberto de Vincenzo (Argentina)	278	Hoylake
1968	Gary Player (South Africa)	289	Carnoustie
1969	Tony Jacklin	280	Royal Lytham
1970	Jack Nicklaus (USA)	283	St Andrews
1971	Lee Trevino (USA)	278	Royal Birkdale
1972	Lee Trevino (USA)	278	Muirfield
1973	Tom Weiskopf (USA)	276	Troon
1974	Gary Player (South Africa)	282	Royal Lytham
1975[11]	Tom Watson (USA)	279	Carnoustie

*Amateur
†Extended to 72 holes, and entry fees introduced
[1] David Strath tied, but refused to play off
[2] After a tie with Bob Ferguson
[3] After a tie with Andrew Kirkaldy
[4] After a tie with John H. Taylor. Replay scores (36 holes) Vardon, 157; Taylor 161
[5] After a tie with Arnaud Massey. The replay was over 36 holes but Massey withdrew after 34 holes
[6] After a tie with Roger Wethered*. Replay scores (36 holes) Hutchinson, 150; Wethered, 159
[7] After a tie with Craig Wood (USA). Replay scores (36 holes) Shute, 149; Wood, 154
[8] After a tie with Harry Bradshaw. Replay scores (36 holes) Locke, 135; Bradshaw, 147
[9] After a tie with David Thomas. Replay scores (36 holes) Thomson, 139; Thomas, 143
[10] After a tie with Phil Rogers (USA). Replay scores (36 holes) Charles, 140; Rogers, 148
[11] After a tie with Jack Newton (Australia). Replay scores (18 holes) Watson, 71; Newton, 72

Popperfoto

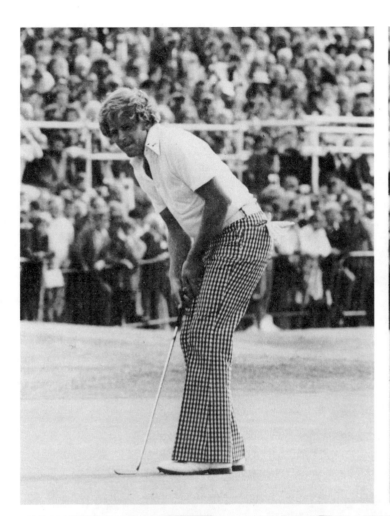

Opposite page, **Jack Newton (left) and Tom Watson tie for the 1975 British Open.** *Top,* **Newton looks pensive during the play-off.** *Below,* **Watson clinches victory.**

A historic picture taken in **1929**. The line-up includes five winners of the US Open (see page **46** for details).

Jack Nicklaus, the 'Golden Bear'—US Open champion in 1962, 1967, and 1972, his first title coming only a year after he had won his second US Amateur Championship.

United States Open Golf Championship

More than any other tournament, the US Open is the one every professional golfer wants to win. It is not just that the prize money is high—there are other tournaments worth more—but in the modern era of big-money golf, winning the US Open will set a golfer on the road to immense wealth. As a result, competition is always intense, and it is not surprising that the pros rate it the most difficult tournament in the world to win.

Like all great tournaments, the United States National Open Golf Championship owes much of its prestige to the courses over which it is played. The United States Golf Association, most conscious of the prestige and tradition of the Open, choose the course with great care, and lay down stringent rules about its condition. Preparations are sometimes begun more than a year before the tournament is played, and the course is always in first-class condition, with carefully

guarded rough, narrowed-down fairways, lengthened tees, and often specially constructed hazards. Not that the championship course always meets the approval of the contestants. In 1970, for instance, when Tony Jacklin became only the fourth man to hold the British and US Open titles concurrently, runner-up Dave Hill described the Robert Trent Jones-designed Hazeltine National course, with its dog-legs and blind greens, as a 'cow pasture'.

The first Open was played in 1895, making the tournament the second oldest in the United States. The Amateur Championship was played just three days before. The Open was a one-day tournament played on October 4 at the Newport Golf Club, Rhode Island, with 10 professionals and a solitary amateur playing four rounds of nine holes each. The winner, a 20-year-old Englishman, Horace Rawlins, shot a score of 173 to win the $150 first prize and a gold medal. Total prize money was $355.

British golfers dominated the early Championships, which from 1898 were played over 72 holes. Willie Smith's victory in 1899 by 11 strokes was a record still standing in 1974, and when Willie Anderson won in 1901 in the

Lee Trevino provides some light relief in the play-off for the 1971 US Open.

tournament's first play-off, it was the first of his four championships in five years, the last three in successive years. Harry Vardon's victory in 1900 had helped create interest in golf in America, but interest grew even greater when Johnny McDermott's victory in 1911 at last broke the British hold. In 1912, there were a record 131 entries, and in winning his second title McDermott became the first man to break par—only officially introduced the previous year—over 72 holes.

The following two years produced two outstanding champions. The 1913 Open is still regarded as the most dramatic moment in American golfing history. The British giants, Vardon and Ted Ray, were expected to sweep all before them, but a 20-year-old local amateur, a former caddie at the Open's venue, the Brookline Country Club, had other ideas. Young Francis Ouimet played the last six holes in two under par to tie the Britons on 304. In the play-off, he demolished them with a 72, beating Vardon by five strokes and Ray by six. Another youngster took the title the next year. After

an opening 68, Walter Hagen led all the way to win with a record-equalling 290.

In 1916, the prize money topped $1,000 for the first time, and, ironically, an amateur emerged as the winner. 'Chick' Evans used his seven hickory-shafted clubs to shoot a record 286 and so become the first man to win both the Amateur and the Open in the same year.

American entry into World War I meant the Open was not played in 1917 and 1918, just as there was no championship between 1942 and 1945. Between the two wars, the event underwent considerable changes. In 1919, when Hagen won again, playing the last six holes in one under fours before winning the play-off by a single shot, the championship was extended to three days and the prize money increased to $1,745. By 1938 it had reached $6,000. In 1922 admission was charged for the first time, and a record entry of 360 in 1923 persuaded the USGA to introduce 'sectional' qualifying the next year. Eastern and western elimination rounds were held, and only the low 40 and ties from each went forward to the championship. By 1936, entries had reached 1,277 and sectional qualifying rounds were being played at 28 different courses. In 1930 the small ball made its last appearance in the Open, and by 1932 the standard ball now in use in the United States had been approved.

The 23 mid-war years produced no less than nine play-offs, the 1920 one involving five players and producing in Ted Ray, at 43, the oldest winner of the title. They also included some remarkable champions.

Gene Sarazen won his first title in 1922, and when he won again 10 years later with a record last round of 66 he became the second man to win both the British and US Open in the same year. The first had been Bobby Jones, who, in 1926, won both Opens and in 1930 won the then grand slam of the British and American Amateur and Open titles, whereupon, at the age of 28, he retired. In all, he won the US Open four times.

The 1935 Open saw the biggest upset in the event's history, when Sam Parks Jr beat Jimmy Thompson and the 43-year-old Hagen with a total of 299. Eleven over par, it was the sole score under 300. Byron Nelson's title in 1939 was also won in interesting circumstances—a double play-off. The first was against Craig Wood and Denny Shute, the second against Wood alone. Wood finally won in 1941, when he also won the Masters title.

For the first Open after World War II, the total purse was increased to $8,000, and by 1957 Dick Mayer, who beat defending champion Cary Middlecoff by seven strokes in a play-off, was taking away $7,200 out of a total purse of $28,560.

Lloyd Mangrum emerged the winner in 1946, after a three-way play-off in which a curious accident robbed Byron Nelson of the title. His caddy accidentally kicked his ball into the crowd, and the former champion incurred a two stroke penalty. Another unusual incident the following year unnerved Sam Snead at the final hole of the play-off. Both he and Lew Worsham had arrived at the 18th green on level terms and both lay about a foot and a half from the flag. As Snead was preparing to putt, Worsham asked that the balls be measured to determine who was away. It was Snead, but when he putted he missed. Worsham made no mistake.

Snead was to finish second on two other occasions, in 1949 and in 1953. The last time he was six shots behind 'The Master', Ben Hogan, who that year led all the way to take his fourth Open title. He also won the Masters and the British Open in what must rank as his finest year. Yet his greatest victory must surely have been in 1950, when, his legs still swathed in bandages from his near-fatal motor accident, he tied with Lloyd Mangrum and George Fazio at Merion, then next day shot a 69 for the title.

During the period from 1947 to 1957, there were only two Open

1 Francis Ouimet's victory in the 1913 Open was a turning point in the history of golf in the United States, for it ended an era of dominance by British golfers. 2 In the 1920s, the great Bobby Jones won the US Open four times, by 1971 a feat only Ben Hogan had emulated. 3 Five former US Open winners meet in 1929: *front row*, (second, third, and and fourth from left) Walter Hagan, Jim Barnes, and Ted Ray; *back row*, Harry Vardon (extreme left) and Fred Herd (third from left). 4 Julius Boros won his first Open in 1952, and then, aged 43, hit the headlines in 1963 when he beat Jacky Cupit and Arnold Palmer (5) in a play-off. For Palmer it meant that he had to be content with his 1960 victory.

finishes in which either Middlecoff, Snead, or Hogan were not involved, the 1952 tournament won by Julius Boros and that of 1954—the first Open to be televised nationally—won by Ed Furgol.

But in 1958, when the winner's purse reached $8,000, the signs of change at the top of the golfing hierarchy were evident. For the first time in 18 years Snead failed to make the 36 hole cut, and a young South African named Gary Player finished second. The tempestuous Tommy Bolt led all the way to win by four strokes, but from then until 1971 there were only five years in which at least one of the five real giants of the modern game were not still in there fighting it out to the finish. In that time, the title was won eight times by either Player, Palmer, Nicklaus, Casper, or Trevino, and on the same number of occasions one of them either forced a play-off or finished in second place. Considering the highly competitive nature of the contemporary golf scene and the vastly increased number of potential winners who start in each tournament, this was a remarkable domination.

On the occasions when these five were not closely involved at the finish, there were two wins by thoroughly experienced players and two by relative newcomers to big-time golf. In 1961, the fluid-stroking Gene Littler—'Gene the Machine'—returned one over par figures to beat Bob Goalby and Doug Sanders, and in 1964, it was the turn of 33-year-old Ken Venturi—and in the most dramatic fashion. In a temperature of 97 degrees and suffering from heat prostration, Venturi staggered through the two rounds of the final day with a doctor in attendance. Yet his 278 total was four shots better than that of Tommy Jacobs, who had equalled the low record of 64 in the second round.

The unexpected victories came from 36-year-old Orville Moody, who two years earlier had given up his 14-year-old army career to try professional golf, and Britain's Tony Jacklin. Moody's 1969 victory was his first on the Tour, and he reckoned later that he had hit only three bad shots in his one-over-par 281. Jacklin's winning margin was the widest since Jim Barnes's nine-stroke victory in 1921, and he became only the second to shoot four sub-par rounds in the Open. He led all the way after an opening 71, the only sub-par round on a day on which gale-force winds forced the scores up—Nicklaus over 80, Palmer 79, Player 80, Casper 75.

But back in 1959, Casper had not allowed bad weather to stop him from winning his first Open. In spite of waterlogged greens on the final day—because of earlier thunderstorms it was a Sunday—he still needed only 114 putts to beat a closely bunched field,

Action Photos

5

U.P.I.

47

establishing his reputation as a putting ace. His second title came in 1966, when he defeated Arnold Palmer in a play-off. This was Palmer's third unsuccessful play-off: in 1963, Julius Boros, at 43, had beaten Jacky Cupit at Brookline to win his second open.

For Palmer, things had been different back in 1960, when, after being seven strokes behind the leaders after 54 holes, he reached the turn in his final round in a record-equalling 30 and finished with a 65 to beat the 20-year-old Jack Nicklaus, whose 282 was the lowest 72-hole score returned by an amateur. Just two years later these two men were involved in a play-off for the title, and this time Nicklaus, in his 'rookie' year as a pro, made no mistake. His 71 gave him victory by three strokes.

Palmer was destined to finish second behind Nicklaus yet again. In 1967, the two giants started the final round a stroke behind the amateur Marty Fleckman. Fleckman soared to an 80, Palmer

managed a 69, but big Jack shot a blazing 65 to break by one shot Ben Hogan's 19-year-old Open record of 276.

In 1965, the Open became a four-day event and the title went outside the States for the first time since 1920. But right up to the closing holes of the play-off there was some doubt as to which country it would go. Gary Player and Australia's Kel Nagle tied on 282 before the South African won the play-off by three strokes. He gave his $25,000 prize money to junior golf and to cancer research.

By the time Lee Trevino won his first Open championship three years later, the prize money had risen to $30,000 out of a total of $190,000. The wisecracking Mexican-American confounded all the experts by becoming the first player in Open history to break 70 in all four rounds and by tieing the record 275 posted by Nicklaus only the year before. Two years later, Trevino established himself among the greats by taking the title again, at Merion, defeating Nicklaus in a play-off. He shot two successive 69s to tie Nicklaus on 280 and went one better in the play-off to win by three shots.

Gary Player caresses the US Open trophy in 1965, when he became the first overseas winner for 45 years.

U.P.I.

UNITED STATES OPEN GOLF CHAMPIONSHIP

Year	Winner	Score	Venue
1895	Horace Rawlins	173	Newport
1896	James Foulis	152	Southampton
1897	Joe Lloyd	162	Wheaton, Ill
1898	Fred Herd	328	Shinnecock Hills, NY
1899	Willie Smith	315	Baltimore
1900	Harry Vardon	313	Wheaton, Ill
1901	Willie Anderson*	315	Myopia, Mass
1902	Laurie Auchterlonie	305	Garden City
1903	Willie Anderson*	307	Baltusrol
1904	Willie Anderson	304	Glenview
1905	Willie Anderson	335	Myopia, Mass
1906	Alex Smith	291	Onwentsia
1907	Alex Ross	302	Chestnut Hill, Pa
1908	Fred McLeod*	322	Myopia, Mass
1909	Geo Sargent	290	Englewood, NJ
1910	Alex Smith	289	Philadelphia
1911	John J. McDermott*	307	Wheaton, Ill
1912	John J. McDermott	294	Buffalo
1913	Francis Ouimet*	304	Brookline, Mass
1914	Walter Hagen	297	Midlothian
1915	J. D. Travers	290	Baltusrol
1916	Charles Evans	286	Minneapolis
1919	Walter Hagen*	301	Brae Burn
1920	Ted Ray	295	Inverness
1921	Jim Barnes	289	Washington
1922	Gene Sarazen	288	Glencoe
1923	Bobby Jones*	296	Inwood, LI
1924	Cyril Walker	297	Oakland Hills
1925	William MacFarlane*	291	Worcester
1926	Bobby Jones	293	Scioto
1927	Tommy Armour*	301	Oakmont
1928	Johnny Farrell*	294	Olympia Fields
1929	Bobby Jones*	294	Winged Foot, NY
1930	Bobby Jones	287	Interlachen
1931	Billie Burke*	292	Inverness
1932	Gene Sarazen	286	Fresh Meadow
1933	Johnny Goodman	287	North Shore
1934	Olin Dutra	293	Merion
1935	Sam Parks	299	Oakmont
1936	Tony Manero	282	Springfield
1937	Ralph Guldahl	281	Oakland Hills
1938	Ralph Guldahl	284	Cherry Hills
1939	Byron Nelson*	284	Philadelphia
1940	W. Lawson Little*	287	Canterbury, Ohio
1941	Craig Wood	284	Fort Worth
1946	Lloyd Mangrum*	284	Canterbury, Ohio
1947	Lew Worsham*	282	St Louis
1948	Ben Hogan	276	Los Angeles
1949	Cary Middlecoff	286	Medinah, Ill
1950	Ben Hogan*	287	Merion
1951	Ben Hogan	287	Oakland Hills
1952	Julius Boros	281	Dallas
1953	Ben Hogan	283	Oakmont
1954	Ed Furgol	284	Baltusrol
1955	Jack Fleck*	287	San Francisco
1956	Cary Middlecoff	281	Rochester
1957	Dick Mayer*	282	Inverness
1958	Tommy Bolt	283	Tulsa
1959	Billy Casper	282	Mamaroneck
1960	Arnold Palmer	280	Denver
1961	Gene Littler	281	Birmingham, Mich
1962	Jack Nicklaus*	283	Oakmount
1963	Julius Boros*	293	Brookline, Mass
1964	Ken Venturi	278	Washington
1965	Gary Player*	282	St Louis
1966	Billy Casper*	278	San Francisco
1967	Jack Nicklaus	275	Baltusrol
1968	Lee Trevino	275	Rochester
1969	Orville Moody	281	Houston
1970	Tony Jacklin	281	Hazeltine
1971	Lee Trevino*	280	Merion
1972	Jack Nicklaus	290	Pebble Beach
1973	Johnny Miller	279	Oakmont
1974	Hale Irwin	287	Winged Foot
1975	Lou Graham	287	Medinah, Ill

*Play-offs:

1901	Willie Anderson 85, Alex Smith 86	
1903	Willie Anderson 82, David Brown 84	
1908	Fred McLeod 77, Willie Smith 83	
1910	Alex Smith 71, John McDermott 75, M. Smith 77	
1911	John McDermott 80, Mike Brady 82	
1913	Francis Ouimet 72, Harry Vardon 77, Ted Ray 78	
1919	Walter Hagen 77, Mike Brady 78	
1923	Bobby Jones 76, B. Cruickshank 78	
1925	William MacFarlane 147, Bobby Jones 148	
1927	Tommy Armour 76, Harry Cooper 79	
1928	Johnny Farrell 143, Bobby Jones 144	
1929	Bobby Jones 141, Al Espinosa 164	
1931	Billie Burke 149-148, George van Elm 149-149	
1939	Byron Nelson 68-70, Craig Wood 68-73 Denny Shute 76—eliminated	
1940	Lawson Little 70, Gene Sarazen 73	
1946	Lloyd Mangrum 72-72, Vic Ghezzi 72-73, Byron Nelson 72-73	
1947	Lew Worsham 69, Sam Snead 70	
1950	Ben Hogan 69, Lloyd Mangrum 73, George Fazio 75	
1955	Jack Fleck 69, Ben Hogan 72	
1957	Dick Mayer 72, Cary Middlecoff 79	
1962	Jack Nicklaus 71, Arnold Palmer 74	
1963	Julius Boros 70, Jacky Cupit 73, Arnold Palmer 76	
1965	Gary Player 71, Kel Nagle 74	
1966	Billy Casper 69, Arnold Palmer 73	
1971	Lee Trevino 68, Jack Nicklaus 71	
1975	Lou Graham 71, John Mahaffey 73	

At Pebble Beach, five years after their Baltusrol classic Palmer again trailed in behind Nicklaus as the blond Californian recorded his third victory, although on this occasion Australian Bruce Crampton pipped Palmer for second spot. In winning Nicklaus was unable to emulate his record-breaking score of 1967 as, buffeted by 30 miles an hour winds and tortured by the lightning fast greens, he could score no better than 290, the highest winning total for nine years. But most of the drama of the championship was provided by the veteran Palmer. After shooting a first round 77 to lie eight strokes off the lead, he came storming back with a superb 68 to pull up to within a stroke of Nicklaus, the joint second round leader. However, Palmer could not sustain his effort and a closing 76 left him four strokes behind Nicklaus.

Not until the following year was the stranglehold the big five had held on the Open at last broken, and it could not have been done in more dramatic fashion. The 1973 Open at Oakmount was in doubt until the last moment. Player opened up a lead after two rounds but crashed with a 77 to allow the indefatigable Arnold Palmer to share the third round lead with two-time winner Julius Boros, and tournament novices, John Schlee and Jerry Heard. Six strokes and a greater number of places behind was 26-year-old John Miller, best known as a protege of Billy Casper. Miller opened his final round with four birdies to bring himself on to the leaderboard, but tension caused him to miss a short putt at the eighth, dropping a stroke. It was his only lapse, for, steadying his nerves, he shot another five birdies to card a record-breaking 63 and snatch the title by one stroke. Miller's victory was all the more remarkable for the list of golfers he overtook in the course of his final round, including, apart from the third round leaders, Player, Nicklaus, Charles, and Trevino.

The next year, when the Open went to Winged Foot, there was a champion as unexpected as Moody had been five years earlier. Bespectacled Hale Irwin, an anonymous but consistent golfer, had played the tour for several years with only mild success, yet in another high-scoring championship, a final round of 73 was enough to win him the title. Once again it was the inexhaustable Palmer who was higher placed, in fifth position, than any previous Open winner.

Hale Irwin played solid but unspectacular golf for a final-round 73 in 1974. It was good enough to get him home by two strokes from Forrest Fezler with a seven-over-par total of 287.

H. W. Neale

U.P.I.

U.P.I.

Scenes from the US Open. The tournament is the one that every professional golfer wants to win, for it sets him on the road to big money.
1 Lee Trevino kicks out as much in relief as exultation as he sinks his putt to par the 14th at Merion in the play-off with Jack Nicklaus for the 1971 US Open. He went on to record a 68 and beat Nicklaus by three strokes to put his name on the trophy for a second time.
2 and **3** Jack Nicklaus in play at Pebble Beach in 1972, where his 290 total was good enough to give him his third championship in 11 years.
4 A moment of muted triumph for Johnny Miller as he pars the final hole at Oakmont in 1973 to card a record 63. One by one the challenges melted in the face of this onslaught, and Miller, who had begun the final round in joint 13th place and six strokes off the lead, beat John Schlee by one for the $35,000 first prize. **5** and **6** There are some illustrious names on the scoreboard as unfancied Hale Irwin lines up and then holes a putt during the final round of the 1974 Open at Winged Foot. A former college football star from Missouri, Irwin had made steady but undramatic progress on the US tour in the 1970s, and this was his first major title.

U.P.I.

BEARD
YANCEY
FEZLER
GRAHAM
PALMER
PLAYER
NICKLAUS
WEISKOPF

Australasian and Far East Golf Circuit

In typical fashion, the Far East golf circuit, once the province of Australia, is now coming under the domination of Japan. By far the most lucrative rewards are to be won under the flag of the Rising Sun, including the richest —though so far not the most prestigious—prize in the world.

For many years Australia and New Zealand were the only spheres of golfing influence in that part of the world, and both countries were able to breed a constant flood of proficient players who eventually headed for the richer pastures of Europe and America. In return, many of the more prominent international golfers would make sporadic assaults on the brief Australian and New Zealand tour.

This was particularly true in the second half of the 1960s when an administrative overhaul relaunched the Australian Professional Golfers' Association as a streamlined body that aggressively pursued sponsorship. The sponsors in turn recognized the value of world stars to whom they offered generous appearance money to play in tournaments, and a thriving circuit was established.

The Australian tour begins in the spring at the end of October and runs over into early February, with the short New Zealand tour sandwiched in the middle. An inevitable difficulty of the circuit has always been the distance between venues, for with 1,500 miles separating the courses of Perth and its closest neighbouring capital, Adelaide, the upheavals and travel involved do not endear it to visiting professionals.

It is not surprising to discover how long the major championships of the two countries remained the monopoly of the home professionals, unbroken for many years except by the globe-trotting South Africans, Bobby Locke and Gary Player. But the prize money offered in Australia almost trebled between 1967 and 1969, and although it has grown at a more moderate pace since, it was enough to persuade such players as Palmer, Nicklaus, and Trevino that Australia was worth a trip during their own closed season.

In the rest of Asia, too, golf has grown apace, and the Australian circuit itself is now only the centrepiece for a larger circuit. From February to April the Asian golf circuit takes place, 10 national Opens offering a total prize money of US $150,000 in 1974, and in July, August, and September the Australian tour is foreshadowed by the Japanese tour, unquestionably the richest

sector of the whole Far East circuit. Five years ago, the Japanese tour had total prize-winnings of £40,000 to be won. In 1974 the Japan Open alone was worth over £42,000.

The greatest barrier the Japanese have found obstructing the growth of their tour as a rival to the American circuit is chronological order. The American tour existed first and has a prestige the most uninhibited prize money in the world would find difficult to equal. In addition, the American PGA retains tight rules that forbid tournament players, with few exceptions, from competing in events overseas when they run concurrently with official American tournaments. At present, the only successful bait the Japanese have offered the United States is an annual stroke-play international between the two countries at the tailend of the American season. Teams of 10 players oppose each other for a team prize, with massive winnings for the best individuals acting as subsidiary inducements.

Nonetheless, the pickings of the Japanese season have deterred many Antipodean stars from making the journeys to Europe and America which would otherwise have been their inevitable fate. Graham Marsh, who would surely be among the top 10 golfers in the world had he chosen to leave Australasia more frequently, is the most notable star to indicate a preference for his enlarged home circuit. He is well supported by others, such as Australia's Billy Dunk and Ted Ball, and Walter Godfrey from New Zealand.

Their numbers are swelled by a new generation of Asian stars. The most famous of these is Lu Liang Huan of Taiwan, who first drew attention for his close pursuit of Lee Trevino in the 1971 British Open. The most regular of the Asian players to compete outside his own hemisphere, the courteous 'Mr Lu' has enjoyed success on almost every continent in the world, a feat still to be emulated by his fellow Asian pros. But Japan's Masashi 'Jumbo' Ozaki, a prodigious prize-winner, and Isao Aoki have already shown in their occasional forays overseas that they have the potential to challenge the best players in the Western world.

The Australian Open, however, still remains the primary star of the Far East tour. Year after year, it draws home local stars like Bruce Crampton, Bruce Devlin, and David Graham, and New Zealander John Lister, from the American tour, anxious to demonstrate their ability to their home crowds. At least a few top Americans are always present as well, while Britain makes a substantial contribution with such players as Maurice Bembridge, a confirmed addict of the Australian tour. And never far away are

Colour Sport

H. W. Neale

4

H. W. Neale

1 The only left-hander in golf's top money-winners, New Zealand Bob Charles is recognized as one of the most skilful putters. He won the New Zealand Open in 1954 and 1966, breaking an Australian monopoly in the event since 1953. 2 American star Jack Nicklaus contributed to the almost complete overseas domination of the Australian Open in the 1960s by capturing it in 1964 and 1968. 3 South African globetrotter Gary Player's record in the Australian Open is even better—four wins in eight years, from 1958 to 1965. He was beaten by just one stroke in 1968 by Jack Nicklaus, but won the Wills Masters later on the tour. 4 Guy Wolstenholme left his native Britain to settle in Australia in the late 1960s and play the Australasian and Far East tours. His consistently high placings made this financially viable. 5 Lu Liang Huan (Taiwan) was one of the first Asian golfers to win world recognition. He came joint third in the 1966 World Cup and joint sixth in 1968. 6 Australian Peter Thomson's successes in his own Open do not compare with his record in the New Zealand Open, which he won 8 times in 16 years from 1950.

6

5

multiple winners and challengers like Peter Thomson, Kel Nagle, and Bob Charles.

The future of the Far East circuit is still uncertain. It has been moulded together over the years as a rich and fluid tour, yet through circumstances, much of it remains closed to the established stars of world golf. It has succeeded in proving how international golf has become; while the calibre of the Australians has never been doubted, the skills of the golfers from Japan and Taiwan, and individuals like the Philippines' Ben Arda have now become known beyond their own continent. But if the Americans and the British refuse to come regularly to the Far East, the question must arise whether the Asian golfers will succumb to the temptation to move west.

AUSTRALIAN OPEN GOLF CHAMPIONSHIP (from 1946)

1946	Ossie Pickworth (Aus)
1947	Ossie Pickworth (Aus)
1948	Ossie Pickworth (Aus)
1949	E. Cremin (Aus)
1950	Norman von Nida (Aus)
1951	Peter Thomson (Aus)
1952	Norman von Nida (Aus)
1953	Norman von Nida (Aus)
1954	Ossie Pickworth (Aus)
1955	Bobby Locke (SA)
1956	Bruce Crampton (Aus)
1957	Frank Phillips (Aus)
1958	Gary Player (SA)
1959	Kel Nagle (Aus)
1960	Bruce Devlin (Aus)
1961	Frank Phillips (Aus)
1962	Gary Player (SA)
1963	Gary Player (SA)
1964	Jack Nicklaus (USA)
1965	Gary Player (SA)
1966	Arnold Palmer (USA)
1967	Peter Thomson (Aus)
1968	Jack Nicklaus (USA)
1969	Gary Player (SA)
1970	Gary Player (SA)
1971	Jack Nicklaus (USA)
1972	Peter Thomson (Aus)
1973	Jesse Snead (USA)
1974	Gary Player (SA)
1975	Jack Nicklaus (USA)

NEW ZEALAND OPEN GOLF CHAMPIONSHIP (from 1946)

1946	R. H. Glading (NZ)
1947	R. H. Glading (NZ)
1948	Alex Murray (NZ)
1949	James Galloway (NZ)
1950	Peter Thomson (Aus)
1951	Peter Thomson (Aus)
1952	Alex Murray (NZ)
1953	Peter Thomson (Aus)
1954	Bob Charles (NZ)
1955	Peter Thomson (Aus)
1956	N. W. Berwick (Aus)
1957	Kel Nagle (Aus)
1958	Kel Nagle (Aus)
1959	Peter Thomson (Aus)
1960	Peter Thomson (Aus)
1961	Peter Thomson (Aus)
1962	Kel Nagle (Aus)
1963	Bruce Devlin (Aus)
1964	Kel Nagle (Aus)
1965	Peter Thomson (Aus)
1966	Bob Charles (NZ)
1967	Kel Nagle (Aus)
1968	Kel Nagle (Aus)
1969	Kel Nagle (Aus)
1971	Peter Thomson (Aus)
1972	Billy Dunk (Aus)
1973	Bob Charles (NZ)
1974	Bob Gilder (USA)
1975	Billy Dunk (Aus)

Above, **Australian Jack Newton.** *Right,* **Masashi 'Jumbo' Ozaki, golden boy of Japanese Golf.**

H. W. Neale

South African and African Golf Circuits

Ambitious plans for the future provide the optimistic keynote for the rapidly developing South African summer professional golf circuit, which grew from humble beginnings into one of the world's leading money-spinners, particularly in the 1960s. Essentially a domestic provincial circuit in pre-World War II years, it developed into one of international stature with prize money rising year after year and with no immediate end in sight.

The 1971 circuit boasted a prize money total of R130,000 (£75,000), which has escalated each year. Even the poorest tournaments were able to offer the 1974 winner a cheque for over £6,000, while tournaments like the Golf Classic—well down in the list of prestige events—cajoled entrants with prizes of over £12,000.

The South African summer circuit usully takes place between December and March with the Natal, Transvaal, Western Province and South African Open championships as the major events. In the later 1960s a number of sponsors came into the game, and among tournaments destined to join the long-life Dunlop Masters event as permanents on the South African

circuit are: the General Motors Open, at Wedgewood near Port Elizabeth, the South African PGA Championships, and the Schoeman Park '4000' in the Orange Free State.

The Transvaal, Natal, and Western Province opens are held in their own domestic provinces each summer. Likewise the General Motors and Schoeman Park opens are held at the same venues each year. The Dunlop Masters and the South African Open are played in a different centre each year, alternating between coastal and inland courses.

Perhaps the development of the South African circuit, which in 1971 comprised 10 major tournaments, including the Swazi Invitational at Mbabane, can best be judged in the growth rate of the Dunlop Masters. In 1923, when Dunlops first backed the South African Professional Match-Play Championship (to become the South African Masters stroke-play even in 1960), prizes were limited to about £50 in sports goods. In 1971 the Dunlop Masters was worth £5,800 with a £1,150 first prize—second only to the South African Open in national prestige value. Yet only three years later, the tournament prize money had again risen out of all proportion to total £22,000, an accurate reflection of the erupting value of the circuit.

The South African Open, backed by the BP Petroleum and Ford Motor companies, had its prize-money trebled from 1965 to 1970. Only the Natal Open lagged behind a trifle, but there were

hopes for a change for the better here as well.

If there remains one doubt about the growing potential of this young giant of the golf scene, it is perhaps South Africa's *apartheid* policy. Domestic pressures may inhibit some of the better American and European golfers from visiting South Africa as the political climate continues to become more heated.

There is also the problem of how golfers are going to have the time and energy to play in South Africa; the circuit overlaps the big American tour, and if the South African circuit were moved so that it began earlier in the year, say in October, it would clash with the Australasian circuit. The problems of making the South African Circuit an integral part of the world golf scene is huge, but many young European professionals have made their names in the lucrative South African tournaments, and others are sure to follow.

A new development has been heralded in Africa in the 1970s, the introduction of a substantial Black Africa circuit. This tour to date has concentrated round Kenya, Zambia, and Nigeria, and consists of about a dozen events including the national open of each country. It follows on from the South African season, and has grown to offer competitive prize money, with cheques for first place rapidly approaching the £2,000 target. Since 1971, the golf administrators from the three countries have been meeting constantly to seek a formula to

From the South African Open. 1 British star Peter Oosterhuis chalked up some of his early successes on the South African circuit. 2 South Africa's Denis Hutchinson won his native Open in 1959.

standardize the tour and attain standards high enough to attract the golfers already drawn to the neighbouring South African tour. Most of their efforts have so far fallen through, but every year about 50 middle-ranking British professionals, with a sprinkling of their more successful fellows and a handful of Commonwealth golfers, winter in these countries and return with sufficient earnings to fund their early weeks on the European circuit.

Contemporary with this move on the part of the African nations was the onslaught of golf in Morocco, on the North African coast. This began as a sudden fettish of the Moroccan king, but golf courses blossomed throughout the country and several events carrying inflated prize money were inaugurated. The richest of these carried a first prize of £8,000 in 1974, and Billy Casper was just one 'name' player making a regular trek to spend a luxurious and profitable week on the Mediterranean in November.

For all this activity, though, the South African circuit remains the premier tour on the African continent. Few golfers would scorn the glory of picking up one of the major South African events, with the Open still an outstanding challenge for any golfer of repute.

South African Open Golf Championship

The annual highlight of the South African circuit is the country's Open championship, carrying prize money of over £20,000. Inaugurated in 1907, the tournament has been remarkable for the domination of three golfers—Bobby Locke, who won it a record nine times; Sid Brews, who won eight times; and Gary Player, who equalled that total in 1972.

The early years of the event meant victory for the Fotheringham brothers: George won in 1908, 1910, 1911, 1912, and 1914, and brother John in 1909. Sid Brews's brother, Jock, was also an outstanding figure in his national tournament, winning four times before World War II.

But the two giants of the modern era are Bobby Locke and Gary Player. Locke first won when he was a slim youngster of 17, in 1935, at Parkview in Johannesburg. Successive wins from 1937 to 1940, and 1946 (the war intervening), and further wins in 1950, 1951, and 1955 stamped him as one of the most consistent golfers of his day. His score of 272 in the 1951 Open at Kensington was still a record for the event in 1971. Locke's final victory, in 1955, was followed by the first win of his successor as South Africa's top golfer—Gary Player, then a stripling barely out of his teens. He won the South African Open from 1965 to 1969, equalling Locke's record of five successive victories.

The 1971 tournament was tinged with controversy. Five strokes down after three rounds, Player swept home with a last round of 65—with seven successive birdies from the 9th to the 15th—but still lost by one stroke to Simon Hobday of Rhodesia. Hobday had been bunkered at the 14th, and in trying to get out he thought the ball might have touched his foot. Spectators claimed the ball could not have touched him, but it was only after a 20-minute debate *in camera* that the South African Golf Union declared him the winner.

With the expansion of the South African circuit, the South African Open became a more important event, with a consider-able challenge from European players wintering abroad. Thus, in 1970 Britain's Tommy Horton had become the first non-South African to win—a sure sign of the times in a game ever becoming more and more international.

Young South African Bobby Cole looked to be taking over Gary Player's mantle in 1974 when he shot a last-round 64 to win by four strokes. But Player served notice at Cape Town a year later with his ninth victory, by six strokes, that he was still in the driving seat, and is not going to give it up easily.

1 Gary Player holes out in 1966 for his fourth title. 2 and 3 Britain's Tommy Horton, the first overseas winner of the title.

SOUTH AFRICAN OPEN GOLF CHAMPIONSHIP
Winners since 1946

Year	Winner	Year	Winner
1946	A. D. Locke	1961	R. Waltman
1947	R. W. Glennie	1962	H. Henning
1948	M. Janks	1963	R. Waltman
1949	S. F. Brews	1964	A. Henning
1950	A. D. Locke	1965	G. Player
1951	A. D. Locke	1966	G. Player
1952	S. F. Brews	1967	G. Player
1953	J. R. Boyd	1968	G. Player
1954	R. C. Taylor	1969	G. Player
1955	A. D. Locke	1970	T. Horton
1956	G. Player	1971	S. Hobday
1957	H. Henning	1972	G. Player
1958	A. A. Stewart	1973	R. Charles
1959	D. Hutchinson	1974	R. Cole
1960	G. Player	1975	G. Player

United States Masters

The United States Master golf tournament stands comfortably as one of the four most important events in the world, the others being the US Open, the US PGA, and the British Open. But only the Masters is played on the same course every year, and it is in many ways a unique tournament. Held early in the American golfing year, in April, it is therefore, depending on the personality of the winner, worth more financially than any of the other three sides of golf's 'quadrilateral'.

From humble beginnings in 1934, the Masters has become the biggest spectacle of all. Colourful azaleas and dog wood provide the floral background to golf's most picturesque setting. No detail of planning is overlooked, and over all broods the spirit of the great Bobby Jones. It was he who, after visiting Augusta, 180 miles north of his home town of Atlanta in Georgia, conceived the idea of building a superlative golf course, one that would at the

This miniature of the Augusta National's Club House serves as the permanent Masters Tournament Trophy. Designed by a firm of silversmiths in Chicago and built by hand in England, this trophy is comprised of 900 separate pieces of silver. On the band around the base of the trophy are the names of the past winners. A small replica of this trophy will be presented each year to the winner of the Masters.

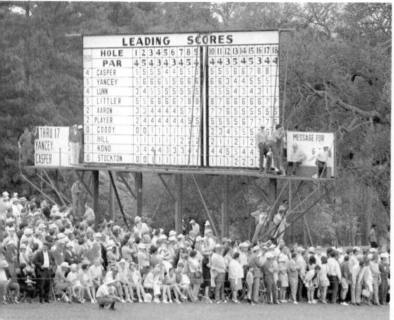

LEADING SCORES

HOLE	1	2	3	4	5	6	7	8	9	10	11	12	13	14	15	16	17	18
PAR	4	5	4	3	4	3	4	5	4	4	4	3	5	4	5	3	4	4
4 CASPER	5	5	5	5	4	4	5	5	6	5	5	6	6	7	8	8		
5 YANCEY	5	6	6	6	5	5	6	6		6	6	3	4	4	5	5	5	
4 LUNN	3	4	5	5	5	5	5	5		5	5	5	4	3	4	3	1	
5 LITTLER	5	5	6	6	6	7	8	8		8	7	6	6	6	6	7		
2 AARON	3	3	4	4	4	4	5	7		7	7	6	5	5	5	5	5	
2 PLAYER	2	4	4	4	4	4	5	5		5	5	5	5	6	7	7	7	5
0 COODY	0	0				1	1	1	1	2	3	4	5	5				
HILL					1	1		2	2	2	1	1	2	2				
KONO	3	4	4	3		3	3		4	4	5	5	4	4				
0 STOCKTON	0	0			1	1	1	1		1	2	2	3					

THRU 17
YANCEY
CASPER

MESSAGE FOR

Above, **The scoreboard at the 18th in 1970, when Billy Casper beat Gene Littler in a play-off.** *Right,* **Gene Sarazen, still going strong in 1970, won the second ever Masters.**

Opposite page, **The Augusta National course provides spectators with a picturesque setting to watch the best golfers battle for the title and the superb trophy** *(below).*

same time test the experts but which the average players could manage and above all enjoy.

A famous Scottish golf course architect, Dr Alister Mackenzie, began work on the course in 1931 under Jones's supervision. The chief features of the Augusta National course are its water hazards, which dominate several of the last nine holes and add to the beauty of the scene. But at the same time they provide for the best players a challenge which is the true secret of the Masters. Boldness is rewarded by birdies at the long holes and by tee shots close to the pin at the short ones, but disaster is never far away. Wide fairways and few bunkers—they number under 40, whereas most championship courses have well over 100—mean that from the forward tees the average player often scores better than the expert in relation to his handicap. Even so, only careful placing of the drive and accurate second shots to undulating greens secure low scores.

The usual length of the course for championship purposes is 6,850 yards. By 1974, only three players had scored 64 on it—Lloyd Mangrum when he was runner-up to Jimmy Demerat in 1940 was the first, and he was followed by Jack Nicklaus as he recorded his second victory in 1965. Nicklaus's round caused Bobby Jones to remark: 'He plays a game with which I am not familiar.' The third 64 was

the most surprising, the last round contribution from Britain's Maurice Bembridge, playing the course for the first time in the 1974 event. Bembridge's score could do no more than pull him into joint ninth position, but when he sank a long, difficult birdie putt on the last green, his ovation from the packed stand was greater than that reserved for Gary Player, the eventual winner.

Over the years the Augusta course has been the scene of some of golf's greatest moments, and of some of golf's finest shots. The best-remembered shot is Gene Sarazen's double-eagle (in British parlance an albatross) at the 520 yard 15th in 1935. Taking a four-wood from 220 yards out he attacked the hole (across a water hazard), and miraculously, holed out. Craig Wood, who in the inaugural Masters the previous year had had victory snatched from him when Horton Smith holed from 20 feet at the 71st hole for a birdie, had completed his four rounds for a total of 282 and was being treated by everyone as the winner, but Sarazen's now-legendary stroke — gaining him three strokes on par—enabled him to catch up and win the play-off.

In 1956, Ken Venturi came near to being the first amateur to win, but Jack Burke made up 8 strokes in the final round as Venturi slumped to 80. Even then, Burke's four-round total of 289 equalled the highest ever winning score.

In 1957 Doug Ford won in the grand manner: a final round of 66 finishing with a birdie at the 18th by means of holing a bunker shot. In 1959 Art Wall made up 6 strokes on Arnold Palmer and Stan Leonard with a final 66, in which he birdied five of the last six holes. In 1968, a year which appeared uneventful up to the last moment, Roberto de Vicenzo, the popular Argentinian, signed

Ed Lacey

Ed Lacey

59

his card incorrectly and lost the chance of a play-off with Bob Goalby, the eventual winner. A birdie of three had gone down on his card as a four at the 17th and, according to the rules, had to stand. De Vicenzo had begun that final round with an eagle two and two birdies.

Much of the drama of Augusta is concerned with low scores and spectacular shots, but tales of woe are not absent from the courses. In 1935 Frank Walsh used up 12 strokes on the par-5 8th. Herman Barron took 11 in 1950 at a short hole, the 6th, and the following year Dow Finsterwald also took 11 at a short hole, this time the 12th. This hole typifies the hazards of Augusta's second nine. It measures no more than 155 yards, but it is half ringed by water and a ditch, and a bunker lies beyond it. The green is only 30 feet in depth, and with the wind swirling in eddies above it because of a nearby tree formation, great accuracy is needed. Severe pin-placing at most holes adds to the difficulties. The greens generally are not too difficult to hit, but unless the approach is unusually accurate and frequently bold, three putts are all too likely on the plush surfaces.

The glamour of the Masters is augmented by the appearance year after year of many of the great names of golf. Jones originally intended to invite some of his friends from among the best amateurs and professionals, but as the event grew it became every golfer's ambition to play in the Masters and even to be invested with the famous green jacket which is annually awarded to the winner. And although the event has fixed conditions of entry, it remains a private competition for which an invitation is needed. It was always Jones's wish that there should be a strong amateur element in the field, and although no amateur has ever won, three have been second—Ken Venturi, (1956), William Patton (1954), and Charles Coe (1961). In the 1960s, Augusta's benevolent dictator, Cliff Roberts, took steps to increase the international representation. Leading professionals in the British Order of Merit appear, as do the leading players from Europe and Asia.

But in the first 38 tournaments, there was only one foreign winner —South Africa's Gary Player, whose first victory in 1961 was said to have earned him a million dollars. It seems, however, that America's monopoly of the Masters could soon be broken, for Player won again in 1974, while the previous year, Peter Oosterhuis had made Britain's strongest ever challenge, leading the tournament by three clear strokes as he entered the final round, only to slip back to joint third position. Bembridge's record equalling 64 in 1974, coupled with some impressive performances

from other guests from Africa, Australia, and the Far East, also indicates that at last the overseas players are beginning to shed their awe of the Masters.

After the tournament, the new US Masters champion is fitted with a green jacket which has to be kept in the clubhouse, for he has a lifelong invitation to return there. This, together with the setting, adds greatly to the atmosphere of the tournament. There is hardly one big name missing from the list of Masters winners—Nelson, Sarazen, Snead, Demaret, Nicklaus, Palmer, Player, and Billy Casper are only a few. Byron Nelson, himself a former Master, takes part in the full programme of television which covers the contest.

Against a background of the old, Colonial-style clubhouse, with its drive lined with magnolia trees and its staff of Negroes, the leading personalities of the golf world meet in weather which has generally maintained a high standard of excellence. The occasion is not spoiled by hordes of spectators, as there is parking space only for 10,000 cars, and thus attendance is limited. All tickets except a few day-to-day tickets are sold months in advance. Because of the warm weather which prevails for the Masters, many spectators sit in stands in the shade at certain vantage points. Others can walk between stately pines, junipers, and flowering peach.

Giant information boards at

intervals round the course keep spectators informed of the hole-by-hole position of the leaders. And the press centre, with about 100 typewriters, is one of the largest and best thought-out in the world. Thousands of agency reports and special articles emanate from there to keep the world informed about the tournament's progress. Bulletins from the tournament committee begin to be circulated early in the year, covering everything from the latest exemptions to the probable state of the azalea blossom behind the 13th green.

However, not everyone has found the tournament idyllic. A few have found the control of the event autocratic. Lee Trevino was, for a time, one of these, and rather than open his mouth too wide in the hushed Georgian atmosphere decided to stay away. Some American professionals think that there should be more of their ilk taking part and not so many outsiders—amateurs and foreigners. There used to be mutterings that the exclusiveness of the Masters extended to colour, but these were silenced in 1974, when Lee Elder, the leading Black golfer on the American tour, qualified by winning the Monsanto Open at the Pensacola Country Club in an emotion-charged play-off with Peter Oosterhuis.

In the event, the strain on Elder was too much for him to produce his best in the 1975 tournament, but what a com-

petition it proved to be. The great Jack Nicklaus emerged from a three-cornered dog-fight with Tom Weiskopf and Johnny Miller to win by one stroke and chalk up his fifth Masters—a record. And Hale Irwin shot a final-round 64 to equal another Masters record.

Elder's appearance in 1975 has strengthened the right of Roberts and his men to invite whom they will and reject any player who does not measure up to the high standard of sportsmanship required. Skill is the first requirement to play in the tournament, but the ability to put the game before the individual is also demanded. That is one reason why no form of advertising is allowed on the course and why prize money is controlled. Every player is assured of a substantial reward, but the real prize for the Masters is merely being allowed to play in it, and the famed green jacket is a bonus for the winner.

Texan Charles Coody won the Masters in 1971, making up for his disastrous finish in 1969, when he blew the lead with bogeys at the last three.

UNITED STATES MASTERS TOURNAMENT

Year	Winner	Score
1934	Horton Smith	284
1935	Gene Sarazen*	282
1936	Horton Smith	285
1937	Byron Nelson	283
1938	Henry Picard	285
1939	Ralph Guldahl	279
1940	Jimmy Demaret	280
1941	Craig Wood	280
1942	Byron Nelson*	280
1946	Herman Keiser	282
1947	Jimmy Demaret	281
1948	Claude Harmon	279
1949	Sam Snead	283
1950	Jimmy Demaret	282
1951	Ben Hogan	280
1952	Sam Snead	286
1953	Ben Hogan	274
1954	Sam Snead*	289
1955	Cary Middlecoff	279
1956	Jackie Burke	289
1957	Doug Ford	283
1958	Arnold Palmer	284
1959	Art Wall	284
1960	Arnold Palmer	282
1961	Gary Player	280
1962	Arnold Palmer*	280
1963	Jack Nicklaus	286
1964	Arnold Palmer	276
1965	Jack Nicklaus	271
1966	Jack Nicklaus*	288
1967	Gay Brewer	280
1968	Bob Goalby	277
1969	George Archer	281
1970	Billy Casper*	279
1971	Charles Coody	279
1972	Jack Nicklaus	286
1973	Tommy Aaron	283
1974	Gary Player	278
1975	Jack Nicklaus	276

*Play-offs:
1935 Gene Sarazen 144, Craig Wood 149
1942 Byron Nelson 69, Ben Hogan 70
1954 Sam Snead 70, Ben Hogan 71
1962 Arnold Palmer 68, Gary Player 71, Dow Finsterwald 77
1966 Jack Nicklaus 70, Tommy Jacobs 72, Gay Brewer 78
1970 Billy Casper 69, Gene Littler 74

United States PGA Championship

The official championship for American professionals and open only to foreign players who are full members of the American PGA, the United States PGA Championship is, with the British and American Opens and the US Masters, one of the Big Four events of golf. In some circles it is also known as the tournament that Arnold Palmer never won.

Prior to 1958, the championship was decided on a match-play basis, but that year it went over to 72-hole medal play and it has remained so ever since. The players were finding the 36-hole matches exhausting, and with the ever-increasing popularity of golf as a television sport the PGA changed to the medal formula.

Played on a different course each year and in a different part of the country, the PGA offers all professionals a fair chance of winning what has always been one of the richest tournaments. For years it led the way in prize money, and even though it has been overtaken by some of the bigger, heavily sponsored events, its prize money of $200,000 is well up with the average. In the 1960s, though, there might have been one or two, especially among the superstitious, who would have thought twice about winning the PGA. With Bobby Nichols, Al Geiberger, and Dave Marr as prime examples, the championship earned a reputation for producing winners who failed to build on their success. But the victories of Julius Boros in 1968 and Jack Nicklaus in 1971 restored the tournament's prestige.

The first winner of the championship, in 1916, was Jim Barnes, a Cornishman who had emigrated to America but later returned to

Britain in 1925 to win the British Open. In the final, Barnes defeated another emigrant Briton, Jock Hutchison, and when the championship was resumed in 1919 he won again, this time from Fred McLeod, an emigrant from Carnoustie. When well into their 80s, Hutchison and McLeod were still seen each year at the Masters tournament where, as a gesture to the past, they opened the tournament by playing nine holes together.

Hutchison's turn came in 1920, somewhat surprisingly as he had failed to qualify for the event and came in only when somebody dropped out. And in 1921, the reign of Walter Hagen made a tentative start. He won the title five times to 1927, but he had to bow to his great friend and rival Gene Sarazen in 1922 and 1923 before winning four in a row. Sarazen was only 20 when he won his first title, and to win his second title he had to eliminate Hagen in the first extra-holes play-off of the championship. Sarazen won the 37th hole after playing out of a cluster of crayfish mounds.

In 1924, Hagen started his historic run that gave him 22 consecutive wins over 36 holes against the elite of American professional golf, which by then had established itself as the best in the world. His performances in the PGA earned him the reputation of being master of match-play. It was one that was well deserved, for not only was he a really great putter and player of recovery shots but he also knew how to assert his authority over any opponent. Barnes was his victim in 1924, and in the following year Hagen's refusal to accept defeat was illustrated by victories at the 39th and 40th holes against Watrous and Diegel on his way to the final. In the final against W. E. Mehlhorn, however, he began with an eagle at the first hole and never looked back.

By 1928, Hagen's attitude to the PGA Championship was becoming casual. Busy giving exhibition matches, he had to be reminded to enter in defence of his title by a telegram from the PGA. And when his long run came to an end in the quarter-finals at the hands of Leo Diegel and the PGA asked for their trophy, Hagen replied with a smile that he was sorry but he had left it in a taxi back in 1925. Fortunately, it was finally recovered.

Diegel went on to his first victory in the championship, playing some of the finest golf of his career. He beat Sarazen 9 and 8 in the semi-final and Al Espinosa by 6 and 5 in the final.

1 A tense Dave Marr watches his putt in the 1965 PGA and **2** relaxes with the spoils of victory—a cheque for $25,000 and the trophy. But Marr's failure to consolidate on his win led to speculation of a jinx on PGA winners.

61

And thanks to two strange strokes of luck he retained his title in 1929. Diegel was one-up on the 27th hole when his opponent, J. Farrell, tried to putt round a half-stymie but succeeded only in knocking Diegel's ball into the hole. Exactly the same thing happened on the next green, giving Diegel two holes and he won by 6 and 4.

These were the years when the championship, dominated by four or five men, built up its reputation, and in 1930 the final produced one of the great matches of all time. The winner was the 'Silver Scot', Tommy Armour, who had already won the American Open in 1927 and was to win the British Open in 1931. His opponent in the final was Sarazen, and they produced some of the finest golf ever played. Sarazen was one-up after 9 holes, Armour one-up after 18, and they were all square after 27. It was only when the Scot holed from 14 feet at the 36th for a birdie that he won. Sarazen just missed from a few inches closer. For the first time

U.P.I.

1 Bobby Nichols, winner in 1964 with a tournament-low 271, was another PGA champion whose promise failed to materialize. **2** Ben Hogan was a merciless winner in 1946 and 1948, years when the title was decided by match play. **3** On the losing end of the 1961 play-off, Don January made the PGA his in 1967 in the event's second play-off.

since 1920 a non-American had won the title, and in the next 40 years only two men were to emulate Armour's victory—the Australian Jim Ferrier in 1947 and Gary Player of South Africa in 1962.

The age of double victories was not quite finished though, and Gene Sarazen returned to win his third PGA in 1933. Paul Runyan, a beautiful player with no great power, won in 1934 at the 38th against Craig Wood, and in contrast beat Sam Snead in 1938 by 8 and 7—the widest margin ever recorded in the final. Those days, however, contrast with more modern times, when in the 21 championships from 1954 there were 18 winners, only Nicklaus and Player able to repeat their victories.

Before World War II interrupted the series, Sam Snead, having been twice runner-up, finally won in 1942. There was no championship in 1943, and when the little-known Bob Hamilton defeated Byron Nelson in 1944 the circuit had not returned to full strength. It had by 1946, when Ben Hogan won his first PGA, after being one down to Ed Oliver after 18 holes in the final. But Hogan played the first nine in the second round in 30 strokes and won by 6 and 4. He was equally merciless in 1948 when he won his second title. Although the PGA

62

In 1951, Snead, then 39, became the oldest champion when he carried off his third title, and seven years later, Dow Finsterwald was the first winner of the PGA under the new 72-hole medal formula, his final round 67 edging out Billy Casper. With the introduction of stroke play, the championship preserved its reputation for five years of producing winners of the highest calibre. Gary Player carried the title back to South Africa in 1962, and the following year the winner was Jack Nicklaus, who became only the fourth golfer to have captured the American Masters, Open, and PGA. He was then only 23, and playing in temperatures of 100°F shortly after returning from a much cooler Britain.

But in the late 1960s, the PGA acquired the unfortunate reputation for producing champions who were then fated to achieve little else of golfing note. Bobby Nichols, Dave Marr, Al Geiberger, and Ray Floyd all failed

Californian Dave Stockton, who pipped Arnold Palmer for the 1970 PGA title.

to build on their PGA success, suffering lean periods for some years after. Geiberger and Nichols had to wait till the 1970s before winning tournaments and coming again to the fore of American golf.

In the 1970s, the PGA regained its merited prestige as the victor's crown again fell regularly into the hands of the big names in golf. Nicklaus reclaimed the title at Palm Beach in 1971, running up a third win at Cleveland two years later, and in between his triumphs, Gary Player scored his second victory, after an interval of 10 years. The 56th championship in 1974 witnessed Lee Trevino scoring his first win in one of the most hard fought contests for years: Trevino birdied the final hole to steal a single-stroke victory from the ever present Nicklaus.

But Nicklaus came thundering back to take the title for a fourth time in 1975, at Akron. He beat Bruce Crampton by two strokes after the Australian had taken a half-way lead of three with a second-round 63, a record single-round score for the championship, and a convincing victory.

Peter Dazely

PROFESSIONAL GOLFERS ASSOCIATION CHAMPIONSHIP

Year	Winner	Score	Venue
1916	Jim Barnes	1 hole	Siwanoy
1919	Jim Barnes	6 and 5	Engineers' Club
1920	Jock Hutchison	1 hole	Flossmoor
1921	Walter Hagen	3 and 2	Inwood Club
1922	Gene Sarazen	4 and 3	Oakmount
1923	Gene Sarazen	at 38th	Pelham
1924	Walter Hagen	2 up	French Lick
1925	Walter Hagen	6 and 4	Olympic Fields
1926	Walter Hagen	4 and 3	Salisbury
1927	Walter Hagen	1 up	Dallas
1928	Leo Diegel	6 and 5	Five Farms
1929	Leo Diegel	6 and 4	Hill Crest
1930	Tommy Armour	1 up	Fresh Meadow
1931	Tom Creavy	2 and 1	Wannamoisett
1932	Olin Dutra	4 and 3	St Paul's, Minn
1933	Gene Sarazen	5 and 4	Milwaukee
1934	Paul Runyan	at 38th	Buffalo
1935	Johnny Revolta	5 and 4	Oklahoma
1936	Denny Shute	3 and 2	Pinehurst
1937	Denny Shute	at 37th	Pittsburg
1938	Paul Runyan	8 and 7	Shawnee
1939	Henry Picard	at 37th	Pomonok
1940	Byron Nelson	1 up	Hershey, Pa
1941	Vic Ghezzie	at 38th	Denver
1942	Sam Snead	2 and 1	Atlantic City
1944	Bob Hamilton	1 up	Spokane
1945	Byron Nelson	4 and 3	Dayton, Ohio
1946	Ben Hogan	6 and 4	Portland
1947	Jim Ferrier	2 and 1	Detroit
1948	Ben Hogan	7 and 6	Norwood Hills
1949	Sam Snead	3 and 2	Richmond, Va
1950	Chandler Harper	4 and 3	Scioto, Ohio
1951	Sam Snead	7 and 6	Oakmount, Pa
1952	Jim Turnesa	1 up	Big Spring, Louisville
1953	Walter Burkemo	2 and 1	Birmingham, Mich
1954	Chick Harbert	4 and 3	St Paul, Minn
1955	Doug Ford	4 and 3	Detroit
1956	Jack Burke	3 and 2	Boston
1957	Jay Hebert	3 and 1	Miami Valley, Dayton
1958	Dow Finsterwald	276	Havertown, Penn
1959	Bob Rosburg	277	Minneapolis
1960	Jay Hebert	281	Akron
1961	Jerry Barber*	277	Olympia Fields
1962	Gary Player	278	Newtown Square
1963	Jack Nicklaus	279	Dallas
1964	Bobby Nichols	271	Columbus
1965	Davie Marr	280	Ligonier, Penn
1966	Al Geiberger	280	Akron
1967	Don January*	281	Denver
1968	Julius Boros	281	San Antonio
1969	Ray Floyd	276	Dayton
1970	Dave Stockton	279	Southern Hills, Tulsa
1971	Jack Nicklaus	281	Palm Beach
1972	Gary Player	281	Birmingham
1973	Jack Nicklaus	277	Cleveland
1974	Lee Trevino	276	Tanglewood
1975	Jack Nicklaus	276	Akron

*Play-offs:
1961   Jerry Barber 67, Don January 68
1967   Don January 69, Don Massengale 71

H. W. Neale

H. W. Neale

Although largely dominated by the United States, Anglo-American golf matches are always keenly contested. The Ryder Cup, for professionals, was first held in 1927, five years after the Walker Cup, its amateur counterpart. The ladies' match, the Curtis Cup, was first staged in 1932. All three fixtures are held every two years, alternately in the United States and the British Isles. 1 A rare triumph is celebrated by the British Walker Cup team in 1971, when they short-headed the Americans by 12 matches to 10 with 2 halved. *Standing,* left to right, Warren Humphries, Rodney Foster, Michael Bonallack (captain), David Marsh, Charlie Green, Hugh Stuart, Roddy Carr; *in front,* Geoff Marks, Scott McDonald, George MacGregor. 2 A rare and famous victory for the British Ryder Cup team at Lindrick in 1957: Dai Rees (captain) displays the coveted trophy. 3 A more usual sight of a victorious American team: Peggy Conley is chaired by team-mates and supporters after clinching the 1964 Curtis Cup match. 4 Barbara McIntyre (US) and 5 Britain's Angela Bonallack, regular Curtis Cup competitors, and familiar faces on the British scene.

3

4

5

Arnold Palmer represented the
United States in six out of the
seven Ryder Cup matches
between 1961 and 1973, with an
outstanding record of 16
victories in foursomes and 6
in singles.

Ryder Cup

The Ryder Cup match, which has focused rivalry between British and American professional golfers since 1927, regained its prominence in 1969, when under the full glare of the television cameras at Royal Birkdale the contest produced the first tie in its history. The occasion was given added dramatic value because the two principal actors in the final scene were the two golfers most in the limelight of world golf at the time.

The British Isles came to the last afternoon and the last series of singles leading by two points, and when every match in that series had been decided except that between Tony Jacklin and Jack Nicklaus, the whole match was level again. Everything de-

pended, therefore, on Britain's Open champion and on the outstanding golfer in America. A distant roar announced to the crowds massed round the last green that Jacklin had holed a long putt to take the 17th and square his match against Nicklaus. The entire encounter was to be decided on the last green of the last match of the final day with the whole of the large crowd accompanying or waiting for it. The desire to beat the Americans is extremely strong—Britain has so often got the worst of it—yet the feeling predominated that a tie was in those circumstances the only possible result. They both made their fours at the last hole, both hitting the green in two. Nicklaus made his second putt of three and a half feet and then, knowing that his country could do

no worse than tie, he conceded the 30 inch putt that Jacklin had left himself, and they left the green with an arm around each other's shoulders.

The scene sealed the popularity of both players in Britain, and the stock of the Ryder Cup itself has never stood higher in Britain than it did at that hour—even during the three spells Britain had held the cup since 1927. The encounter between professionals of both countries on which the series is based took place in 1926, but is not included in the official records. It was played at Wentworth and resulted in victory for the home team by the remarkable margin of 13 matches to one. There were two big American names of the day: Jim Barnes, a lanky, sardonic Cornishman who had gone to live in the United States, had won its Open championship, and was at the time reigning British Open champion; and Walter Hagen, also a winner of the Open on both sides of the Atlantic. These two, however were beaten by 9 and 8 in the foursomes by Mitchell and Duncan, and were also beaten by them respectively by 8 and 7 and 6 and 5 in the singles. Present at that match was Samuel Ryder, head of a large seed firm, who has taken to golf only at the age of 40 but who, under constant instruction from Abe

Royal Birkdale, destined to witness the first tied Ryder Cup, watches Jack Nicklaus putt against Tony Jacklin.

Mitchell, had quickly lowered his handicap to single figures. He offered to put up a cup, and the Ryder Cup contest was born.

Since 1927 the competition has been scheduled for every second year and held alternately in the two countries. It consisted of four 36 hole foursomes and eight 36 hole singles until 1961. That year the format was changed to twice the number of matches—cut to 18 holes—and two years later an extra day was added during which eight four-ball matches were played, increasing the number of points to be scored from the original 12 to 32. Although the match was usually close in Britain, it tended to be one-sided in the Americans' favour when they were at home. Interest dwindled and the changes reflected the attempt to revive interest and

Left, **Samuel Ryder, who gave his name and the trophy** *(right)* **to the biennial match between English and American professionals. It was first contested in America in 1927.**

Radio Times Hulton Picture Library

Fox Photos

1 course with a stick after his near-fatal car accident. Their scoring in the singles was sensational: Dutch Harrison led the way with crushing figures against Max Faulkner in the top match, and only Rees and Jimmy Adams scored for Britain. The United States eventually won by 7-5.

After the customary defeat for Britain in America in 1951 (9½-2½) came the frustration of the 1953 match at Wentworth, when a British victory slipped away at the last moment. The result was the more cruel because the full burden fell on two newcomers to the team, Peter Alliss and Bernard Hunt. The other newcomer was Eric Brown, whose last-hole victory over Lloyd Mangrum, the American captain, marked the beginning of a notable run of victories in the event. Another outstanding performer was Fred Daly; in an all-Irish partnership with Harry Bradshaw he holed a

1 A loyal crowd see Dai Rees beat Byron Nelson in the first of his 9 consecutive Ryder Cup contests, in 1937.
2 Walter Hagen, who lost only 1 of his 9 Ryder Cup games.
3 Peter Alliss, Max Faulkner and Rees after Britain's only post-war victory, in 1957.

3 in a row to bring his match with Densmore Shute back to all square on the 36th tee. Both were bunkered with their drives and both reached the green in three. Shute charged the hole with his first putt and missed the one back from 18 inches; Easterbrook manfully got down in two, and the cup was back in Britain.

In 1935 at Ridgewood, New Jersey, the Americans won comfortably against what was considered one of Britain's strongest teams, although Henry Cotton (who the year before had broken the American domination of the British Open), was not in the side. Thumping defeats in the first three foursomes set the tone for the whole match. Two years later Britain suffered their first home defeat, the Americans winning the last four singles. But there were hopeful signs in the British performance, for the new names had acquitted themselves well: Dai Rees halved his foursome in partnership with Charlie Whitcombe, and beat Byron Nelson in the singles. World War II, which caused the cancellation of the 1939 and ensuing matches, damped any hope of reivival, however, and proved a much greater setback to British golf than to the American game.

The contest resumed in 1947 at the Pacific sea-port of Portland, Oregon, at the invitation of Bob Hudson, who had come to the financial rescue of the event. Britain lost all the foursomes (the top pair of Cotton and Arthur Lees going down by 10 and 9) and only Sam King won a point in the singles. Britain had reached their lowest ebb.

They did, however, make a better showing at Scarborough two years later, gaining a 3-1 lead in the foursomes. But the Americans made a fine recovery thanks mainly to the inspiring leadership of non-playing captain Ben Hogan, who hobbled round the

attract the television companies. The increased amount of play led to the teams being increased in 1969 to 12-a-side, although the number of matches played at any one time remained the same.

The Americans were not slow to take revenge for their 1926 defeat, winning by 9½-2½ at Worcester, Massachusetts, in 1927, in the first of the official Ryder Cup encounters. But Britain continued to hold their own at home for another two contests. In 1929 at Moortown,

after trailing in the foursomes, they won five of the eight singles and Walter Hagen took another beating from his fellow captain George Duncan, this time by a margin of 10 and 8. The British victory at Southport in 1933 produced the last exciting match in the series for 20 years. Britain were captained by the legendary figure of J. H. Taylor, and the two teams stood level at 5½ points each with one single still to be decided. In this, Britain's Syd Easterbrook had holed three tremendous putts

long putt on the last green to win their foursome and then crushed Ted Kroll by 9 and 7 the next day. Not the least notable winner was Harry Weetman, turning four down with six to play to gain victory on the last green against Sam Snead—one of the greatest collapses by a star player there has ever been in the Ryder Cup. If Alliss, one down and one to play, could halve, and Hunt, one up with one to play could win, the cup would return to Britain. In the full glare of publicity, which made a lasting mark on Alliss, he took four from close to the green for a six (when a five would have won the hole), and Hunt took three putts and a six when a five would have won him his match and tied the contest.

The match showed once again the closeness of the contest in Britain, and this was emphasized in 1957, when at Lindrick the British won for the first time in 24

4 Britain lost the foursomes 3-1 in 1957, but pulled back in the singles to win 7½-4½.
5 Spectators have a fine view of yet another American win, at Royal Birkdale in 1965.
6 Tony Lema (blue) follows Neil Coles' ball during a 1965 four-ball foursome.

years. It was not the strongest of American teams, and the atmosphere left much to be desired, for there was a row between two members of the British team and the Americans were discontented with the arrangements made for them. The visitors, however, won the foursomes 3-1 and nobody gave the British team a chance on the second day. That they did win was a triumph for the captain, Dai Rees, who had won the solitary foursome with Ken Bousefield and who refused to give up hope. A great send-off was given to the home side in the singles by Eric Brown with another of his four singles victories, this time over the fiery Tommy Bolt; and behind him Peter Mills, making his only Ryder Cup appearance, disposed of a worried American captain, Jack Burke, by 5 and 3. Gradually it became apparent that Britain could win, and the long afternoon at Lindrick was punctuated by cheers as British putts were put away and holes won. The infection of victory could be felt spreading through the team, and in the end Peter Alliss was the only one of the eight British players to lose his single.

American supremacy continued in their own country, and they

won comfortably at Californian desert venues in the 1955 and 1959 matches. From the British point of view these were notable only for individual efforts. The 1955 match included two players, John Jacobs and Johnny Fallon, who had not played before (and have not played since) and who were unbeaten in the matches they played. In 1959 the British team included Norman Drew, one of a select band of golfers who have played for their country at both amateur and professional level. Townsend, Oosterhuis, and

Clark later joined them. The 1959 team was caught in a ferocious thunderstorm while flying to Palm Springs and they all thought their last hour had come: they formed a club with a tie to mark the event.

In 1961 the 18 hole matches were introduced. They were successful in quickening public interest in the event, but they did not improve the British chances. Against an immensely powerful side, which included Arnold Palmer and Billy Casper for the first time, the issue was never really in

Ray Green

doubt. The four-ball matches (introduced mainly for the benefit of American audiences, who have no experience of foursomes), had the effect of strengthening the Americans' hand. Those matches have also been criticized on the grounds that there is hardly enough time so late in the year to complete them—in 1967 car headlights were switched on to enable last putts to be holed—and that they make for too much golf.

The introduction of 18 hole contests has lessened the impact of individual matches, which tend to get swallowed up in the general picture, but the 1960s have enhanced some reputations in this match. In 1967 Dai Rees made his 10th Ryder Cup appearance, covering 30 years as player and captain. He handed over the captaincy in 1969 to Eric Brown, who won four consecutive singles in the 1950s. In that decade Peter Alliss built up an enviable record in singles, having lost only 3 out of 11, winning four and halving the remainder.

In Britain the home team continued to make an excellent fight of it. Increasing emphasis was put on the event as a spectacle, and at Royal Birkdale in 1965 a high level of presentation was reached, the costs of the meeting have been underwritten by private enterprise. The result was much closer than the final score of 19½-12½ to America suggests, and the match was notable for the high standard of play, although in the four-ball matches there were two notable British landslides. Dave Thomas and George Will, four up against Dave Marr and Palmer with seven to play, lost by one hole, and Lionel Platts and Peter Butler could only halve after being dormy four on Casper and Gene Littler. But some 50,000 people had watched the contest and a new zest had been injected into the series—one that was powerfully reinforced in 1969.

The fighting quality of the British golf was maintained in both the 1971 and 1973 encounters, enabling the public involvement to be consolidated. Both matches in the end went comfortably to the United States, but it was not until the final day's singles in each case that the issue was put beyond doubt.

In 1971 at St Louis, Britain made a brilliant start to take the two-ball foursomes by 4½ to 3½, the highlight of the day's play coming when Jacklin holed a 50-foot pitch to enable Huggett and him to halve their match against Trevino and Mason Rudolph at the 18th. Unluckiest pair for the British Isles were Peter Oosterhuis and Peter Townsend, shooting the best British golf of the day in each of their rounds while falling in both series to Arnold Palmer and Gardener Dickinson. Townsend was to play superb golf throughout the match without ever

managing a win.

On the second day, in company with Scotland's Harry Bannerman, he had a betterball outward half of 29 against the mighty Palmer and Nicklaus, yet the British pairing still conceded defeat on the 18th green. By the end of the day, the position was reversed and the United States held a four-point lead, which they were able to increase comfortably in the singles.

The same story was repeated at Muirfield two years later when the Ryder Cup visited Scotland for the first time. The British team swamped the Americans on the opening day to lead by 5½ points to 2½, with the top pairing of Bernard Gallacher and Brian Barnes leading the way with victories over Trevino and Casper in the morning, and Tommy Aaron and Gay Brewer after lunch. Jacklin and Oosterhuis produced the most sensational golf, opening the afternoon with seven successive birdies against Casper and Tom Weiskopf. 'I guess you're enjoying this', a despondent Casper remarked to Jacklin, whose reply is not on record.

But tragedy struck the British camp the next day when Gallacher was confined to bed with illness, and his vital partnership with Barnes was split up. The lack of depth in the British team was quickly exposed as the Americans levelled the match. Most successful of the British were the old-timer, Huggett, and the newcomer Maurice Bembridge, who followed their dramatic victory over Palmer and Nicklaus the previous day with a win and a half in the four balls. Again, however, it was the singles that proved Britain's downfall. In the morning only Jacklin could win, and despite three halved matches, the United States swept into a commanding position that the British could not overcome in the afternoon.

The disparity in the standard of golf between the two countries was never demonstrated more than at Laurel Valley, Pennsylvania, where the 1975 clash took place. The Americans, under Arnold Palmer as non-playing captain, fielded perhaps their strongest ever side – all 12 had been winners on the US tour that year, 6 of them more than once, making a collective 23 victories. The British team could boast only three players with wins in Europe in 1975, and a total of just four victories. Comparison of career winnings was even more revealing, the US team having won nearly $30,000,000 to the British total of just over $1,000,000. So the Americans, on a course ideally suited to their brand of power golf, started as hot favourites not just to win, but to win easily. And so it turned out, for they finished the four rounds of foursomes and four balls on the Friday and Saturday

with an almost unassailable nine point lead.

However, thanks to some sterling individual performances in the singles on Sunday, the British team averted the expected massacre and salvaged a great deal of their pride. The two largely responsible for this were Brian Barnes and Peter Oosterhuis. Barnes, who amused the galleries by smoking his pipe while putting, did not amuse his redoubtable opponent Jack Nicklaus when he sank 18-foot birdie putts on the first two greens. He merged a sensational 4 and 2 winner over the American Masters and PGA champion, who had been having his best ever season. So when the same pair came out after lunch for a return match, and Nicklaus birdied the first two holes, it

looked as if the impertinent Scot was going to be put in his place. Barnes had other ideas, though, and playing imperturable golf, squared at the turn and then powered to a 2 and 1 win to accomplish the most remarkable Ryder Cup double in years. Oosterhuis also completed a double, beating the great Johnny Miller in the morning and Jesse Snead in the afternoon, to maintain his unbeaten singles record in Ryder Cup matches.

After Britain's 21-11 defeat, there were the usual cries from critics who felt it was time to scrap the fixture. But, as US captain Arnold Palmer pointed out, everyone who mattered wanted the Ryder Cup to continue, although possibly with a revised format in its grand tradition.

3

4

Colour Sport

Colour Sport

1 Billy Casper, who with Gene Littler was an ever-present in the United States team from 1961 to 1973, was second only to Palmer in matches won, with 13 foursomes and 5 singles to his credit. 2 Peter Townsend celebrates one of his putts at Birkdale in the tied match in 1969. 3 Two young Ryder Cup stalwarts for Great Britain, Peter Oosterhuis and Tony Jacklin. (*Inset,* The Ryder Cup trophy). 4 The famous American partnership of Jack Nicklaus (crouching) and Arnold Palmer study the line of a putt in the 1973 match.

RYDER CUP

Year	Venue	Winners	USA Fours	Singles	Total	Britain Fours	Singles	Total	USA	Captains Britain
1927	Worcester, Mass.	USA	3	6½	9½	1	1½	2½	W. Hagen	E. Ray
1929	Moortown, Leeds	Britain	2½	2½	5	1½	5½	7	W. Hagen	G. Duncan
1931	Scioto, Ohio	USA	3	6	9	1	2	3	W. Hagen	C. Whitcombe
1933	Southport, Lancs.	Britain	1½	4	5½	2½	4	6½	W. Hagen	*J. H. Taylor
1935	Ridgewood, New Jersey	USA	3	6	9	1	2	3	W. Hagen	C. Whitcombe
1937	Southport, Lancs.	USA	2½	5½	8	1½	2½	4	*W. Hagen	C. Whitccmbe
1947	Portland, Oregon	USA	4	7	11	0	1	1	B. Hogan	T. Cotton
1949	Scarborough, Yorks.	USA	1	6	7	3	2	5	*B. Nelson	*C. Whitcombe
1951	Pinehurst, N. Carolina	USA	3	6½	9½	1	1½	2½	S. Snead	*A. Lacey
1953	Wentworth, Surrey	USA	3	3½	6½	1	4½	5½	L. Mangrum	*T. Cotton
1955	Palm Springs, Calif.	USA	3	5	8	1	3	4	C. Harbert	D. Rees
1957	Lindrick, Sheffield	Britain	3	1½	4½	1	6½	7½	J. Burke	D. Rees
1959	Palm Desert, Calif.	USA	2½	6	8½	1½	2	3½	S. Snead	D. Rees
1961	Lytham St Annes, Lancs.	USA	6	8½	14½	2	7½	9½	J. Barber	*J. Fallon
1963	Atlanta, Georgia	USA	12	11	23	4	5	9	A. Palmer	*J. Fallon
1965	Royal Birkdale, Lancs.	USA	9	10½	19½	7	5½	12½	*B. Nelson	*H. Weetman
1967	Houston, Texas	USA	13	10½	23½	3	5½	8½	*B. Hogan	*D. Rees
1969	Royal Birkdale, Lancs.	(tie)	8	8	16	8	8	16	*S. Snead	*E. Brown
1971	Old Warson, St Louis	USA	10	8½	18½	6	7½	13½	*J. Herbert	*E. Brown
1973	Muirfield, Scotland	USA	8	11	19	8	5	13	*J. Burke	*B. Hunt
1975	Laurel Valley, Penn.	USA	12½	8½	21	3½	7½	11	*A. Palmer	*B. Hunt

*non-playing captain

Radio Times Hulton Picture Library

Gerry Cranham

Walker Cup

From a glance at the results, it would appear that the biennial match for the Walker Cup between the amateur golfers of the United States and those of Great Britain and Ireland has been one of the most one-sided in the history of international sport. The matches have, however, often been closer than the figures suggest, with the issue remaining in doubt until the last few games have been decided, and it is a fixture neither side is ready to drop. The Walker Cup provides a goal for aspiring young golfers on both sides, and in 1971, when Great Britain and Ireland won for only the second time, the match was very much alive.

The first international match between the two sides was in 1921. The previous year, an American, Bob Gardner, had reached the final of the British Amateur against Cyril Tolley, and a handful of British players had taken part in the American Amateur. In 1921, several leading Americans went to Hoylake for the British Amateur and, with international golf in the air, a meeting between the two countries was a natural outcome. The match was played before the championship was completed in one day, with the Americans, whose team included three US Open champions in Bobby Jones, Francis Ouimet, and Chick Evans, winning comfortably.

When a British team went to America the following year, a vice-president of the United States Golf Association, Cyril Walker, put up a cup, and so the Walker Cup competition was born. There were, however, none of the elaborate preparations of modern times. For example, when the British captain was taken ill, his place was taken by Bernard Darwin, who was covering the match for *The Times*. This match was played at Long Island on August 29, and resulted in a win

for the Americans, a precedent that was to be continued until 1938. The home side, should, perhaps, have won the second contest, at St. Andrews in 1923, but the Americans came with a rush in the singles, Ouimet winning the last three holes to halve his match with Roger Wethered, and America won 6-5.

When the matches resumed after World War II, Britain slipped back into her old position. In the early 1950s, training programmes and a generally more positive effort brought about an increase in the standard of amateur golf in Britain, though the results were not so apparent in the Walker Cup. Hopes were high for a British victory in 1959, but the Americans, with two young unknowns—Deane Beman and Jack Nicklaus—shattered these by winning all four foursomes on the first day. Britain did, however, manage to force a tie in America in 1965 when Clive Clark holed from 33 feet on the last green.

The 1967 Walker Cup saw

1 Francis Ouimet (left) was in the American team and Roger Wethered in Britain's when the two countries met at Long Island, New York, in 1922 for the first Walker Cup contest. Ouimet played in 8 Walker Cup matches in all, but this was passed by Ireland's Joe Carr

3 with 10 from 1947 to 1967. The splendid Carr, however, was never fortunate enough to finish on the winning side, and it was not until 1971 that American supremacy was broken. Fittingly, Joe Carr's son Roddy **2** was a member of the victorious British team.

Gerry Cranham

WALKER CUP									
Year	Venue	Winners	USA			GB & Ireland			Matches
			Fours	Singles	Total	Fours	Singles	Total	halved
1922	Long Island, NY	USA	3	5	8	1	3	4	–
1923	St Andrews	USA	1	5	6	3	2	5	1
1924	Garden City, NY	USA	3	6	9	1	2	3	–
1926	St Andrews	USA	3	3	6	1	4	5	1
1928	Wheaton, Ill	USA	4	7	11	0	1	1	–
1930	Royal St George's, Sandwich	USA	3	7	10	1	1	2	–
1932	Brooklyn, Mass	USA	4	4	8	0	1	1	3
1934	St Andrews	USA	3	6	9	1	1	2	1
1936	Pine Valley	USA	2	7	9	0	0	0	3
1938	St Andrews	GB & I	1	3	4	2	5	7	1
1947	St Andrews	USA	2	6	8	2	2	4	–
1949	Winged Foot, NY	USA	3	7	10	1	1	2	–
1951	Birkdale, Lancs	USA	2	4	6	0	3	3	3
1953	Marion, Mass	USA	3	6	9	1	2	3	–
1955	St Andrews	USA	4	6	10	0	2	2	–
1957	Minikahda	USA	2	6	8	1	2	3	1
1959	Muirfield	USA	4	5	9	0	3	3	–
1961	Seattle, Wash	USA	4	7	11	0	1	1	–
1963	Turnberry	USA	6	6	12	1	7	8	4
1965	Baltimore	Tied	3	8	11	4	7	11	2
1967	Royal St George's, Sandwich	USA	4	9	13	3	4	7	4
1969	Milwaukee	USA	3	7	10	3	5	8	6
1971	St Andrews	GB & I	2	8	10	5	7	12	2
1973	Brookline, Mass	USA	6	6	12	0	8	8	4
1975	St Andrews	USA	5	9	14	3	4	7	3

Ireland's Joe Carr play in his last Walker Cup. He had appeared in every match since World War II, setting a record that passed even the many appearances of the American giants, Jesse Sweetser and Francis Ouimet. But the Carr name was not absent from the competition for long. Joe's son, Roddy, was a last-minute selection in 1971, and he achieved something his father had never done when Great Britain and Ireland won. It was an unexpected victory, for the home side at St. Andrews was largely untried, whereas the Americans had one of their strongest teams. They had shown their supremacy the previous year in the world team championship, and their defeat was a boost for both the competition and amateur golf in Britain.

Britain's triumph did not look possible until the very last moment. After winning every one of the first morning's foursomes on either the 17th or 18th, they crashed in the singles to finish the day only a point behind. Hugh Stuart was the only winner, though Roddy Carr salvaged a half-point from the formidable veteran, 'Big Bill' Hyndman, who had never lost a Walker Cup singles. After the second day's foursomes, Britain had fallen a further two points behind, and when Bonallack went down to the brilliant Watkins in the opening singles, their cause seemed doomed. However, hopes

were revived as Stuart and Warren Humphries beat Vinny Giles and Steve Melnyck respectively, though Gordon Marks flattered against Tom Kite. Then three more victories suddenly shot Britain into the lead, and David Marsh approached the last green requiring a half against the invulnerable Hyndman to confirm victory. His jubilant team-mates hoisted him aloft as he won his match to return the Walker Cup to British hands after a gap of 33 years.

The United States inevitably regained the trophy in 1973, but not before the British Isles demonstrated that their 1971 win had reawakened their belief in themselves. This time the Americans completely dominated the foursomes, losing not a single match. But the British battled till the very end, actually coming out on top in the singles, a feat that had escaped them even in the heady days of 1971. Despite the lures of professional golf which were tempting more young players to abandon the amateur game earlier than ever, the new life in the Walker Cup had done much to restore the prestige of amateur golf.

1 A scene from the 1971 match, also at St Andrews, where Great Britain achieved a rare win.
2 The victorious US Walker Cup team at St Andrews in 1975 after their 14-7 triumph.

Curtis Cup

The biennial golfing fixture between the ladies of the British Isles and the United States, known as the Curtis Cup has resulted in a total of 14 wins for the United States, 2 for the British Isles, and 2 matches tied from its inception in 1932 to the present. When one learns that, in addition, no British team ever recorded an outright victory in America so far, the whole affair might begin to look like a one-horse race. But in defence of Britain's women golfers it can be said that their record at least bears comparison with that of both their amateur and professional male counterparts, and any suggestion that the Americans should be given a tougher test by including Commonwealth or European players has received little support.

Although the Curtis Cup was the last of the three regular golf matches between Great Britain and the United States to come into being—the official opening match was played at Wentworth in 1932 —the seeds of the contest were sown in 1905 when a party of American women golfers came to play in the British championship at Royal Cromer, and, before the

Opposite page. **Ann Irvin, the 1967 English Ladies' champion, was unbeaten in her four matches in the 1968 Curtis Cup at Royal County Down.**

event, took part in a match against the strongest British golfers available. Among the visitors were two sisters from Boston—Margaret and Harriet Curtis—and it was by their initiative that the idea of an official match between the two countries later took shape. The sisters were distinguished figures in New England life and between them won four American championships. In 1907 they returned to Britain for another championship, dressed, according to the records of the day 'exquisitely in the latest fashions which consisted of wasp waists and tiny hats

perched on elaborately coiffed hair'.

The original intention of the Curtis Cup matches was 'to stimulate friendly rivalry among the women golfers of many lands'— the inference being that the example of Britain and the United States would induce other countries, particularly France who took part in the preliminary discussions, to join later.

Since 1964 the matches have been decided by two series of three foursomes and six singles, making 18 games in all, played over two days. The gap between the first

meeting in 1905 and the inaugural match 27 years later was a result of World War I, and the financial difficulties that arose in Britain.

Although the British team had won the match at Cromer 6-1, the years between were formative ones in women's golf in the United States. In 1932 their team arrived in Britain a week in advance and practised hard. The British team included such formidable figures as Joyce Wethered, Enid Wilson, and Diana Fishwick, but over confidence proved to be their downfall, and after losing all three foursomes—a form of the game almost unknown to the Americans —they were beaten 5½-3½. A draw at Gleneagles in 1936 was the best the British team could record up to World War II. In those days matches were played over 18 holes and on that occasion the contest was finished in one day. With one match to be completed America led by one point; in the last one, Miss Jessie Anderson, who as Mrs Valentine played a conspicuous part in post-war matches, holed from 21 feet on the last green to win her match against Mrs L. D. Cheney and halve the contest.

Two years later the British team lost a chance to win in America. They were ahead by 2½-½ in the foursomes but lost five of the six singles. Here again the contest was decided by the last match and finished on the last green. Britain's Miss Nan Baird was two up with three to play but her opponent, Miss Charlotte Glutting, won the

1 Joyce Wethered. **2** Diane 'Di' Fishwick, and **3** Enid Wilson were members of the strong British team that were expected to win the inaugural Curtis Cup competition at Wentworth. However, the Americans won by 5½ matches to 3½ and began their long run of success in this ladies' transatlantic match. **4** 'Bunty' Stephens, later Mrs Frances Smith, was one of Britain's leading Curtis Cup players. She played in six matches, and captained the team in the United States in 1962. **5** Ireland's Philomena Garvey also played in six matches, from 1948 to 1960, and was a member of the team that won the Cup at Muirfield in 1952. **6** Britain's Mrs Spearman won both foursomes and halved her singles in the 1964 match. **7** Jessie Valentine played in seven Curtis Cup matches, the first in 1936, the last in 1958. In 1959, she was awarded the MBE.

last three holes and the match.

In the first two encounters after the war the Americans appeared to have regained their early supremacy, thanks in part to the inspiring example of Babe Zaharias who later started up the professional circuit. But in the 1950s a small group of British golfers put a very different complexion on the series. With only nine matches being played—between 1950 and 1964 matches were over 36 holes—a handful of talent was all that was needed to swing the advantage, and Britain found that nucleus in Miss Frances Stephens, Mrs George Valentine, Miss Philomena Garvey from Ireland, Miss Elizabeth Price, Miss Jeanette Robertson (later Mrs Wright), and, towards the end of the decade, Miss Angela Ward (later Mrs Michael Bonallack). The result was that in the 10 years from 1950, the British players gave as good as they got.

For Britain's first victory in that particular series much credit must go to Lady Katherine Cairns who by her drive and confidence inspired the members of her team. She issued instructions, that they were, amongst other things, to practise their bunker play—and she went round seeing that her instructions were carried out. The British won the foursomes at Muirfield 2-1 and it was Miss Price's victory at the bottom of the singles that secured the trophy. Miss Jean Donald, a magnificently powerful striker of the ball, was beaten on the last green in the top match after being five up with 11 to play.

Britain still could not win away from home but, after surprisingly losing the three foursomes two years later in America, they halved the singles—Miss Stephens maintaining her unbeaten record in the singles by beating Miss Lena Faulk on the last green.

The history of the Curtis Cup revolves around memorable individual matches, and one of the greatest of these was that between Miss Stephens and Miss Polly Riley in 1956. Both players were unbeaten in singles up to that point, which added spice to the contest, which as it turned out, decided the entire match. The pressure could not have been greater. The match was all square at lunch, Miss Stephens having lost a four-hole lead. She became two up again and held that for a time but was back to all square after missing the 13th and 14th greens. They exchanged the 15th and 16th holes and halved the 17th, coming to the last all square with everything (and how much it was!) to play for. Miss Riley's second missed the putting surface and her approach gave her no chance of a four, but Miss Stephens from the longer drive found the centre of the green. She won her match and with it the contest.

Two years later these two met again in America. This time Miss

Stephens needed to win to save Britain from defeat, and again she did it, striking a two-iron at the last hole well onto the green. The Curtis Cup has produced outstanding players on both sides representing all that is best in women's golf, but none has had more courage or better concentration that Mrs Smith (as Miss Stephens later became), who remained unbeaten in her five singles matches.

In the 1960s the pendulum swung back to the United States. It was their turn to find a nucleus of exceptional players. Miss Jo Anne Gunderson (later Mrs Carner), Miss Anne Quast (later Mrs Welts), and Miss Barbara McIntyre won nine American championships between them in 12 years, and not even Mrs Bonallack's brilliantly competitive spirit could overcome the genius of 'Gundy' on the three occasions that they met. Britain, holders of the trophy, went to the 1960 contest at Lindrick with high hopes, but they never looked like winning. In subsequent years they did better, but only at home. The outstanding golfers that must be able to stand up to the heat in the United States and to opponents who can produce their best on the day were not there in sufficient numbers, but that did not prevent some thrilling individual performances.

In 1964 and 1968 Britain caught a glimpse of victory but could not quite clinch it. Both these matches produced great individual performances—by Mrs Marley Spearman on the first occasion and Miss Ann Irvin on the second. In 1964 Mrs Bonallack was still playing, although she had three children in the nursery and another on the way, but leadership in the field naturally fell to Mrs Spearman, a player of great spirit who just

lacked the guns of her colleague. Nevertheless she won great credit for holding Miss Jo Anne Gunderson, and Miss Barbara McIntyre, America's two best, to halve matches at the top.

A less happy year for Britain was 1966. They were severely beaten in America where the heat and difficulty of the Broadmoor greens were altogether too much for an inexperienced side. British chances did not look bright in 1968 but the choice of venue, Royal County Down, where the Curtis sisters had played 41 years before, combined with the wonderful example set by Miss Irvin, who was undefeated in all four matches, made it one of the best of recent years. In the absence of Mrs Bonallack and Mrs Spearman, Miss Irvin played quite heroically at the top, exhausting herself completely in the process.

The British ladies demonstrated their inability to adjust to American courses yet again in both the 1970 and 1974 encounters. In 1970, after winning the opening morning's foursomes, they could win only one of the afternoon singles and were never able to recover. The story was the same at San Francisco four years later, when the 1966 score was repeated. The British team had been criticized for omitting 1973 British Amateur champion, Anne Stant, while mother of three Angela Bonallack, who had lost in the final of the 1974 British championships to American Carol Semple, withdrew from the team in protest at the tournament's declared mandatory number for the British squad in the run-up to the match.

In 1972 it was a different story, for the flat open course of Western Gailes in Ayrshire inspired Britain to produce the hardest fought match since the 1958 tie. Britain took the morning

1 Angela Bonallack chips from the edge of the 9th green at Lindrick where she partnered Elizabeth Price to Britain's only win in the 1960 Curtis Cup foursomes. 2 An anxious Isabella Robertson, a member of the 1968 British team. 3 Mrs Evelyn Monsted, non-playing captain of the US team in 1968, takes the Cup in hand for two years. It was America's fifth successive victory. 4 The Mountains of Mourne form a backdrop to the 1968 Cup at Newcastle in Co Down. 5 Shelley Hamlin, baby of the 1968 US team.

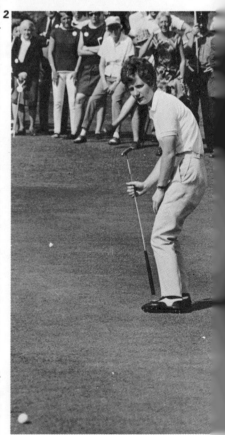

| THE CURTIS CUP British Isles v United States ||||
Year	Winners	Score	Venue
1932*	United States	5½-3½	Wentworth
1934	United States	6½-2½	Chevy Chase
1936*	tied	4½-4½	Gleneagles
1938	United States	5½-3½	Essex County Club
1948*	United States	6½-2½	Birkdale
1950	United States	7½-1½	Buffalo
1952*	British Isles	5-4	Muirfield
1954	United States	6-3	Merion
1956*	British Isles	5-4	Prince's, Sandwich
1958	tied	4½-4½	Brae Burn GC
1960*	United States	6½-2½	Lindrick
1962	United States	8-1	Colorado Springs
1964*	United States	10½-7½	Porthcawl
1966	United States	13-5	Hot Springs, Virginia
1968*	United States	10½-7½	Newcastle, Co Down
1970	United States	11½-6½	Brae Burn, Mass
1972*	United States	10-8	Western Gailes
1974	United States	13-5	San Francisco
* Played in the British Isles			

3

Syndication International

Syndication International

4

Fairway & Hazard

singles with two victories to one, including a 2 and 1 win by Belle Robertson and Diane Freason over Jane Booth and Barbara McIntire, who had been three up after 10 holes. Again Britain could only win one singles and they finished the day two points behind. The highlights of the afternoon's play was the battle between the two teenage heroines of the match, Britain's Michelle Walker and Laura Baugh of America. In halving their match, both girls were round in 75.

On the final day the foursomes were shared, then Laura Baugh crushed Britain's Belle Robertson in a David and Goliath battle to win the first of the final series of singles. However, against all odds, Mary Everard, Michelle Walker, and Mary McKenna recorded victories against the three golfers who formed the heart of the team to bring the match back to level. To hope for victory in the end was too much, but for the British team there was the consolation that they instilled an unexpected tension and excitement into the match, restoring some of the stimulus that had ebbed away from the Curtis Cup over the previous decade.

1

2

The Piccadilly World Match Play Championship, held annually at Wentworth since 1964, regularly produces fine golf from the world's leading players and has a reputation for nail-biting finishes. **1** Australia's Graham Marsh, playing out of a bunker at the fourth in the 1973 final, was involved in the most nerve-racking of all of them, for players and spectators alike, when he took Gary Player to the 40th hole before the little South African got the better of him. **2** Bob Charles of New Zealand hits an iron shot from dry ground during a very wet opening to the 1968 series, in which he reached the final only to lose to Player at the last hole in another very tight finish. **3** Britain's Neil Coles reached the first Piccadilly final, in 1964, losing 2 and 1 to Arnold Palmer. By the mid-1970s he was still the only Briton to have reached a final. Some of the leading players had been losing interest in the event, but it was hoped to remedy this situation by increasing the prize money. The sponsors more than doubled the prizes for 1976, raising their total stake from £30,000 to £75,000, allowing £5,000 each for the first-round losers, and £25,000 for the champion.

H. W. Neale

H. W. Neale

H. W. Neale

80

Piccadilly World Match Play Champion- ship

Second only to the Open in its appeal to the British golfing public, the Piccadilly World Match Play Championship is the 'raw blood and guts' of match play featuring the finest players in the world and one of the finest courses, Wentworth. In fact, such is its popularity that one year the swarming crowds did such damage to the West Course that it took a year and thousands of pounds to repair.

One look at the list of winners since its inception shows why the Piccadilly match play has drawn the crowds. Arnold Palmer, Gary Player, Bob Charles, and Jack Nicklaus have all won the championship, which has also been graced with such names as Peter Thomson, Gene Littler, Lee Trevino, Tony Jacklin, and Roberto de Vicenzo.

Yet it is not merely the star names that people go to watch. One of the great joys of match play is that it produces incidents without number. When two men are out on the course each determined to do the other down, tensions run high and on occasions in the Piccadilly's history tempers have gone perilously close to being lost.

Perhaps the most sensational incident was Jack Nicklaus' disagreement with the match referee, Col A. A. Duncan, in 1966. Nicklaus, the British Open champion, was playing Gary Player in the final and at the long ninth drove into a position where he considered a distant hoarding obstructed his line to the hole. His request for a favourable drop was refused, and after various exchanges he played the ball as it lay. Col Duncan, however, felt unable to continue as referee and was replaced by Gerald Micklem. The incident did not affect Player, though, and producing wonderful golf he won 6 and 4.

The other incidents also involved the controversial Player, for whom at times it seems as if match play might have been invented. His 1968 semi-final with Tony Jacklin produced perhaps the most unfortunate. The match had gone to the 37th, and Player,

hitting a shortish putt for a birdie four, thought he heard a woman spectator saying 'Miss it, miss it'. The ball went in, and then he walked over to remonstrate with the spectator concerned. This was understandable, but many people thought he should have waited until Jacklin, who had a putt for a half, had himself putted. Jacklin took five and lost the match.

A previous incident was not so serious though. In the first round of the 1967 championship Gay Brewer, the pair had reached the 39th in what at the time was still the longest World Match-Play game—when Brewer noticed the pin had been removed from its original position. He demanded it be replaced, and there was the

slightly comic spectacle of referee Michael Bonallack cutting out the hole with a penknife. Brewer need not have bothered: he took 6 to Player's 4 and lost the match.

In 1969 and 1970, the finals produced magnificent golf. Bob Charles' putting in 1969 was almost unbelievable. One down to Gene Littler he holed putts of 35, 30, and 45 feet at the 8th, 9th, and 10th respectively to go two up, and when Littler looked set to win, he holed a 27-footer at the 36th to save the match. Not surprisingly, perhaps, he beat a shaken Littler on the 37th.

In 1970, Nicklaus and Trevino fought their way to the final with Trevino, having played superb golf throughout, a warm favourite.

But he could not match a Nicklaus determined to add the Piccadilly to his second Open victory, and after one of the finest finals of all, Trevino succumbed at the 35th.

The 1971 and 1973 competitions were dominated by Gary Player. The final was the most memorable event of the 1971 championship, for Player covered the first 18 holes in 68, only to be one down to Nicklaus. But a charge over the first nine holes of the afternoon saw the position change, and Player, out in 32, went on to a 5 and 4 victory. Two years later, he again occupied the victor's rostrum after a nail-biting thriller against Australian Graham Marsh.

In between, Tom Weiskopf had claimed a win by beating Trevino 4 and 3. But the 1972 Piccadilly will always be remembered for the classic semi-final battle between Trevino and Tony Jacklin. Shooting a superb 67, Trevino had opened up a four hole lead on Jacklin when he adjourned for lunch. All seemed over, yet after nine holes of the second round, Jacklin was in the lead, thanks to seven-under-fours. Not until the last green was the match decided in favour of Trevino, despite a round of 63 from Jacklin.

In 1974 the championship seemed certain to fall to Player for the sixth time as he faced American Hale Irwin in the final. A comparative stranger to Britain, Irwin, despite his victory in the American Open earlier in the year, was given little chance against the experienced South African, but he dumbfounded the critics by playing skilful and steady golf to win on the 35th green, preserving the Piccadilly's reputation for the unpredictable.

Irwin returned in 1975, this time as favourite, a position he confirmed immediately with a crushing 9 and 8 defeat of Peter Oosterhuis. He went on to beat Australia's Jack Newton 4 and 3 in the semi-final, and his compatriot Al Geiberger 4 and 2 in the final for a really comprehensive victory. And he promised to defend his title the following year, when the first prize would be increased from £10,000 to £25,000 in an attempt to attract the world's top golfers again.

1 Master of the Match Play, Gary Player sinks a long one against Bob Charles in the 1968 final. **2 and 3** Jack Nicklaus, disgruntled over the lie of his ball, asks for a favourable drop and is shown the rules by Col Duncan, the match referee. **4** 1969 winner Bob Charles, concentrating on his shot.

PICCADILLY WORLD MATCH PLAY CHAMPIONSHIP

Year	Winner	Runner-up	Score
1964	Arnold Palmer	Neil Coles	2 and 1
1965	Gary Player	Peter Thomson	3 and 2
1966	Gary Player	Jack Nicklaus	6 and 4
1967	Arnold Palmer	Peter Thomson	2 up
1968	Gary Player	Bob Charles	1 up
1969	Bob Charles	Gene Littler	at 37th
1970	Jack Nicklaus	Lee Trevino	2 and 1
1971	Gary Player	Jack Nicklaus	5 and 4
1972	Tom Weiskopf	Lee Trevino	4 and 3
1973	Gary Player	Graham Marsh	at 40th
1974	Hale Irwin	Gary Player	2 and 1
1975	Hale Irwin	Al Geiberger	4 and 2

Played over 36 holes

1 The American pair Arnold Palmer and Jack Nicklaus receive the Canada Cup after their 1963 victory at Saint-Nom-la-Breteche. Heavy mist curtailed the event to 63 holes (3). **2** Encouraged by his home crowds, Roberto de Vicenzo took the individual prize in 1960 and 1970.
4 Christy O'Connor who, with Harry Bradshaw, in 1958 led from the second round and won a surprise result for Ireland.
5 In 1968, Al Balding won the individual and, with George Knudson, won the trophy (now the World Cup) for Canada.
6 Peter Thomson, architect of two Australian victories.

World Cup
(Canada Cup)

Professional golf's international competition, the World Cup came into being as the Canada Cup after American scientist and industrialist John Jay Hopkins had decided, in 1952, to use golf as a medium to promote international good will. More and more countries were playing golf, but what international contests existed, such as the Ryder Cup, involved only two or three countries. Hopkins wanted a competition open to the whole world, and from humble beginnings in 1953, when only seven teams entered, the World Cup has become just that. Backed by powerful commercial groups, it has been played in most of the main regions in the world, often in exotic settings, and has been instrumental in developing the game in widely scattered countries.

Each team comprises two players, who play one round a day for four days, the combined total determining the winning nation. Because of the small financial rewards to be won from it, and because it involves much travel, some professionals have shown reluctance to appear in the World Cup year after year. Nevertheless, many of the world's greatest golfers have appeared in the competition, and their presence has roused great interest in the countries where it is played. The extraordinary growth of golf in Japan, for example, with driving ranges springing up where land is limited, can be largely attributed to the Canada Cup being held there in 1957.

The United States, being able to call on their best players, and hence most of the world's best players, has dominated the event almost since its inception. Canada staged the first two events, with Argentina emerging the winner ahead of Canada, the United States, Australia, Germany, Mexico, and a combined team of England and South Africa. And the next year 1954, Peter Thomson and Kel Nagle won for Australia. But in 1955 the venue

moved south of the border and the host nation emerged victorious. The following year, it crossed the Atlantic to Britain, where spectators were given the rare chance of seeing Ben Hogan at his best. He and Sam Snead retained the cup for the United States, and the Canada Cup made history by being the first golf event held in England on a Sunday.

The Canada Cup continued its travels in 1957, going even farther afield to the Far East—to the Tokyo course of Kasumigaseki with its female caddies. With Snead and Demaret in the United States team, an American hat-trick was confidently expected. Instead, to the delight of a curious audience and of millions watching golf for the first time on television, Torakichi Nakamura and Koichi Ono won the event for Japan, showing, like so many orientals, a phenomenal touch round the greens.

The following year it was Ireland's turn to win, their victory coming in Mexico City through Christy O'Connor and Harry Bradshaw. There had been some doubts about Bradshaw's selection to play in the rarefied atmosphere, for he was no longer young and was no lightweight. As events turned out, he tied with Sebastien Miguel of Spain in the individual, only to lose the play-off, after he and O'Connor had taken the team lead in the second round and were never caught. The individual prize has always held an uneasy place in the tournament, for the Canada Cup was, in its origin, a team event. But over the years, with such an impressive line-up of talent competing, it has proved impossible to ignore the leading individual scorer.

Australia's early Canada Cup success was recognized when the tournament was taken to Melbourne in 1959, and the global nature of the tournament was illustrated by Indonesia's appearance for the first time. Neither Salim nor Sjamaudin had ever worn spiked shoes before and each carried only four clubs—Salim three woods and an iron; Sjamaudin three irons and a

putter. But their debut was truly shattering, Salim driving his first ball through a plate-glass window of the clubhouse. At the end of the tournament, the pair were honoured with cigarette cases inscribed 'to the players who tried the hardest'. The main prize went to the Australians, again Thomson and Nagle, who were well supported by the home crowd, some 60,000 turning out over the four days. There was another play-off for the individual honour —Canada's Stan Leonard defeating Peter Thomson.

The 1960 Canada Cup saw Arnold Palmer and Sam Snead begin a run of American victories that lasted well into the 1960s. Meanwhile the number of entrants continued to grow, with more than 30 countries represented in 1962. That year Snead and Palmer won again for America, dragging a large gallery along behind them as they moved to victory ahead of Argentina. But there was some consolation for the Buenos Aires crowd when their own hero, Roberto de Vicenzo, came storming home to capture the individual prize.

A new course outside Paris— St-Nom-la-Breteche — was the scene of the tournament's first visit to the Continent of Europe, in 1963, and though heavy early mist caused the event to be limited to 63 holes, Jack Nicklaus, with a run of five successive birdies in the final round, caused plenty of excitement. Here again the event achieved a pioneering role, for France had never witnessed such a large-scale tournament before.

A year later, players from 32 nations arrived in Hawaii armed with supplies of the small ball to counter the trade winds they expected, but never experienced. The natives said this was a miracle; the mayor of Maui attributed it to divine providence, having asked in advance the members of 14 religious faiths to pray for good weather. Victory went to the United States for the fifth consecutive time, Nicklaus finishing just ahead of Palmer to take individual honours for the second year running.

With the Canada Cup's return to Europe, however, there was a change of possession. Gary Player and Harold Henning at last broke the dominance of the United States to register South Africa's first win, thanks largely to a winning individual total of 281 by Player. Spain, maintaining the tradition that the host country makes a good showing, finished second, and for the first time Czechoslovakia entered a pair, their two amateurs receiving a great ovation.

Because of the popularity of the event when it first visited Tokyo, a return visit was made in 1966, but this time the Americans Palmer and Nicklaus were at the top of their form, setting a new aggregate record of 548 for

the four rounds—28 under par. They also became the first team, as distinct from the first country, to win the event three times. In the individual, the host professional Hideyo Sugimoto tied with Canada's George Knudson but lost the play-off, the fourth in the 14-year history of the event, which was the last to go under the name of the Canada Cup. That championship also

Ed Lacey

marked the emergence of the Formosan Liang Huan Lu, who finished equal third with Nicklaus with a last round 65.

In 1967, now the World Cup, the tournament revisited Mexico City where Palmer and Nicklaus won a fourth time and Palmer at last won the individual. It had eluded him since he had first appeared in the tournament in 1960, although since then he had won four Masters, two British Opens, and one US Open.

It was slightly ironic that almost as soon as the event discarded its original name, Canada won. In Rome, Al Balding and George Knudson were chased home by a new personality to world golf—Lee Trevino, winner of that year's US Open, who, with Julius Boros, only just failed to tie with the Canadians on the last green. But Trevino's turn came the next year when, with Orville Moody, he won the event in Singapore, having jumped on a plane immediately after losing the Alcan tournament in Portland, Oregon, in dramatic fashion.

But though the United States won the World Cup, the tournament showed clearly the increasing standards of the Oriental countries. Japan finished second and Thailand and Formosa distinguished themselves by finishing equal fifth. There were many notable occurrences that year— Trevino holing from 30 feet on the last green to avoid a play-off with de Vicenzo; and Welshman Dave Thomas holing in one on a 224-yard hole—but the lasting memory will probably be that of Sukree Onchum, the 'toy tiger' from Thailand. Just 5 ft. 2 in. tall and weighing slightly over 8 stone, he failed to tie for the individual only at the last hole. At the end of his round, he was then hoisted

WORLD CUP*

Year	Venue	Winners		Score	Individual Winner	Score
1953	Toronto	Argentina	(A. Cerda & R. de Vicenzo)	287	A. Cerda (Argentina)	140
1954	Montreal	Australia	(P. Thomson & K. Nagle)	556	S. Leonard (Canada)	275
1955	Washington	United States	(C. Harbert & E. Furgol)	560	E. Furgol (USA)†	279
1956	Wentworth	United States	(B. Hogan & S. Snead)	567	B. Hogan (USA)	277
1957	Tokyo	Japan	(T. Nakamura & K. Ono)	557	T. Nakamura (Japan)	274
1958	Mexico City	Ireland	(C. O'Connor & H. Bradshaw)	579	A. Miguel (Spain)‡	286
1959	Melbourne	Australia	(P. Thomson & K. Nagle)	563	S. Leonard (Canada)‡‡	275
1960	Portmarnock	United States	(S. Snead & A. Palmer)	565	F. van Donck (Belgium)	279
1961	Puerto Rico	United States	(S. Snead & J. Demaret)	560	S. Snead (USA)	272
1962	Buenos Aires	United States	(S. Snead & A. Palmer)	557	R. de Vicenzo (Argentina)	276
1963	Paris	United States	(A. Palmer & J. Nicklaus)	482**	J. Nicklaus (USA)	237**
1964	Hawaii	United States	(A. Palmer & J. Nicklaus)	554	J. Nicklaus (USA)	276
1965	Madrid	South Africa	(G. Player & H. Henning)	571	G. Player (South Africa)	281
1966	Tokyo	United States	(A. Palmer & J. Nicklaus)	548	G. Knudson (Canada)††	272
1967	Mexico City	United States	(A. Palmer & J. Nicklaus)	557	A. Palmer (USA)	276
1968	Rome	Canada	(A. Balding & G. Knudson)	569	A. Balding (Canada)	274
1969	Singapore	United States	(L. Trevino & O. Moody)	552	L. Trevino (USA)	275
1970	Buenos Aires	Australia	(D. Graham & B. Devlin)	545	R. de Vicenzo (Argentina)	269
1971	Palm Beach	United States	(J. Nicklaus & L. Trevino)	555	J. Nicklaus (USA)	271
1972	Melbourne	Taiwan	(Lu Liang Huan & Hsieh Min Nan)	438—	Hsieh Min Nan (Taiwan)	217—
1973	Nueva Andalucia	United States	(J. Nicklaus & J. Miller)	558	J. Miller (USA)	277
1974	Caracas	South Africa	(R. Cole & D. Hayes)	554	R. Cole (SA)	271
1975	Bangkok	United States	(J Miller & L. Graham)	554	J. Miller (USA)	275

*Known as the Canada Cup from 1953 to 1966. †After a play-off with P. Thomson (Australia) and F. van Donck (Belgium). ‡After a play-off with H. Bradshaw (Ireland). ‡‡After a play-off with P. Thomson. **Over only 63 holes. ††After a play-off with H. Sugimoto (Japan). —Over only 54 holes.

into the air by the American pair and carried off the green.

In 1970, Australia, represented by Bruce Devlin and David Graham, who finished second and third respectively in the individual, had a runaway win by 10 strokes from Argentina. Once again, however, there was consolation for the populace of Buenos Aires in the victory of Roberto de Vicenzo in the individual event.

It was Australia's third victory, but inevitably, in the hot Florida sun the following year, the United States reasserted their supremacy through the powerful team of Nicklaus and Trevino. South Africa opened a lead on America in the first round and held on to it at the halfway stage, but in the third round Nicklaus roared into full gear with a score of 63 that pulled his team away from all the others. Solid scoring in the final round left the Americans 12 strokes ahead of the field with Nicklaus, unsurprisingly, winning the individual title by a massive seven strokes.

This result was repeated almost exactly two years later in Spain, when the partnership of Nicklaus and Johnny Miller won by six strokes from South Africa. On this occasion, Miller won the individual event, with Gary Player again the runner-up.

In stormbound Melbourne in 1972, the Asian countries had at last made their long-awaited leap to the forefront in a tournament curtailed to three rounds. The opening day was beset by chaos, with some rounds taking six and a half hours, to the dismay of the established stars in particular. More protests were raised at the decision to restrict the event to three rounds after thunderous rain caused the postponement of the second round. Through it all, it was the teams from Asia that weathered the conditions and the controversies best of all. Japan led in the early stages, but the team from Taiwan, consisting of Lu Liang Huan and Hsieh Min Nan, emerged as the eventual winners, taking the World Cup to Asia for the first time. A final round of 78 was insufficient to deprive Hsieh Min Nan of the individual title. The Asians, displaying new found skill and temperament, had firmly arrived on the world golfing scene. John Jay Hopkins could look at the material achievements of the smaller golfing nations, and feel with some pride that his competition was accomplishing its original purpose.

1 Lu Liang Huan, who with Hsieh Min Nan won the shortened World Cup competition for Taiwan (Formosa) in 1972. **2** Johnny Miller (USA) won the 1973 World Cup with Jack Nicklaus, and also finished as leading individual. He is tipped as heir apparent to Nicklaus.

2

H. W. Neale

Vardon Trophy

Named after the famous British golfer Harry Vardon, the Vardon Trophy is much coveted by professional golfers. There are, in fact, two Vardon Trophies, one in Britain, and another in the United States, and both are among the most respected, but least publicized, awards in professional golf.

The trophies are awarded annually, and in the modern era of big-money golf they provide a welcome relief from the constant emphasis on money winnings and the almost obsessive attempts of golf writers, promoters, and the public to classify golfers as 'great' or otherwise solely according to the tournaments they win and the money they earn. Golf is basically a contest between the player and the course, with a round below par indicating a victory for the player. The professional aims to beat par as often as possible, and

Ed Lacey

is concerned above all with consistent low scores. In this respect the Vardon Trophy is the ultimate professional award: it is awarded to the professional on each side of the Atlantic whose stroke average in regular tournament play is the lowest for the year.

This makes the Vardon Trophy winner a sort of professionals' professional. In America the winner must play at least 80 rounds in PGA sponsored or co-sponsored events. This 80-round minimum was introduced in 1962. Before that a 60-round minimum had been necessary since 1948.

The Vardon Trophy itself, a bronze-coloured plaque measuring 39 in. by 27 in. was first introduced, on both sides of the Atlantic, in 1937. In the United States it succeeded the Harry A. Radix Trophy which had been awarded annually since 1934. It was not always awarded on a stroke-average basis; from 1937 to 1941 the winner was decided on a points basis whereby the leading players in each event received a predetermined number of points.

In the 32 times the Vardon Trophy has been awarded in the United States between 1934 and 1970, only 13 times has it been won by the top money winner of the same year. Five of these double wins came in successive years after World War II, but only

four came in the years 1951-70.

Between 1938 and 1950, the American averages were dominated by Sam Snead, Byron Nelson, or Ben Hogan, who topped the table 10 years out of 12 between them, and they also led the list of money winners 9 times —a fair reflection of their supreme position in world golf then.

In the nine years from 1960 to 1968, Arnold Palmer (four) and Billy Casper (five) shared the trophy. Casper twice won the trophy with averages below 70, and this points out the injustice of his belated acceptance by the game's fans. Professionals questioned on the fans' neglect of Casper during this period used to shake their heads and talk with awe of his Vardon Trophy averages.

The British Vardon Trophy was, until 1971, awarded on the basis of stroke averages, though the players on the British circuit do not play in as many events as their American counterparts. No individuals have predominated as they have in America. From the 1971 season, the Vardon Trophy was awarded to the leader of the Order of Merit points table.

1 Sam Snead and 2 Billy Casper both won the Vardon Trophy several times.

Ray Green

VARDON TROPHY				
Year	American winner	Score	British winner	Score
1934	Ky Laffoon[1]	72.20		
1935	Paul Runyon[1]	72.29		
1936	Ralph Guldahl[1]	71.63		
1937	Harry Cooper*	500 pts	Charles Whitcombe	71.62
1938	Sam Snead*	520 pts	Henry Cotton	72.87
1939	Byron Nelson	473 pts	R. A. Whitcombe	73.00
1940	Ben Hogan*	423 pts	not awarded	
1941	Ben Hogan*	494 pts	not awarded	
1942	Ben Hogan*		not awarded	
1943	not awarded		not awarded	
1944	Byron Nelson[2]*	69.67	not awarded	
1945	Byron Nelson[2]*	68.33	not awarded	
1946	not awarded		Bobby Locke	73.00
1947	Jimmy Demaret*	69.90	Norman von Nida	71.25
1948	Ben Hogan*	69.30	Charles Ward	71.29
1949	Sam Snead*	69.37	Charles Ward	70.77
1950	Sam Snead*	69.23	Bobby Locke	70.03
1951	Lloyd Mangrum*	70.05	John Panton	71.51
1952	Jack Burke	70.54	Harry Weetman	71.34
1953	Lloyd Mangrum	70.22	Flory van Donck	71.06
1954	E. J. Harrison	70.41	Bobby Locke	71.00
1955	Sam Snead	69.86	Dai Rees	71.85
1956	Cary Middlecoff	70.35	Harry Weetman	71.06
1957	Dow Finsterwald	70.29	Eric Brown	70.09
1958	Bob Rosburg	70.11	Bernard Hunt	71.67
1959	Art Wall*	70.35	Dai Rees	—
1960	Billy Casper	69.95	Bernard Hunt	70.29
1961	Arnold Palmer	69.82	Christie O'Connor	70.80
1962	Arnold Palmer*	70.27	Christie O'Connor	71.25
1963	Billy Casper	70.58	Neil Coles	71.73
1964	Arnold Palmer	70.01	Peter Alliss	72.48
1965	Billy Casper	70.59	Bernard Hunt	71.40
1966	Billy Casper*	70.16	Peter Alliss	70.51
1967	Arnold Palmer	70.18	Malcolm Gregson	71.11
1968	Billy Casper*	69.98	Brian Huggett	71.65
1969	Dave Hill	70.34	Bernard Gallacher	71.96
1970	Lee Trevino*	70.64	Neil Coles	70.88
1971	Lee Trevino	70.41	P. A. Oosterhuis†	—
1972	Lee Trevino	70.91	P. A. Oosterhuis†	—
1973	Bruce Crampton	70.69	P. A. Oosterhuis†	—
1974	Lee Trevino	70.53	P. A. Oosterhuis†	—

*Also leading money winner on US circuit.
[1]Won Harry A. Radix Trophy.
[2]Unofficial: Trophy not awarded.
†Leader of Order of Merit points table

Golfer of the Year Championship

The idea of bringing together the golfers of the world to decide who was the best 'golfer of the year' was first considered by two Canadians, sportscaster Doug Smith and publisher Hilles Pickens when they were stranded in a motel after their car had broken down. Their concept was thought ideal by Alcan Aluminium Limited, a Canadian metal concern who in 1966 were seeking to extend their industrial image to the domestic market. Alcan contracted with the British PGA to hold the tournament for four years, and of these one could be held outside Britain —the 1969 championship that was held in Portland, Oregon.

All golf promoters try to lure the best possible field to their meetings. The Alcan team were prepared to donate enormous amounts of prize money to make it a greater attraction, while the invited players would be the most consistent golfers in certain major tournaments on both sides of the Atlantic. But for all Alcan's efforts, some of the best golfers— including the 'Big Three', Jack Nicklaus, Arnold Palmer, and Gary Player—either did not play in the qualifying events or were otherwise committed at the time of the tournament. But a brief examination of the qualifying tournaments and the qualifiers for the first Alcan in 1967 reveals what the organizers were trying to do.

The first Alcan field was intended to consist of 15 golfers from the American circuit and 7 from the British. Twelve would be those who had scored the lowest aggregates in any three of four particular American tournaments—the Colonial National, the Cleveland Open, the Western Open, and the Philadelphia Classic. Three more would be chosen from the leading money winners on the US circuit who accepted the invitation. Five players from the British circuit to qualify would be those with the lowest aggregates in any three of four tournaments: the Agfacolor at Stoke Poges (a parkland course), the Martini International at Fulford (heathland), the Carrolls International at Woodbrook (seaside pasture), and the Dunlop Masters at Royal St Georges (true golf links). The two top British money winners were also to be invited. This method of invitation was, in theory, to ensure that the world's best all-round golfers were competing. The entrants would have proved their ability on courses of different characteristics, and would also be the most consistent.

The second 'Golfer of the Year

Championship' was held at Royal Birkdale, near Liverpool. This time the scope of the tournament had been widened to include Australia's Peter Thomson, New Zealand's Ted Ball, Cobie Legrange from South Africa, Kenji Hosoishi of Japan, and Canada's Alvie Thompson. It was, therefore, a truly international tournament, and not confined to the prominent members of the American and British circuit elites.

For the 1969 Alcan, the course

1 Billy Casper won the 1969 Alcan, beating 2 Lee Trevino in one of golf's most dramatic finishes. 3 The 1967 and 1968 winner Gay Brewer with caddie Alfie Fyles, who got a £1,000 tip after each victory.

chosen was at Portland, Oregon. The winners of the Spanish, French, German, and Swiss Open championships were added to the list of qualifiers, thus opening up the field still more. In 1970, winners of certain events in South Africa were made eligible.

Despite the initial teething troubles, the Alcan Golfer of the Year Championship has become one of the highlights of the international golf circuit. The very first championship at St Andrews in 1967 produced a tie between Americans Billy Casper and Gay Brewer, who both shot four-round totals of 283 on the Old Course. In the play-off Brewer grabbed a 4-stroke lead with an opening burst of 3-4-4-3-4 and held on to win by those four strokes. In the supporting Alcan International Championship competition, which

was held over the same course at the same time, Peter Thomson returned a score of 281—a feat that rather took the edge off Brewer's victory. But Brewer repeated his success in 1968, on a Royal Birkdale course that was almost awash as a result of exceptionally heavy rain. It had to be dried out by Bert Flack, the groundsman at Old Trafford cricket ground. After four soggy days, Brewer retained his title with a total of 283 strokes, with Britain's young Peter Townsend three strokes in arrears. For the second time Brewer rewarded his caddie Alfie Fyles with a £1,000 tip out of his prize—£19,754 in 1967 and £23,025 in 1968. The international Championship, for non-qualifiers, was won jointly by Bill Large and Christie O'Connor, each with 288 strokes. This

tournament was played from different tees to avoid comparisons and was dropped for 1969.

Possibly the most dramatic finish in the 1969 golf season came in the Alcan at Portland. With three holes to play, Lee Trevino was leading Billy Casper by six shots. But Casper played like a man inspired to 'birdie' the final three holes while Trevino unaccountably took six strokes at the short 17th. It was one of the most surprising reversals in the history of golf, and a drama that assured the Alcan of a prominent place in golfing history. Alas it was indeed to be only in history, for although Australian Bruce Devlin won another titanic struggle with thrilling golf in 1970, this tournament tolled the death knell for the Alcan. The huge cost of holding it, when balanced

against the difficulty of slotting it into an already overcrowded golf season, persuaded the sponsors that it was no longer a viable commercial proposition.

Today, the vast prizes that were the undoubted derivation of the Alcan's extraordinary spectator appeal seem common-place. For example, the first 'World Open', held at Pinewood in the United States in 1973, offered winnings to a grand total of half a million dollars. But the Alcan was a memorable experiment which almost succeeded, but at the very least, established a niche for itself in golfing lore.

Billy Casper, who lost the 1967 Alcan in a play-off with Gay Brewer, but made up seven strokes in the last three holes to pip Trevino in 1969.

1 John Panton (GB) defeated Sam Snead (USA) 3 and 2 in 1967 to end an eight-year run of American success. 2 Sam Snead blasts out of a bunker during his 1965 match with Charlie Ward, whom he eventually beat on the 37th.

World's Seniors Golf Championship

A matchplay event held annually over 36 holes, the World's Seniors Golf Championship is a head-to-head duel between the PGA senior champions of the United States and Great Britain. These two final contestants are the winners of their respective country's own 72-hole stroke-play tournament for professionals over 50 years of age.

Commercial sponsorship brought the championship into being and has determined its form since it was first played in 1954 under the sponsorship of the distilling company, William Teachers. Then the winner of the US PGA Seniors Championship played a golfer nominated by the British Association of Golf Writers, an arrangement that lasted until 1957, when the British Senior Professional Championship was inaugurated. Teachers continued their sponsorship until 1968, and until that time the world event was always played over a British course to give the American finalist an opportunity to compete in the British Open. In 1969 the championship came under the joint sponsorships of the Ford Motor Company, who sponsored the American event, and Pringle of Scotland, who sponsored the British. Also that year the World's Senior moved to the United States.

The event started out rather modestly with a £500 first prize, but by 1971 it had grown considerably in prestige, attracting a number of former United States and British Open winners, and in value, the winner taking £2,000 and the loser £1,000.

First winner of the championship was Gene Sarazen, who beat Percy Alliss, and it was not until the third final, in 1956, that the British golf writers finally nominated a winner in Bob Kenyon. In 1957 John Burton justified his earlier selection by winning the first British championship, only to be hammered 7 and 6 by Al Watrous, and the following year saw the championship change countries again when Norman Sutton beat Sarazen, who had become the first player to capture two national seniors titles.

The event really came of age in 1964, when Sam Snead competed for the first time and picked up the title two years in succession. His first win was an easy romp over Syd Scott, but his second came after the championship's first call for extra holes. Snead came to the 34th tee three up on Charlie Ward and a seemingly certain winner. Ward, however, finessed his way to take the last three and tie after the regulation 36 holes, only for Snead to win the 37th.

Fred Haas Jr managed to halt Snead's run in America in 1966, but Slammin' Sam was back again the following year, only to lose to Scotsman John Panton. Panton putted like a man possessed, and his performance so impressed the British Golf Writers that they voted him '1967 Golfer of the Year'.

The world event was played in the United States for the first time in 1969, with 'Tempestuous' Tommy Bolt living up to his reputation before finally defeating Panton at the 39th. Bolt, one up at the time, hotly disputed the referee's ruling that his ball had moved during address at the 34th hole. The Rules Committee overruled the referee and Bolt went on to halve the hole, only to lose the 36th. The next year saw Snead take the title for a third time, helped by both the heat, which exhausted Max Faulkner after he had been 5 up after 15 holes, and the controversial 'croquet' style of putting that was declared illegal later that year.

WORLD'S SENIORS GOLF CHAMPIONSHIP

Year	Winner	Runner-up	Score
1954	Gene Sarazen (USA)	Percy Allis* (GB)	4 & 3
1955	Mortie Dutra (USA)	John Burton* (GB)	2 up
1956	Bob Kenyon* (GB)	Pete Burke (USA)	4 & 3
1957	Al Watrous (USA)	John Burton (GB)	7 & 6
1958	Norman Sutton (GB)	Gene Sarazen (USA)	2 & 1
1959	Willie Coggin (USA)	Arthur Lees (GB)	5 & 3
1960	Dick Metz (USA)	Reggie Horne (GB)	2 & 1
1961	Paul Runyan (USA)	Sam King (GB)	3 & 1
1962	Paul Runyan (USA)	Sam King (GB)	2 & 1
1963	Herman Barron (USA)	George Evans (GB)	3 & 2
1964	Sam Snead (USA)	Syd Scott (GB)	7 & 6
1965	Sam Snead (USA)	Charlie Ward (GB)	37 holes
1966	Fred Haas Jr (USA)	Dai Rees (GB)	3 & 2
1967	John Panton (GB)	Sam Snead (USA)	3 & 2
1968	Chandler Harper (USA)	Max Faulkner (GB)	2 up
1969	Tommy Bolt (USA)	John Panton (GB)	39 holes
1970	Sam Snead (USA)	Max Faulkner (GB)	3 & 2
1971	Kel Nagle (Aus)	Julius Boros (USA)	4 & 3
1972	Sam Snead (USA)	Ken Bousfield (GB)	3 & 2
1973	Sam Snead (USA)	Kel Nagle (Aus)	41 holes
1974	Roberto de Vicenzo (Arg)	Eric Lester (GB)	5 & 4

*Selected by British Association of Golf Writers.

The Players

1 Bobby Jones, 2 Peter
Oosterhuis, 3 'Old Tom' Morris,
4 Arnold Palmer, 5 Tony Jacklin,
6 Gary Player, 7 Jack Nicklaus,
8 Bernard Gallacher (left),
9 Lee Trevino, 10 Ben Hogan,
11 Johnny Miller.

Central Press

Peter Dazely

Radio Times Hulton Picture Library

Ray Green

U.P.I.

Archer

George (1939–)

When George Archer won the US Masters in 1969 at the age of 29, it was his first major championship success. He had been among the leading money winners on the American golf circuit for a number of years, and this victory established him in the top rank of world golf.

Considered by many experts to be the best putter on the American tour, Archer possesses a smooth blend of technical proficiency and unflappable temperament. He would be conspicuous in tournament play irrespective of his merits, for at 6 ft 6 in he is the tallest United States professional.

Archer was born in California. After high school, he took a job on the ranch of retired brewery and cattle baron Eugene Selvage, who gave him sufficient time off to polish his game, and offered to be his sponsor. Archer met with success as an amateur, but had the good sense to wait to join the professional tour until he was sure that his game would stand up under pressure. He put in the better part of a year at the ranch hitting hundreds of practice shots a day, and only then told Selvage that he was ready.

As a consequence, Archer's professional record has not been marked by the abrupt peaks and valleys that characterize so many young players' performances. In 1964, his first year on the tour, Archer earned $15,000. He doubled that sum the following year, and then soared to $45,000 in 1966, $84,000 in 1967, and $151,000—including three victories—in 1968. His 1968 earnings put him third in the world rankings. By then his fellow professionals were saying that it was only a matter of time before Archer won one of the big ones. And at the 1969 Masters he fulfilled their predictions.

ARCHER George

Major victories

1965	Lucky International
1967	Greensboro Open
1968	Pensacola Open
	New Orleans Open
1969	US Masters
1971	Andy Williams-San Diego Open
1972	Greater Greensboro Open
	Los Angeles Open

Armour

Tommy (1895-1968)

Tommy Armour lost the sight of one eye in World War I, but went on to win every major golf championship. As an amateur, he played for Britain against the United States, and as a professional for the US against Britain —a unique achievement.

Armour was born in Edinburgh, Scotland. He played in the first international match against the United States in 1921, and settled in America in 1922. He turned professional in 1924, and played for the United States against Britain at Wentworth in 1926. The next year, he captured the US Open boldly making a treacherous putt on the final green to force Lighthorse Harry Cooper into a play-off, which Armour won by three strokes. In 1930 he beat Gene Sarazen in the final of the American PGA tournament, and a year later overcame a five-stroke deficit in the last round to beat Jose Jurado of Argentina in the British Open.

A superb shot-maker, Armour's strong suit was his iron play; he had, however, no weakness as a golfer. His massive hands contributed to his exquisite control. Known as the 'Silver Scot' by millions of sports fans, Armour was a meticulous player who would sometimes waggle the club as many as 20 times before launching into a shot.

His tournament playing days behind him, Armour forged a reputation as a teacher even more formidable than the one he enjoyed as a player. He was sought out by golfers as diverse as Bobby Jones and Richard Nixon. A stickler for the rules, Armour once saw an opponent tee up the ball in the rough. He strode over and trod the ball into the ground with his spiked heel. 'Play it from there', he barked. The fellow played it from there.

ARMOUR Tommy

Major victories

1927 United States Open, Canadian Open
1930 United States PGA Championship, Canadian Open
1931 British Open
1934 Canadian Open

1 The tallest golfer and possibly the best putter on the US tour in the late 1960s, Californian George Archer won the US Masters in 1969. **2** Tommy Armour was coming to the end of his competitive career when the first Masters was staged in 1934, but despite the loss of an eye he won every major title open to him. A Scot, he played for Britain against the USA in 1921 before settling in America and playing for the USA against Britain. He was popularly called 'the Silver Scot'.

Balding

Al (1924-   )

The best came late for Al Balding, the rangy, silver-headed Canadian golfer who won the International Trophy, symbol of individual supremacy in World Cup play. This was in 1968, when he was 44. His 274, with rounds of 68, 72, 67, and 67, was 14 under par at the wooded Olgiata course near Rome. And he combined with George Knudson to give Canada the team championship as well. Balding had been beset by pain in his shoulder, on which he had surgery in 1965. He still managed to play marvellously consistent golf to defeat leading professionals from 42 nations.

Balding was the first Canadian to win on the United States circuit, capturing the 1955 Mayfair Inn Open, and taking three other American tournaments. A force in Canadian national championships, he rivalled Stan Leonard and George Knudson for top honours in the late 1950s and the 1960s.

Balding's is an unusual success story. He never played competitive amateur golf nor belonged to a golf club. From 1941 to 1949 he did not swing a club. He drove trucks for a brewery and worked at weekends as a starter on a Toronto course, eventually becoming an assistant pro.

A pleasant, approachable man, Balding earned a reputation for helping young professionals (and some not so young) with their game. In the late 1960s he left the tournament circuit for a club job.

1 John Ball, 2 Al Balding, and 3 Pam Barton.

Ball

John (1861-1940)

John Ball was the supreme amateur golfer of the generation before World War I. Between 1888 and 1912, he was British amateur champion eight times, five with the gutty ball and three with the new rubber-core ball. In 1890, he became the first amateur to win the British Open, and remains the only British golfer to hold the Amateur and Open titles in the same year.

The story of this remarkable man is almost synonymous with that of Hoylake. The Royal Liverpool club was founded in 1869, eight years after Ball's birth on Christmas Eve 1861 in the Royal Hotel, which was owned by his father and which used to overlook the links by the 17th green. At 15 he finished eighth in the Open at St Andrews, accepting a prize of ten shillings. This provoked discussion as to Ball's status when he entered for the first Amateur championship in 1885, but there never was a truer amateur, and he was allowed to play.

It was said that Ball was the first golfer to develop accurate long-iron play to the flag; a rare control of his backswing enabled him to play every kind of half-shot. He had a wonderful facility for stopping pitches, even out of bunkers, with the straight-faced clubs of the day, His swing, effortlessly rhythmic, grooved, and powerful, gave that doyen of golf writers Bernard Darwin more 'aesthetic ecstasy' in the watching than those of either Bobby Jones or Harry Vardon.

Ball was a formidable competitor—a silent man, modest and retiring, but shrewd and resolute. He often emerged victorious from the most unpromising situations, notably in the famous amateur final at Prestwick in 1899 when he went 5 holes down to F. G. Tait but won at the 37th. Ball played his last championship in 1921 before retiring to his farm in Wales.

BALL John	
Major victories	
British Open	1890
British Amateur	
Championship	1888, 1890, 1892, 1894, 1899, 1907, 1910, 1912
Irish Open Amateur	
Championship	1893, 1894, 1899

Barton

Pamela (1917–1943)

Pam Barton was a golfing prodigy. When she was in form no other woman could touch her. She was the youngest player ever to represent Britain in the Curtis Cup, and in 1936 won both the British Open Championship and the American Women's Amateur Championship. Only one other player has achieved that double in one season, and that was Dorothy Campbell as long ago as 1909.

Born in London, Pam Barton made her debut in championship golf at 17, when she was beaten finalist at Royal Porthcawl, in

May 1934. Six weeks after she first came into prominence she was chosen to play for Britain against France. She won her first championship—the French Open —at Le Touquet in July 1934. And later that year she represented Britain against Canada at Montreal, and played in the Curtis Cup Match at Chevy Chase, Washington.

Miss Barton was again runner-up for the British title in 1935, and later that season travelled to Australia and New Zealand with the first Ladies' Golf Union team to tour there. But her really big year was 1936. In that year she established herself as a truly great golfer when she won the British Open Championship at Southport and Ainsdale, and the American Women's Amateur Championship at Canoe Brook Country Club, New Jersey. She notched a second win in the British championship at Royal Portrush in 1939, and again tried for the double, but lost in the third round of the American.

Pam Barton was killed in a flying accident at Manston, in November 1943, while serving as a flight officer in the Women's Auxiliary Air Force.

The stocky, freckle-faced red-head from Royal Mid-Surrey had a wonderful temperament which allowed her to play her own game even when she was out-hit. She had an exceptionally good short game for such a young player, and her outstanding powers of recovery enabled her to fight her way out of many tricky situations.

Her death was a major blow for British women's golf.

BARTON Pamela
Major victories
1934 French Open
1936 British Women's Championship, American Women's Championship
1939 British Women's Championship
Internationals
1934 v USA, v Canada, v France
1935 v Australia, v New Zealand, Home Internationals (England)
1936 v USA, v France, Home International
1937 v France, Home Internationals
1938 v France, Home Internationals
1939 v France, Home Internationals

Berg
Patty (1918-   )

Patty Berg burst on to the golfing scene in 1935 at the age of 17, when she reached the final of the US Women's Amateur championship at her first attempt. She made the Curtis Cup team the following year, and in 1938 won the amateur championship. She turned professional in 1940, and in 1946 became the first US Women's Open champion. She was voted American Woman Athlete of the Year three times—in 1938, 1943, and 1955—and won the Women's World Golf Championship four times—in 1953–55 and 1957.

Miss Berg was born in Minneapolis, Minnesota. Conspicuous with her copper-coloured hair, enormous freckles, and snub nose, she was a great favourite

with the crowds. Starting with a basically sound swing and style, she put everything into hitting the ball. She won more than 80 tournaments and topped $100,000 in prize money, a record for a woman golfer.

After turning professional, Miss Berg travelled extensively throughout the world holding clinics, playing exhibitions, and taking part in tournaments. A natural mimic, she enlivened her golf clinics with impressions of the hackers and the 'rabbits'. And her love of the game was demonstrated in 1948 after she had won the Western Open for the third time; she returned the $500 prize to the organizers to be used for the promotion of junior golf.

BERG Patricia Jane
Major victories
1938 USA Ladies' Amateur
1941 Western Ladies' Open
1943 All-American Ladies' Open, Western Ladies' Open
1945 All-American Ladies' Open
1946 National Open
1948 Western Ladies' Open
1951 Western Ladies' Open
1953 World Championship, All-American Ladies' Open
1954 World Championship
1955 World Championship, All-American Ladies' Open, Western Ladies' Open
1957 World Championship, All-American Ladies' Open, Western Ladies' Open
1958 Western Ladies' Open
1936 American amateur (Curtis Cup) team member
1938 American amateur team member, voted woman athlete of year
1943 Voted woman athlete of year
1951 American professional team member
1954 LPGA leading money winner
1955 Voted woman athlete of year, LPGA leading money winner
1957 LPGA leading money winner

Bonallack
Michael (1935-   )

Michael Bonallack, top British amateur golfer of the post-war years, won every major title in Britain during the 1960s. British champion for the fifth time in 1970, the following year he led the British Walker Cup team that won the trophy for the first time since 1938, at St Andrews.

Born into a wealthy Essex family, Bonallack learned his golf on holiday in Devon. At Haileybury School he was such an outstanding cricketer that he was invited to play for Essex Colts side. But after he had beaten Alec Shepperson for the 1952 boys' championship he forsook cricket for golf.

Bonallack's wife (formerly Angela Ward) twice won the English women's championship, and his sister Sally also won the title. Bonallack himself has remained unchallenged in the amateur ranks during a period in which many of his rivals have turned professional. In 1968 he made a strong bid for the US amateur

title; beat Joe Carr (who, with American Bill Joe Patton, had the greatest influence on his career) for his third British amateur title; and in the English championship at Ganton in Yorkshire, returned an unofficial record 61 against David Kelly.

In the Milwaukee Walker Cup Match in 1969, in which Britain were narrowly defeated by 10 matches to 8, Bonallack, tensed with the burdens of captaincy, turned on the full power of his golfing genius. On the Friday he had played below standard to lose his foursome with Tom Craddock. But worse was to come. Playing against American amateur Champion Bruce Fleisher, he was 5 up after 9 holes, but allowed his commanding lead to dwindle to a halved match. The following day, with great courage, he chose as his partner for the second foursomes the relatively untried youngster Peter Tupling. Stiffened by this faith in his abilities, Tupling played his part well, and the British pair won by 4 and 3. With that hurdle surmounted, Bonallack crushed the formidable Fleisher in the return singles by 5 and 4.

Bonallack admits that he has a swing 'more suited to shovelling coal'. But this very unorthodoxy, with an attendant wildness, has made him the finest exponent of the short game in the British ranks—paid or amateur. The secret of his success is his flawless play on and around the green. His main problem was to retain his enthusiasm. For this reason he even tried to change his swing in 1968.

Bonallack has said; 'When I was young enough, I wasn't good enough to turn professional. Now that I'm good enough, I am too old'. Such is the verdict of one of the last of the dedicated and successful amateurs.

BONALLACK Michael
Tournaments and awards
1961 British Amateur
1962 English Amateur
1963 English Amateur
1964 English Amateur stroke-play
1965 English Amateur, British Amateur, St. George's Challenge Cup
1967 English Amateur, Golf Illustrated Gold Vase, Prince of Wales Challenge Cup
1968 English Amateur, British Amateur, English Amateur stroke-play, Golf Writers' Trophy*, Golf Illustrated Gold Vase
1969 British Amateur
1970 British Amateur
1973 Lytham Trophy
Representative appearances
Home Internationals: 1957 1958 1959 1960 1961 1962 1963 1964 1965 1966 1967 1968 1969 1970 1971 1972 1972
Great Britain v USA (Walker Cup): 1957 1959 1961 1963, 1965, 1967, 1969, 1971, 1973
British Commonwealth Team: 1959, 1963, 1967
Great Britain v Rest of Europe: 1958, 1960, 1962, 1964, 1966, 1968, 1970, 1972
*For greatest contribution to golf in the year

Associated Press

Braid

James (1870-1950)

James Braid was one of the evergreen 'Big Three' that dominated the British professional golf scene from 1894, when J. H. Taylor won the first of his five Open championships, until 1914 when Harry Vardon became champion for the sixth time.

Although he was the same age as his two celebrated rivals, Braid was still pursuing his trade as a joiner, and playing as an amateur, while they were established professionals. Eventually he became a club-maker at the Army and Navy Stores in London, and while there halved an exhibition match with Taylor. Although his reputation grew, he did not win the Open until 1901—the last victory with the gutty (gutta-percha) ball. Nine years later he became the first man to win the event five times.

During this period Braid also won the professional match-play championship four times, and was the master of his great contemporaries. Thereafter his eyesight troubled him, but he still remained a fine player, if not quite a winner of championships. And he was good enough to reach the match-play final at the age of 57.

A tall, lean, powerful man, Braid was an attacking golfer, lashing the ball with a 'divine fury'. He was a long driver, and a masterly player of irons and all kinds of recovery shots. He was also blessed with exceptional calm and judgement, impassive in the face of disaster. In 1908 the 'Cardinal' hole at Prestwick cost him an 8 in the third round, but he showed no sign of disturbance, and his winning score of 291 remained the record until Bobby Jones beat it in 1927.

No professional ever commanded deeper respect and affection, nor served the game with greater loyalty and dignity. He gained an enduring reputation as a golf-course architect, was a founder member of the Professional Golfers' Association, and served as professional for

1 Michael Bonallack, leading British amateur from the late 1950s to the early 1970s.
2 Julius Boros, who won two US Opens and a US PGA Championship over a 17-year period, the PGA at the remarkable age of 48.

Boros

Julius (1920-   )

In 1968, at the age of 48, Julius Boros became the oldest man to win the United States Professional Golfers' Association Championship. He had previously become the oldest winner of the US Open, and has now captured over 20 major titles in all, although he did not turn professional until he gave up his accounting career at the age of 30. A top-line contender in major events, Boros earned nearly $150,000 on the US tour in 1968, and since reaching the age of 40 has earned half a million dollars on the links.

An unflappable, laconic, shuffling bear of a man, Boros probably has the perfect temperament for golf—a game that demands perfection but never permits it for very long at a time.

Boros's technique involves ambling casually to his ball on the fairway, and addressing and hitting it quickly with his lazy, fluid swing, having analysed the possibilities while approaching the ball. His swing is unusually wristy but beautifully synchronized, and grooved by years of repetition. His relaxed rhythm has contributed heavily to his protracted success.

Relaxation seems to be the Boros philosophy of life, which he practises on the golf course, and while fishing from the sea wall near his Florida home. He will often fish the ponds on a tournament course for several hours after completing a round—to relax. He prefers summer tournaments because the heat lubricates his stiffening muscles—and because the fishing is better.

Boros practises sparingly, bothered as he is by a catalogue of ailments, some of which he is not sure have been named. 'If I don't know how to play by now', he says with a half grin, 'it's too late to learn'.

BOROS Julius

Tournaments and awards
1952	US Open
	Old 'World' Championship
	US PGA Player of the Year
1954	Ardmore Open
	Carling Open
1955	Old 'World' Championship
1958	Carling's Tourney
1959	Dallas Open
1960	Colonial Tourney
1963	US Open
	Buick Open
	US PGA Player of the Year
1964	Greensboro Open
1967	Buick Open
	Phoenix Open
	Florida Citrus Open
1968	US PGA Championship
	Westchester Classic

Representative appearances
USA v Great Britain (Ryder Cup) 1959, 1963, 1965, 1967

45 years at Walton Heath where, even in his last years, he frequently beat his age.

1

Brewer
Gay (1932-   )

Gay Brewer's swing is almost universally regarded as the worst among the leading golfers of his day, as far as accepted style is concerned. He takes the clubhead away from the ball on an excessively upright path, his right elbow flying out away from his body. At the top of his swing he makes a distinct looping motion, then he lunges through the ball, finally following its flight by peering back over his shoulder.

But Brewer's swing works for him. He won the US Masters in 1967 and the rich Alcan Golfer of the Year Tournament in 1967 and 1968. He has gone from near-poverty to financial comfort with his funny-looking swing. Brewer broke his elbow at the age of 7 playing football, and in order to hit a golf ball had to let his elbow fly out from his body. This then, is his natural swing, and he has described the path of the clubhead as 'a sort of figure 8'.

Brewer's Masters victory is a great comeback story. In the 1966 tournament he missed a short putt on the last hole that would have given him the championship. Forced into a playoff on the following day, he finished a poor third to Jack Nicklaus and Tommy Jacobs. Such a setback might have seriously affected the confidence of a lesser man, but Brewer set his heart on the Masters, and won it the very next year.

Brewer is noted for his candour and willingness to express his views. When the 'Big Three' (Arnold Palmer, Jack Nicklaus, and Gary Player) were carrying all before them in the golfing world, Brewer ventured the opinion that they were the product of the business manager they had in common, and that other good players would beat them regularly. This came to pass in the late 1960s, and Gay Brewer had his share of the spoils.

He received the recognition he sought when he was selected for the American Ryder Cup squad in both 1969 and 1971. He remains, however, a mercurial golfer; as likely to miss the cut on a tournament as to win it, devastatingly good or notoriously erratic. Fortunately he wins sufficiently often to confirm the belief that he is primarily a golfer of genuine ability and finesse.

**1 Five times champion James Braid was still playing in the British Open in his late fifties.
2 Gay Brewer (USA), twice Alcan champion.**

Brown
Eric Chalmers (1925-   )

Scottish golfer Eric Brown has a record in Ryder Cup matches that is not even remotely approached by any other Briton. On each of the four occasions he played against the Americans in this competition, he won his singles match. And in 1969, he was non-playing captain of the British side that figured in the only tie in the history of the match.

Brown won the Scottish Amateur Championship, a match-play event, in 1946 and turned professional the same year. But he had to wait until 1953 for his first Ryder Cup badge. It was a successful debut for him and, although the Americans won the match at Wentworth by 6–5 with one halved, Brown beat Lloyd Mangrum by two holes.

He went to Palm Springs, California, in 1955 with the next side, and beat Jerry Barber 3 and 2. Then in 1957, the year he came third in the Open, he was a member of the side that won 7–4 at Lindrick, in Nottinghamshire—the first British side to win the Ryder Cup since 1933. Brown's match was against the temperamental Tommy 'Thunder' Bolt. Much depended on him, as the Americans had already won the foursomes and a win by Brown would be a boost to the others in

Bradford Telegraph and Argus

Colour Sport

their singles matches. Bolt lived up to his reputation, but Brown remained calm throughout a tempestuous match and won 4 and 3.

The 1958 Open at Royal Lytham was Brown's best. His 279—including a brilliant third-round 65—left him sharing third place, just one stroke behind the leaders.

Brown's final appearance in the Ryder Cup as a player was in 1959 at Palm Desert, California, where he beat Cary Middlecoff by 4 and 3. He was the only singles winner in the British side, which lost the cup, but he had at least maintained his unbeaten record.

Brown has always risen to the challenge offered by the man-to-man combat of match play. But his record in stroke play, for such an accomplished golfer, is not nearly as good as many of his contemporaries. Yet because of his Ryder Cup achievements, he will be remembered long after they are forgotten.

London Express News and Feature Services

BROWN Eric Chalmers
Tournaments and awards
1946 Scottish Amateur
1951 Swiss Open
1952 Italian Open
1953 Irish Open
Portuguese Open
1957 Dunlop Masters
Harry Vardon Trophy
1959 Golf Writers' Association Trophy
1960 News of the World Match Play
1962 News of the World Match Play
Represenative appearances
Great Britain v USA (Ryder Cup): 1953, 55, 57, 59. Non-playing captain, 1969
World Cup (Scotland): 1954, 55, 56, 57, 58, 59, 60, 61, 62, 66, 67

1 Eric Brown (right), as non-playing captain of the British Ryder Cup team in 1969, exchanges cards with Sam Snead after the only tie in Ryder Cup history. **2** and **3** Peter Butler on his way to victory over Ray Floyd in that classic Ryder Cup match.

3

Butler

Peter (1932-   )

Ask most British professionals whom they would back to play a par round in a golf tournament and many of them would name Peter Butler. He is the complete professional—sound in technique and solid in temperament.

Crowds do not flock to watch him except in his native Midlands, because he is not one for the spectacular shots, the impossible recoveries, the match-winning chips. But he does produce the dependable strokes, and possibly only Butler of the British professionals could, as he did in 1968, score 24 consecutive tournament rounds of par or under. During that period he won the Penfold, Wills, and French Open tournaments and headed the Order of Merit.

Butler is not a long hitter. He prefers to fade the ball into the fairway and to reach the green in regulation figures. Once there he uses a formidable putting technique—one which prompted Eric Brown, his Ryder Cup captain in 1969, to label him the best putter in Britain.

In the 1969 Ryder Cup at Royal Birkdale, Butler was the only player—British or American—to win both his singles matches on the last day, when the pressure was really on, a performance that included the defeat of Ray Floyd, US PGA champion. In his modest way, he refused to see anything remarkable in this. 'I just tried my hardest', he said. Butler was less successful in the 1973 Ryder Cup, though, losing each of his three matches. However, he made his mark on the series by holing out from the tee on the 16th at Muirfield, the first time this feat had been performed in the history of the cup.

He was the first British player to compete six successive times in the American Masters, to which he went direct from his Parisian club, St Cloud, where he spends the winter teaching. In the summer he is at he Harborne club, Birmingham—his first and only British club.

Today, while not the prolific winner he once was, Butler does not lack success. Forays to the Caribbean have twice resulted in wins in the Grand Bahamas Open, despite the presence of formidable American rivals. Butler has also established himself as a teacher and adviser to the younger generation of tournament professionals, and his influence on British golf will be felt for many years yet.

BUTLER Peter
Tournaments won
1959 Swallow-Penfold
1963 PGA Close Championship
Bowmaker
1965 Martini
Piccadilly Stroke Play
1967 Piccadilly Stroke Play
Bowmaker
1968 French Open
Penfold
Wills Open
1969 RTV Rentals
1971 Classic International
Grand Bahamas Open
1972 Grand Bahamas Open
1974 Sumrie-Bournemouth
Representative appearances
Great Britain v USA (Ryder Cup): 1965, 1969, 1971, 1973
World Cup (England): 1969

Carr

Joseph Benedict (1922-)

Irishman Joe Carr was the biggest name in British post-war amateur golf until the coming of Michael Bonallack. His three victories in the British amateur championship were unparalleled in modern golf, again until the advent of Bonallack. In the 20 years from 1947 he took part in more Walker Cup matches against America than anyone in the history of that event. He played in the first world team championship in 1958, and captained the victorious Great Britain and Ireland team in 1964.

Above all a great match player, Carr was ruthless in victory, capable when down of reversing a dangerous situation with a devastating shot or a brilliant recovery. His putting was no more than adequate, but in playing from sand he was almost without equal. He had a distinctive flailing action, but realizing that this might not last he worked tirelessly at controlling his great and sometimes wayward length.

Carr won several stroke-play events, and was leading amateur in the 1956 and 1958 Opens. His most striking achievements were against professionals. In the 1958 Masters at Portmarnock, when it seemed that the whole of Ireland was at his heels, and in the 1963 PGA close championship, he came within a stroke or two of beating the best on the British circuit.

His popularity, not only in Ireland where he is life member of at least two dozen clubs and has been honoured by most of the rest, but also among players and crowds all over the world, is enormous. The tall lanky Carr attracted spectators as much through his gay and out-going personality as through the excitement of watching his game.

CARR Joseph	
Tournaments and awards	
1946	Irish Open Amateur
1950	Irish Open Amateur
1951	Golf Illustrated Gold Vase
1953	British Amateur
	An Tostal Golden Ball trophy
	Golf Writers' Trophy*
1954	Irish Close Amateur
	Irish Open Amateur
1956	Irish Open Amateur
1957	Irish Close Amateur
1958	British Amateur
1960	British Amateur
1961	USGA R. T. Jones Award†
1963	Irish Close Amateur
1964	Irish Close Amateur
1965	Irish Close Amateur
1967	Irish Close Amateur
	Walter Hagen Award‡
Representative appearances	
Great Britain v USA (Walker Cup):	
1947, 49, 51, 53, 55, 57, 59, 61, 63	
(captain)	
*awarded to the person who has done most for golf during the year	
†for outstanding sportsmanship in golf	
‡for contribution to international golf	

H. W. Neale

Casper

Billy (1931-)

California's Billy Casper is, in the opinion of his fellow professionals on the American golf circuit, the most consistently outstanding player of his time. He has been among the top four money winners in all but 4 of his first 14 years on the tour, and has won the Vardon Trophy for the best scoring average no less than five times.

Though he had already won the US Open twice, the outwardly bland Casper gained really widespread attention from the golfing world only in 1968, when he won six major tournaments, set a money record of $205,168, and had the lowest stroke average at 69.82. Not surprisingly the American golf writers voted him Player of the Year. Such statistics are difficult to ignore, but even then most followers of the game were reluctant to elevate him to a class with Arnold Palmer, Jack Nicklaus, and Gary Player, and his remarkably successful figures failed to command half the attention of Palmer's celebrated slump.

To the fickle galleries, Casper is the quiet man who eats exotic foods such as buffalo meat to combat a recurring allergy problem, is a convert to Mormonism, and is an excellent putter. But he has not always been placid—as a younger player he was as wild as anyone, and an undisciplined urge to eat made him fat. While he has always possessed a smooth putting action, the rest of his very underrated game was developed through assiduous practice. He would spend two-thirds of a day on his driving. Even when he won the US Open in 1959 he was the subject of a strange mixture of mean remarks about his figure and more pleasant ones about his performance on the greens.

Casper admits that the taunts needled him—he was a shambling and incomplete player. He set about rectifying the situation. He went on a diet and lost 55 pounds, developed his game into the all-round equal of any, and became a steadier player. As a Mormon he claimed a new peace of mind and improved family life (a family of six children, three of which the Caspers adopted) that enabled his golf to benefit.

But old images die hard, and while nobody could now refute his trimness, many hesitated to concede that he was anything more than a great putter.

Casper nurtured his putting skill as a youngster, practising at night on an unlit green near his San Diego home. As he could not see the hole, he learnt to judge speed and distance with canny precision. He sharpened his eye by shooting pool at every opportunity.

Casper was the second golfer, after Palmer, to take his tournament winnings to one million dollars, a fact that surprised American golf fans. His early ambition of retiring as the all-time leading money-winner has been tempered today, for he now restricts his tournament appearances to a limited number. Yet, in spite of this apparent handicap, it is rare to find Casper far from the top ten money-earners on the US tour, and his income is consistently bolstered by victories in Europe, Africa, and the Far East.

He remains a pleasure to watch, no less so because of the speed at which he plays, a trait that has

1 Joe Carr, Irish amateur star for more than 20 years after World War II. 2 Billy Casper, one of the most consistent American golfers since the mid-1950s, failed to get the public acclaim he deserved despite over 50 big wins. 3 Bob Charles, the only world-class left-hander.

earned him the reputation of being an impatient golfer. Casper's practice is to step straight up to the ball, taking a solitary practice swing before playing his stroke. Today, when golfing ability is so geared to equipment and psychological devices, Casper is living proof that skill and technique are the ultimate barometer.

CASPER William

Tournament and awards

1956	Labatt Open
1957	Phoenix Open
	Kentucky Derby Open
1958	Brazilian Open
	New Orleans Open
	Buick Open
	Havana International
	Bing Crosby National
1959	US Open
	Brazilian Open
	Portland Open
	LaFayette Open
	Mobile Open
1960	Portland Open
	Hesperia Open
	Orange County Open
	Vardon Trophy
1961	Portland Open
1962	Doral Open
	Greensboro Open
	500 Festival Open
	Bakersfield Open
1963	Bing Crosby National
	Insurance City Open
	Vardon Trophy
1964	Doral Open
	Colonial National
	Seattle Open
	Alamaden Open
1965	Bob Hope Desert Classic
	Insurance City Open
	Sahara Invitational
	Western Open
	Vardon Trophy
1966	US Open
	San Diego Open
	500 Festival Open
	Western Open
	Vardon Trophy
	US PGA Player of the Year
1967	Canadian Open
	Carling World Open
1968	Los Angeles Open
	Colonial National
	500 Festival Open
	Greater Hartford Open
	Greensboro Open
	Lucky International
	Vardon Trophy
1969	Bob Hope Desert Classic
	Western Open
	Alcan Golfer of the Year
1970	Philadelphia Classic
	Arco Classic
1972	Lancombe Trophy
1973	Western Open
	Morocco GP
	Greater Hartford Open
1974	Lancia D'Oro
	Lancombe Trophy
1975	Greater New Orleans Open
	Italtan Open

Representative appearances
USA v Great Britain (Ryder Cup): 1961 1963 1965 1967 1969 1971 1973 1975

Colour Sport

Syndication International

Charles
Bob (1936-   )

A tall, lean, quiet New Zealander, Bob Charles is the first golfer from his country and the first left-handed professional of undisputed world class. His achievement is even more impressive when the scarcity of left handers is considered. For when something goes wrong with his golf—his swing is inclined to let him down at vital moments—Charles has to sort out for himself what is misfiring in his game.

But his putting, always outstanding and sometimes breathtaking, rarely lets him down. And when his driving fails him, as it did in the 1969 Open at Royal Lytham and St Annes, he is apt to comment: 'I have trouble getting started but I can usually finish off'. A good many judges are prepared to call Charles the finest putter in the world, and the American star Gene Littler would go along with that. In the final of the 1969 Piccadilly World Match-Play Championship, Charles was outgunned by Littler from tee to green, but he performed such prodigies on the greens that he eventually won on the 37th. On three successive greens, he holed birdie putts of 45, 36, and 54 feet to go from one down to two up.

Charles, who is considerably more forthcoming than he at first appears to be, made his international name when he won the 1963 Open at Royal Lytham and St Annes. At the beginning of the last round, Charles was leading by two strokes thanks to a brilliant third round 66, but as the round progressed he slipped slightly. The American Jack Nicklaus, trailing behind fellow American Phil Rodgers and Charles, thought he could get fives at the 17th and 18th, which he did, and still win. But both Charles and Rodgers rallied to finish level on 277, one shot ahead of Nicklaus.

In the 36-hole play-off, Charles played like a man determined, and destined, to win. He was three ahead at lunch, and Rodgers, possibly realizing that nothing could deter the fanatical looking New Zealander, crumbled completely in the afternoon to lose by eight strokes.

That win brought Bob Charles £1,500. But, perhaps more important to him, it brought world-wide recognition and also furnished proof that his win in the 1954 New Zealand Open, as an 18-year-old amateur, was no fluke.

Charles left Britain to try for the big prizes of the American circuit. But he did not win as much money as his putting said he ought to, and it was not until 1966 that he really showed the world what he was capable of.

That year, he won four New Zealand tournaments, finished seventh in the individual section of the World Cup, and beat

Arnold Palmer in a four-match exhibition series. Like Palmer, Nicklaus, and Gary Player, Charles was by this time under the management of American lawyer Mark McCormack.

Bob Charles has not always won tournaments, and so has not always made the headlines. But he is never far behind the leaders, having finished second in both the 1968 and 1969 Opens, and in the 1968 United States PGA Championship. No matter what the tournament, competitors know he is one of the men they have to beat, and his deadly putting rarely makes it easy.

Syndication International

CHARLES Robert
Tournaments won
1954 NZ Open
1961 NZ Professional
Bowmaker
Caltex (NZ)
1962 Swiss Open
Engadine Open
Daks
Caltex (NZ)
1963 British Open
Houston Classic
Watties Open (NZ)
1965 Tucson Open
1966 NZ Open
Watties Open (NZ)
Forest Products (NZ)
(tied, no play-off)
Metalcraft (NZ)
1967 Atlanta Classic
Watties Open (NZ)
Caltex (NZ)
Wills Masters (NZ)
1968 Canadian Open
Watties Open (NZ)
Caltex (NZ)
1969 Piccadilly World Match-Play
1970 NZ Open
1972 John Player Classic
Dunlop Masters
1973 SA Open
Scandinavian Enterprises Open
NZ Open
City of Auckland Classic
1974 Greater Greenboro Open
Swiss Open

Cole

Bobby (1948-   )

Some golfers take a long time to make a name, others explode on to the golfing scene, as did South African Bobby Cole in the 1966 British Amateur golf championship at Carnoustie. Almost unknown at the time, except to those who had heeded Gary Player's warning of a rising young star, Cole was just 18 when he beat Ronnie Shade in the final. Only 1956 winner John Beharrell has won the title at a younger age, and only a few hours separate the two.

The son of a mining foreman in a small town outside Johannesburg, Cole showed an early natural talent for the game. At 15, he won the junior national championship and the Transvaal Amateur, before setting off for Britain, backed by a rich South African. His patron's faith in him was not misplaced, as his British Amateur victory showed. Later in the year, he represented South Africa in the Eisenhower Trophy, in which, coincidentally, the best individual scorer was Ronnie Shade.

After the Eisenhower Trophy, Cole turned professional and joined the group managed by Mark McCormack. At the American professional school that qualifies recruits for their tour, he finished top in 1967, ahead of Deane Beman, Bob Murphy, and Tony Jacklin among others. And although these three may have won more money since. Cole has played regularly on the tough American circuit with sufficient success to enable him to return year after year, although a victory still eludes him. His best performance to date came in 1974, when a series of consistent scores kept him in a healthy position in the money-winners' table.

Away from the American circuit, Cole spends his winters profitaby in his homeland, where a constant number of tournaments fall to him each year. In 1974, he tasted the sweetness of

Ed Lacey

his first victory of international renown when he swept away with the South African Open. He is still younger than many of the other leading modern golfers were when they achieved a significant breakthrough, and every year Cole seems to move closer to his own. When he does, his future is assured. A classic swinger of the club, he combines youthful good looks and a personable appearance to attract the support of the gallery. Slim and supple, he is nonetheless one of the longest drivers in golf, a useful attribute to add to the more readily obvious of his manifold abilities.

COLE Robert

Major victories
1969 Natal Open
        Dunlop Masters (SA)
1972 Transvaal Open
        Rhodesian Masters
        Natal Open
1974 Vavasseur International (SA)
        SA Open

Coles

Neil (1934-   )

By modern standards, British golfer Neil Coles matured slowly. His first noticeable success was winning the Hertfordshire Open championship in 1955. A year later, he won the assistant professionals' championship, but it was another five years before he broke through.

1 New Zealander Bob Charles during the 1969 British Open.
2 South African Bobby Cole in the 1966 British Amateur.
3 Neil Coles (GB) in the 1969 Open. **4** Britain's Henry Cotton in the 1948 Open, on the way to his third victory.

There were several factors holding Coles back. One was a looseness at the top of his swing, and another was a fiery temperament that he eventually subdued. His temperament, combined with a deep concentration, give him an engagingly sultry manner on course.

When Coles finally did break through, however, it was in a sensational manner. Playing in the 1961 Ballantine tournament, in which an American-sized ball was used, he shot a final-round 65 to win the £1,500 first prize, the biggest ever offered in Britain up to that time. The following year he showed this was no flash in the pan by winning the £2,000 first prize in the Senior Service tournament.

Coles visited America twice, and finished well in one tournament in 1961. But he did not enjoy the life, and, at about this time he developed an aversion to flying, he decided to play most of his golf in Britain. In fact, most of his subsequent successes have been achieved within 50 miles of London. Notable among these have been the *News of the World* Match-Play championship in 1964 and 1965, and victories in the Daks Tournament in 1963, when he tied with Peter Alliss, and 1964. In 1964 he also finished runner-up to Arnold Palmer in the Piccadilly World Match-Play championship, and finished the year with a new British record in earnings, which approached the £8,000 mark.

Coles best performance in the British Open was in 1973, when a last round of 66, which would have been a course record for Troon had not Jack Nicklaus shot 65 a few moments earlier, tied him with Nicklaus for second place behind Tom Weiskopf. Coles has also enjoyed an un-interrupted run in Britain's Ryder Cup team since 1961, establishing himself as the most successful British golfer since the series began with a list of victories bettered only by the Americans, Palmer, Casper, and Littler.

As the British Ryder Cup team is selected from the leaders in the Order of Merit, this is testimony to the position Coles has occupied in British golf for so many years. Every season, he does not fail to win at least one of the top prizes in Europe and can never be discounted when the others are being disputed. His skill and energy have shown no sign of declining now that he has reached his 40th birthday, and had he achieved the belief in himself that his playing record merits, he might deservedly have attained the status internationally that he has in Britain.

COLES Neil

Tournaments and awards
1961 Ballantine
1962 Senior Service
1963 Daks (shared with P. Alliss)
        Martini International (shared with C. O'Connor)
        Harry Vardon Trophy
1964 Daks
        Bowmaker
        PGA Match Play
1965 PGA Match Play
        Carrolls Sweet Afton
1966 Pringle
        Dunlop Masters
1970 Carlyon Bay Hotel Tournament
1971 Penfold Tournament
        Carrolls International
1972 Sunbeam Scottish Open
1973 Spanish Open
        Sumrie Bebler-Ball
        Benson & Hedges Match-Play
        Kennedy Pro-Am
1974 Wills Open
Representative appearances
Great Britain v USA (Ryder Cup): 1961
1963 1965 1967 1969 1971 1973

Cotton

Thomas Henry (1907-   )

In an age when no other Briton won the Open Golf Championship more than once, Henry Cotton, three times holder of the title, stood out like a colossus. The victories added lustre to his reputation. In 1934 at Sandwich he put an end to 10 years of American domination of the event, and his opening rounds of 67 and 65 were so devastating that after a third round of 72, he was 10 strokes ahead of the field. Before the final round he had an attack of stomach cramp, but despite a round of 79 he still won by five strokes.

Three years later at Carnoustie he won from a field that contained the entire American Ryder Cup team. His last round of 71, played in belting rain on a waterlogged course, was one of the finest ever played. It was surpassed in his own career only by the 66 that set a new course record for Muirfield and gave him his third victory, in 1948. Between 1930 and 1948 he was only once outside the leading 10 players in the Open.

Cotton was not naturally gifted. He reached the top by his intelligence and by intensely hard practice, which, as a young man, sometimes left his hands sore and blistered. Once he had left Alleyn's School, Dulwich, with the decision that golf was to be his life, it was character that brought him success. And when he had achieved it, he was shrewd enough to use it to the full.

His position as the greatest British golfer of his age rests on more than his record of achievement. As teacher, writer of several books, and inventor, he exploited the full range of his talents. His

Central Press

belief that the public would pay well for what professionals had to offer opened up new fields for his colleagues and extended the work of emancipation started by Walter Hagen. Cotton has an original and inquiring mind, and probably no Briton has studied the game in greater depth. By his fastidious way of living and the ease with which he mixed with all kinds of people, he brought style and dignity to his profession. In all these things he has been staunchly supported by his Argentinian-born wife, Toots, a fine golfer in her own right.

After turning professional at 17, Henry Cotton was assistant at Fulwell, Rye—where he even practised by moonlight—and Cannes, before being appointed, at the age of 19½, professional to the Langley Park Club.

In 1933 he went to the Waterloo club in Belgium for four years, a move that marked the beginning of an association with the Continent that has lasted all his life. Particularly in the 1960s, he has spent much time abroad.

Before his second victory in the Open in 1937 he was back in England at Ashridge. The war interrupted his career at its peak—his services to the Red Cross in raising funds were recognized by

the award of the MBE. He was with the RAF for a time, but although physically very strong—he was a great believer in muscle-building exercises—he was not so constitutionally, and was invalided out. When golf resumed he soon showed that his game had not suffered. He had very strong hands and his three-quarter swing was full of grace and power. On his first visit to America, in 1928, he had played frequently with Tommy Armour, and changed his game by learning to draw the ball (hit it from right to left) to gain length.

Notable among many other victories besides the Open were his pre-war wins over several of the leading players of the day in challenge matches; three victories —1932, 1940, and 1946—in the PGA match-play championship (an event in which he was also three times runner-up), and at least 15 Continental championships. He played in the Ryder Cup matches of 1929, 1937, and 1947, and he was captain both in that last year and in 1953. At the age of 47 he won a five-round tournament at Wentworth. Final proof of his fitness and the soundness of his technique came in 1956, when in his 50th year he tied sixth in the Open at Hoylake.

COTTON Thomas Henry	
Tournaments and awards	
1930	Mar-del-Plata Open (Argentina)
	Belgian Open
1931	Dunlop Southport
1932	Dunlop Southport
	PGA Match Play
1934	British Open
	Belgian Open
1936	Italian Open
	Dunlop Metropolitan
1937	German Open
	British Open
	Czechoslovak Open
	Silver King Tournament
1938	Belgian Open
	German Open
	Czechoslovak Open
	Harry Vardon Trophy
1939	German Open
	Daily Mail tournament
	Penfold League (shared)
1940	PGA Match Play
1946	French Open
	Vichy Open
	PGA Match Play
1947	French Open
	Spalding
1948	British Open
	White Sulphur Springs Invitational
1953	Dunlop 2,000 Guineas
1954	Penfold 1,000 Guineas

Representative appearances
Great Britain v USA (Ryder Cup) 1929, 1937, 1947 (captain); (non-playing captain 1953).

Crampton
Bruce (1935-   )

In 1957, Bruce Crampton, then a slightly built young man with the appearance of an angry cherub, shouldered his golf clubs, boarded an aircraft in Sydney, and began his invasion of the United States. If he had hoped for easy success he was to be disappointed, for a long way of attrition lay ahead. But, some 17 years later, there could be no doubt that he had conquered.

By then, he had built the unenviable record of being the greatest living golfer never to have won a major golfing championship. And those who question the validity of this opinion will find some confirmation in the fact that Crampton, in 1974, stood as the fifth biggest money winner in the history of golf, ahead even of Gary Player. His achievement is all the more spectacular when one remembers that Crampton was one of the first overseas players to commit himself to the rigorous American circuit.

Sydney born, Crampton decided while still a youth that he enjoyed golf sufficiently, and was good enough at the game, to make it his career. He did

Australian News and Information Bureau

Associated Press

not take long to justify his self-confidence, for at the age of 20 he emerged as winner of the Australian Open. On the strength of that, he accepted an invitation to the Masters in Augusta, a whole continent away, and although not earning enough to pay for his journey, he quickly decided that his future lay in the United States.

Crampton's first few years on the American tour scarcely paid his living expenses as he finished annually about 60th on the prize list. But in 1961 came his break-through when he snatched the Milwaukee Open, following this up the next year by taking the Motor City Open to leapfrog to 13th place in the money table. In 1965 he won three events and total prize money of 56,024 dollars, over 50,000 dollars more than he had gathered only five years earlier.

For the next two years he slumped again, but then in 1968 he topped the 100,000-dollar earnings for the first time, his takings boosted by a tournament win in the Bahamas. The next year he repeated this performance, and with his first victory on the US tour for five years finished among the top 10 money winners for the first time. Yet despite these sporadic victories, Crampton developed the reputation of being the best loser on the circuit, the man who finished high with increasing regularity yet could never pull out that little extra for a victory.

Crampton answered his critics in 1973 by winning five tournaments and 273,918 dollars, a figure only Jack Nicklaus could beat with a surge at the end of the year. At last he had shown signs that he possessed the final resolution needed to claim one of the big classics, the determination to stake a place in golf's Hall of Fame.

Over the years, Crampton has sojourned on the brief Australian tour in the winters, but most of his success today is confined to America. More than any of the Australians on the US circuit he has become Americanized, though in those early days he was often misunderstood, going to great lengths to help those who tried to figure him out. There was a singleness of purpose about him that caused Americans to refer to the fiery Australian as a 'cat who walks alone'.

One of the most modest and articulate golfers around, Cramton once summed up the all-round golfer as requiring four ingredients. He must be able to play well enough; be able to

produce; have good luck; and finally must have good nerves. Three of these attributes Cramp-ton certainly has. If luck sided with him more frequently, he might well obtain the rewards ability merits.

CRAMPTON Bruce

Major victories
1957	Australian Open
1961	Milwaukee Open
1962	Motor City Open
1964	Texas Open
1965	Bing Crosby Invitation
	Colonial National Invitation
	'500' Festival
1968	West End Classic
1969	Hawaiian Open
1970	Westchester Classic
1971	Wills Masters (Aus)
	Western Open
1973	Phoenix Open
	Deans Martin-Tucson Open
	Houston Open
	American Golf Classic
1975	Houston Open

Daly
Fred (1911-   )

Fred Daly was the first Irishman and one of the few Britons after World War II to win the British Open Golf Championship. He was the Professional Golfers' Association matchplay champion in 1946, 1948, and again in 1952 when he and Alan 'Tiger' Poulton set a record by going to the 30th hole in their third-round match, and was eight times Ulster champion.

Born at Portrush in Northern Ireland, Daly served as a caddie on the local links at the age of 9, and at 17 turned professional. Few saw his great Open victory at Hoylake in 1947, because, un-

like today when the leaders go out last, he was an early starter before the crowds gathered. He had slipped with 78 in round three, but he scored a final 72, then waited in the clubhouse to see if his total of 293 would be good enough. It was. Britain's Reg Horne and American amateur Frank Stranahan finished on 294. His remarkable consistency in the Open made him runner-up the following year, third in 1950 and 1952, and 4th in 1951.

Daly played in four Ryder Cup matches for Britain, scoring a 9 and 7 victory over Ted Kroll at Wentworth in 1953. He also captained a touring team to South Africa in 1950–51, but ill health cut short his career at the top.

A natural golfer, with a relaxed and carefree style, he had a habit of whistling throughout the whole of a game. Daly's waggle—a tapping in front of and behind his ball before putting, became his trademark. He often indulged this idiosyncrasy a dozen times before stroking the ball into the hole.

DALY Frederick

Year	Tournament victories
1940	Irish Native Professional
1946	Irish Open
	Irish Native Professional
1947	British Open
	PGA Match Play
1948	PGA Match Play
	Penfold
	Dunlop Southport
1950	Lotus
1952	PGA Match Play
	Irish Native Professional
	Daks

Representative appearances
Great Britain v USA (Ryder Cup): 1947, 1949, 1951, 1953
Great Britain tour of South Africa 1950-51 (non-playing captain)

---

de Vicenzo
Roberto (1923-   )

Big, amiable, Argentine profes-sional golfer Roberto de Vicenzo began to hit the headlines as far back as 1944, but he will best be remembered for the incident that shattered his chances in the 1968 United States Masters' Tourna-ment at Augusta, Georgia.

In the final round, American Ryder Cup player Tommy Aaron, with whom he was paired, mis-takenly marked a 4 on de Vicenzo's card for the 17th hole—thousands of course spectators and millions watching on tele-vision had seen him score a 3. His actual round score was 65, which would have given him a tie for first place with the American Bob Goalby. But de Vicenzo signed for the incorrect total of 66 and, according to the rules, that figure had to stand as returned.

Such a trivial yet basic mistake meant a tragic second place. It cost him a play-off with Goalby for the $20,000 victory cheque, many thousands of dollars more in contracts and endowments, and a classic 'double' after his victory in the British Open Championship the previous July. His comment at the presentation ceremony: 'What a stupid I am.'

Golf enthusiasts everywhere shared the disappointment of the big man's loss. His warm, friendly personality and great sense of humour had gained him universal affection and respect. Britain was no exception, though success in the Open eluded him for many years. De Vicenzo had already won more than 130 tournaments in 16 countries when in 1967 he became, at the age of 44, the

1 and 2 A consistent performer on the US tour, Australian Bruce Crampton won $131,356 in 1974 without winning a tournament. **3** Fred Daly became the first Irishman to win the British Open, in 1947.

1 Looking thoroughly rueful, and with every reason to be, Roberto de Vicenzo (left) sits next to the new US Masters champion Bob Goalby. Had the Argentinian not overlooked an error on his scorecard, he would have forced a play-off with Goalby. **2** Another moment of anguish in de Vicenzo's career as he misses a vital putt.

oldest winner of the coveted championship. In 20 years of trying for the British title he had finished second in 1950, third four times, fourth, and sixth. En route to his victory at Hoylake (by two strokes from Jack Nicklaus) he became, with his third round of 67, the first Hoylake winner to break 70 in an Open Championship.

A native of Buenos Aires, de Vicenzo learnt the game as a boy caddie. A big hitter with a classically simple swing, he mellowed a Latin temperament to achieve success as a golfer. He once explained, in his fractured English: 'When I was young I sometimes lose temper, lose strokes, lose tournament, lose friends and lose money. So I tell myself, this is no good. You got to keep calm or your swing lose rhythm.'

In 1964 de Vicenzo adopted a new grip and putting action. He moved his left hand on the shaft, gripping the club in the palm instead of with the fingers. This cured a persistent hook which, he claimed, had cost him a great deal of prize money. He increased his putting control by restricting the bend back of the right wrist.

One of the most widely travelled professional golfers, de Vicenzo has also, at one time or another, won the open titles of Argentina, Brazil, Chile, Colombia, Jamaica, Mexico, Panama, Belgium, France, the Netherlands, and Spain. And in 1953, he and countryman Antonio Cerda won the inaugural Canada Cup (now World Cup) tournament for Argentina.

DE VICENZO Roberto	
Year	**Tournaments and awards**
1944	Argentine Open
1946	Chilean Open
1947	Colombian Open
1949	Argentine Open
	Uruguayan Open
1950	French Open
	Dutch Open
	Belgian Open
1951	Argentine Open
	Mexican Open
1952	Panamanian Open
	Argentine Open
1953	Canada Cup (with A. Cerda)
	Mexican Open
1954	Brazilian Open
1956	Jamaican Open
1957	Brazilian Open
	Jamaican Open
1958	Argentine Open
1960	French Open
	Brazilian Open
1962	Canada Cup individual title
1963	Brazilian Open
1964	Brazilian Open
	German Open
1965	Argentine Open
1966	Spanish Open
	Greater Dallas Open
	Los Logartos Open
1967	British Open
1968	Houston Champions International
	Los Logartos Open
1970	USGA R. T. Jones Award*
1971	Panama Open
1972	Caracas Open
1973	Caracas Open
	Panama Open
	Brazilian Open
1974	Panama Open
	US Seniors' Championship
	World Seniors
Representative appearances	
World Cup (Argentina): 1953, 1954, 1955, 1962, 1963, 1964, 1965, 1966, 1968, 1969, 1970, 1971, 1972, 1973, 1974	

*For outstanding sportsmanship in golf

Devlin
Bruce (1937-   )

American pressmen seem intrigued by the fact that Australian golfer Bruce Devlin was once a plumber. In the mass interviews that are part of the United States tournament ritual, someone invariably refers to his aptitude with a stillson wrench. After the second round of the 1969 Masters, when he was joint leader with Billy Casper, Devlin was asked whether he still kept up his membership of the Master Plumbers' Union. He replied that he did, saying: 'Golf's an uncertain game. I might have to fall back on mending leaky faucets for a living one day.' There seems little justification for this precaution. By the end of that year, he had won more than £41,000 on the United States circuit, the high point of a remarkably consistent season being his victory in the Byron Nelson Classic. And on his return home he won three Australian events in five weeks and was voted the Australian Golfer of the Year.

Born at Goulburn, New South Wales, Devlin began his golfing career playing against his father (also a master plumber). In 1958,

he laid some claim to being considered the best amateur medal player in the world when, at the inaugural Eisenhower Cup, at St Andrews, his scores laid the basis for an Australian victory and won him the individual title. The following year he won the Australian amateur championship. Then, in 1960, he climaxed his brilliant amateur career with a flourish by winning the Australian Open against a powerful international field. He was the first amateur to take the championship since early in the century.

Immediately after winning the Open, Devlin turned professional, playing in Australia until he felt he had refined his scoring technique sufficiently to take on the Americans on their home ground. Even then, his early ventures on the United States circuit were sporadic, though not discouraging. It became clear, however, that he would have to play there regularly to make a worthwhile career. So in 1964 he played the full circuit and took home a good profit from consistent, if unexceptional, performances. By the end of the following season, the unobtrusive Australian had played in 36 consecutive tournaments without missing the money, at that time a record, and was third in prize winnings, with £24,000. Yet he had not won a single tournament!

In 1966, he established himself among the golfing elite by winning the Colonial Invitation in the United States and the Carling in England, the latter then the richest tournament in the world. But the following season may account for Devlin's keeping his union dues up to date for he could not even cover expenses. Nevertheless he made a decision to take his family to America during the United States season,

Australian Bruce Devlin was a consistent money-winner on the US tour in the late 1960s.

Australian News and Information Bureau

Ray Green/Transworld

instead of his constant commuting between Australia and America and it worked wonders. He was back in the money in 1968, and may have won the Masters but for a lack of caution when a bold shot to a tight pin placement put him in a water hazard. The eight he ran up made an ugly bulge in his score and he eventually finished third, just two strokes behind the winner Bob Goalby.

Lean, laconic, and amusing, Devlin is a daring player who hits the ball as far as anyone, including Jack Nicklaus, when he cuts loose, and he likes to live dangerously by attacking the pin when he reckons he has a gambler's chance. An indication of his success is the great respect he commands from his American colleagues who rate him a potential winner in any tournament, and against any opposition.

Faulkner
Max (1916-   )

Max Faulkner's victory in the 1951 British Open at Portrush, with a score of 285, stood as the last win by a British golfer in that event for 18 years until the success of Tony Jacklin in 1969. This gave him a rare distinction—he became (once Fred Daly, the 1947 winner, had retired) the only Open champion from the British Isles still in serious competition.

He carried the honour well. Tall and imposing, with a magnificent physique that in his later years put younger men to shame, he was invariably well turned out. If at times some found his colour schemes too flamboyant, his example did lead the way to a revival in brighter dress that was given a powerful boost by the coming of colour television.

Born in Bexhill, in Sussex, Faulkner began winning major events in the late 1940s. His record contains a unique achievement: he is the only player to have won the Open (1951), the PGA Match-Play championship (1953), and the Dunlop Masters tournament (1951)—three of the biggest events on the British circuit.

The most impressive parts of his game were his woods and long

Right and below, **The immaculate Max Faulkner dazzled crowds with his splendid attire as well as his excellent golf.**

Colour Library International

Action Photos

irons. Although a rigid, crouched stance gave his swing a rather awkward look, it was rhythmic, powerful, and controlled. He experimented with many types of putter, and the more unconventional their shape the more likely they were to please him. Ceaseless attempts to find the one that suited best testified to the growing difficulties he found in that department of the game. In the 1960 Dunlop Masters, in which he tied for second place, he used a putter with a home-made head attached to an old hickory shaft. It was typical of his restless enthusiasm for the game.

This zeal was much in evidence when he made his fifth and final appearance in a Ryder Cup match in 1957, the year Britain won at Lindrick. Though dropped in the singles, he gave cheerful support to his fellow members on the course and contributed to the remarkable turning of the tables on the Americans. A touch of the clown in his manner, combined with an easy, likeable personality, must have suited him for the music-hall had he not turned to golf. But for all his carefree extrovert manner, he felt the strain of competing as strongly as anyone though as late as 1968, at the age of 52, he won the Teacher British Senior Professional Championship at Aldeburgh.

FAULKNER Max

Tournaments and awards

1949	Lotus
	Penfold
	Dunlop Professional
1951	British Open
	Dunlop Masters
	Golf Writers' Association Trophy
1952	Spanish Open
	Dunlop Professional
1953	PGA Match-Play
	Spanish Open
1957	Spanish Open
1959	Irish Hospitals £5,000
1968	Teacher Senior Professional

Representative appearances
Great Britain v USA (Ryder Cup):
1947 49 51 53 57

Gallacher

Bernard (1949-   )

In only his second season as a professional, at the age of 20, Bernard Gallacher quietly emerged as the leading golfer on the British circuit. While Tony Jacklin was winning the Open Championship, the headlines, and the glory, Gallacher was finishing high up in tournament after tournament, to such effect that he won the Harry Vardon Trophy awarded to the leader of the PGA Order of Merit.

These performances automatically put Gallacher into the 1969 British Ryder Cup team. And what a baptism of fire this proved to be for the Scot from Bathgate,

Young Scot Bernard Gallacher (right), a competitive golfer who excels in match-play.

for this was the dramatic tied match. The youngest player ever to represent Britain in the Ryder Cup, he played with calm assurance throughout. And he beat Lee Trevino 4 and 3 in the final round, stemming the tide just when the Americans appeared to be getting on top.

Gallacher is one of the game's thinkers. He sets great store on the tactical side of golf, and this, allied to a determination to perfect his game, makes him a formidable competitor in match or medal play. His international career has been somewhat curtailed by love of his homeland, and he has perhaps not yet fulfilled his early promise. But 1974 saw a return to his 1969 form, highlighted by a sudden-death play-off win over Open champion Gary Player in the Dunlop Masters. Then in 1975, he became the first man to defend this title successfully, and he had another fine Ryder Cup, halving his two singles matches, with Lee Trevino and Al Geiberger.

GALLACHER, Bernard

Tournaments and awards

1969	Schweppes
	Wills Open
	Harry Vardon Trophy
1971	Martini International
1973	Coca-Cola Young Professionals
1974	Carrolls Celebration
	Dunlop Masters
1975	Dunlop Masters

Representative appearances
Great Britain v USA (Ryder Cup) 1969,
71, 73, 75
World Cup (Scotland) 1971, 74

Peter Dazely

Gardner

Robert (1890-   )

To be American amateur golf champion at the age of 19 years and world record holder in the pole vault less than three years later was the unique accomplishment of Robert Gardner.

Gardner went to Yale University in the autumn of 1908, and the next September he won the United States amateur golf championship when he beat H. C. Egan 4 and 3 in the final. In the championships of those days all the competitors played 36 holes of stroke play with the best 32 qualifying for the knock-out proper.

Because of the rules regarding sport in American universities, men in their first year could not represent their universities in senior competitions. But in 1910, 1911, and 1912, Gardner regularly competed in the pole vault for Yale, and captained the team in his last year. By 1912 he was consistently clearing 12 feet, but there were nearly a dozen American vaulters capable of that height. In the inter-collegiate championships Gardner was up against Harry Babcock (the eventual gold medallist at Stockholm later in the year). The bar was at 12 ft $9\frac{1}{2}$ in, and Babcock cleared it at his first try, Gardner at his second. At 13 ft 1 in, Babcock failed, and Gardner soared over for a world record at his third attempt. It stood for just one week: in the Olympic trials Marc Wright vaulted 13 ft $2\frac{1}{2}$ in—a record that lasted seven years. Though offered the opportunity of representing the United States in the Olympics, Gardner declined. The Games were not so important then.

Golf was really Gardner's first love. In 1915 he again won the American amateur championship, and the next year he beat the 15-year-old Bobby Jones 4 and 3 in the third round, only to lose the final by a similar margin to Chick Evans, who that year also won the US Open Championship. In 1920 Gardner tried his luck in the English amateur championships, and in one of the most exciting finals seen at Muirfield succumbed to Cyril Tolley at the 37th hole.

Gardner represented the United States four times in the Walker Cup, and was captain of the team on three of those occasions. He lost only two of his eight matches, each time in a foursome.

GARDNER Robert

Won USA Amateur Golf Championship
1909, 1915
United States Walker Cup team
1922, 23, 24, 26

Walter Hagen attacks the 14th hole at Muirfield in 1929 on the way to winning his fourth British Open.

Left, **Robert Gardner, US amateur champion in 1909 and 1915, took time off in 1912 to break the world pole vault record.** *Right,* **Precocious South African star Dale Hayes.**

Radio Times Hulton Picture Library

Hagen

Walter (1892-1969)

American golfer Walter Hagen meant much more to the sport than the fact that he was a great champion. He was the most gregarious golf hero ever, and the man who took his fellow professionals out of involuntary servitude. As two-time United States Open champion Gene Sarazen said: 'All the pros who have a chance for the big money today should say a silent prayer to The Haig. He made it all possible.'

Hagen's record was brilliant. He won the British Open four times, the United States Open championship twice, and five United States PGA titles, at match play. Four of his PGA crowns came in consecutive years, from 1924 to 1927, and during one incomparable stretch he won 22 individual matches in succession. He won dozens of lesser tournaments, including the Western and Canadian Opens—respected titles in their own right. To Hagen

though, one of his most satisfying accomplishments was disposing of Bobby Jones by the considerable margin of 11 and 10 in a 72-hole challenge match in 1926. The following year, he captained the United States team in the first ever Ryder Cup tie.

Hagen excelled at match play, and his success was due in no small part to his confessed gamesmanship. A master showman, he loved to lull his opponents into a false state of security by making easy shots appear difficult—and then dupe them by making difficult ones appear easy. His confidence was unmatched, and so too was his short game. He was perhaps at his best at the touchy little recovery shots from around the green, and he was a fearless putter. His short game more than offset his swaying, often 'scattershot' driving.

Until Hagen's dominance in the 1920s—the famed Golden Era of Sport—golf professionals were simply hired hands at clubs. But after Hagen, they entered, as the saying went, through the front

door. When the tall, handsome, debonair Hagen went to England to play in the 1920 British Open, pros went in the back door of the clubhouse at Deal and dressed in an old shack nearby. Hagen jolted the British establishment by arriving in a chauffeur-driven limousine and dining in it on champagne delivered from the front door of the clubhouse. Two years later, when he won, the ex-caddie from Rochester, New York, was entering through the main door at the British Open. Soon after, so were the other players.

Hagen earned a million dollars and he enjoyed spending every cent of it. He once said, 'Be sure to smell the flowers along the way' —and Walter Hagen made sure he did.

HAGEN Walter Charles

Major tournament victories
1914	US Open
1916	Western Open
1919	US Open
1921	US PGA championship
	Western Open
1922	British Open
1924	British Open
	US PGA championship
1925	US PGA championship
1926	US PGA championship
	Western Open
1927	US PGA championship
	Western Open
1928	British Open
1929	British Open
1931	Canadian Open
1932	Western Open

Representative Appearances
USA v Great Britain* 1921, 26, 27†, 29†, 31†, 33†. Non-playing captain 1937

*Ryder Cup from 1927. †Captain.

H. W. Neale

Hayes

Dale (1952-   )

Few amateurs can have made such a storming impact on every shore of the golfing world as South African Dale Hayes did between 1968 and 1969. And what made his performance all the more outstanding was the fact that he was only 16 at the time. Visiting America, he won the World Junior title, which he followed up the next year by winning the Scottish Amateur championship and reaching the semi-finals of the British Amateur. He picked up the German title as well, before making a detour on his way home to pocket the Brazilian championship.

Not surprisingly, Hayes turned professional six months later and quickly put his first tournament victory behind him by winning the 1971 Newcastle Open in Natal. The same year, on his first trip to Europe as a professional, he repeated the smash and grab image he had created as an amateur by winning the Spanish Open. Despite the continual flow of tournament successes in his home country, however, this has been Hayes' solitary victory abroad. The blame for this must lie on his temperament, rather than his proficiency, for he has never been far off the lead in any tournament, nor out of the top half-dozen in the European order of merit.

Hayes, though completely committed to the game—he is a member of a professional golfing family—is too easily distracted from the purpose of winning. Deliberately or not, he imparts an attitude which suggests that he is making quite enough money at any given moment to satisfy his needs, and that he has enough time in the years ahead to concenrate on winning tournaments.

His forecast is almost certainly accurate. Tall, strong, and one of the most infectiously good-humoured professionals playing today, Hayes seems guaranteed of a long career of fame and fortune. His easy nature may be his stumbling block, but if he can conquer that—on the golf course at least—he has already developed the other attributes he promised as a teenager. Hayes' avowed intention is to strive for his American tournament card when he is 23.

In 1974 Hayes enjoyed his best year to date, winning three tournaments in South Africa and the Coca-Cola Young Professionals in Britain, overhauling the leaders with a majestic closing-round 65. And he partnered Bobby Cole in South Africa's World Cup victory at Caracas. Another fine season in 1975 saw him win the Vardon Trophy by topping the British PGA Order of Merit.

Henning

Harold (1936-   )

Affectionately called 'The Horse' by his colleagues, South African golfer Harold Henning is probably the third best golfer to emerge from that country, behind Gary Player and Bobby Locke. He is one of five golfing brothers, two of whom, Alan and Graham, joined Harold in making an impact on the professional circuits of the world. Harold, however, is the only one to have succeeded in America.

And it was there that he was subjected to a number of threats from militant anti-apartheid factions. One telephone call told him he would have his hands blown off if he touched another club in America. Henning replied by winning the 1970 Tallahassee Open shortly afterwards—his first victory on the tour since 1966 when he won the Texas Open. The closest he had come to winning an event after 1966 was in 1969 when he tied for the Los Angeles Open and then lost to Negro golfer Charlie Sifford.

Henning began his professional golf career by winning the South African Open in 1957, and on the strength of a successful year he began playing on the Continent and Great Britain, where he created an immediate stir with his so-called 'pendulum' putting method. Holding both arms straight down in front of him, he swung the putter just like a pendulum. But however strange the method may have seemed, it worked magnificently for him and he won three tournaments in England and France in 1959.

But for his biggest success he did not need his putter at all. Playing in the 1963 Esso Golden tournament at Moor Park, he holed in one at the 18th, winning a special prize of £10,000. His caddy, Denis Hutchinson, was just as delighted as Henning, for together with another South African, Trevor Wilkes, they were sharing all expenses—and all winnings. The prize was split three ways, and Henning used his share to travel to America, where he did well enough to stay for many years. Recently he has returned to South Africa, where his guile and experience ensure that he remains a dominant figure in South African golf. And when he does make occasional trips overseas, he still cannot be dismissed as an opponent unworthy of consideration.

HENNING Harold	
Tournaments won	
1957	South African Open
	Italian Open
	Transvaal Open
	Natal Open
	Western Province Open
1958	French Open
	Daks
	Spalding
1959	Western Province Open
	Cock o' the North
1960	Swiss Open
	Danish Open
1962	South African Open
1964	Swiss Open
	Danish Open
1965	Swiss Open
	Danish Open
	German Open
	South African PGA
1966	South African PGA
	Texas Open
	Engadine Open
1970	Tallahassee Open
Representative Appearances	
World (Canada) Cup*: 1957, 58, 59, 61, 65	
1972	South African PGA
	General Motors Invitation (SA)
Representative appearances	
World (Canada) Cup: 1957, 58, 59, 61, *65	
*Won with Gary Player	

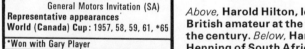

Above, **Harold Hilton, leading British amateur at the turn of the century.** *Below,* **Harold Henning of South Africa.**

Hilton

Harold Horsfall (1869-1942)

One of the greatest figures in British amateur golf, Harold Hilton held the unique record of winning the British Open twice (1892 and 1897), the British Amateur four times (1900, 1901, 1911, and 1913), and the United States Amateur, in 1911, at the age of 42.

Born at West Kirby near Hoylake and the historic links of Royal Liverpool, Hilton won several club competitions as a boy. In an age of great amateurs, though, he usually took second place in match play to John Ball and Freddie Tait, and it was not until they were away at the Boer War that he won his first Amateur. But stroke play was his forte, and he was the first amateur to win the Open over 72 holes. This performance was, however, considered something of a fluke, for Muirfield was well dried up at the time. But five years later, he won the event again against the pick of the professionals, including the Great Triumvirate—Braid, Taylor, and Vardon. A year later he narrowly missed

winning it again, and as late as 1911 was well in the hunt until the last hole.

Powerfully built and 5 ft 7 in in height, he was a master at imparting backspin and was a brilliant shot maker, whose swing developed from a slow start into a whirlwind finish. A scientific golfer, he possessed a great knowledge of the game, which made him a gifted teacher. And he also made a name for himself as a writer, being at times editor of *Golf Illustrated* and *Golf Monthly*.

Hogan
Ben (1912-   )

That Ben Hogan was one of the most dedicated golfers the game has seen is obvious from his record, his technique, and his personality. Between 1946 and 1953 he achieved immortality by winning the US Open four times, the Masters twice, the American PGA twice, and the British Open once. His feat of winning in one year—1953—the Masters and the US and British Opens is unmatched.

During that time he was the man everyone else had to beat—it was Hogan against the field. He became justifiably known as the outstanding athlete of the post-war period, and was acknowledged as a legend while still at the prime of his career, which started early but did not bloom quickly: Hogan was 40 when he won the three big events in 1953. The first full-length film ever made about a professional golfer, *Follow the Sun* (starring Glenn Ford), was shot in 1951, when his best was yet to come. It featured Hogan's remarkable recovery from injury.

Having started in golf at the age of 11 as a caddie at Fort Worth, Texas, Hogan struggled for several years on the tournament circuit. He did not win a professional event until he was 27, when hard years of day-long practice to develop a firm, compact, repeating swing finally bore fruit. During the war he gradually asserted himself, and in 1946 he won his first major title, the PGA championship at Portland. His career was ended, according to the vast medical opinions, in a hideous motor accident on a foggy Texas highway in 1949. But after a year's absence the slight Hogan battled back to the pinnacle of his sport and if anything improved. He was the dominant force in American golf in the early 1950s, and continued to play on through middle-age—as late as 1967 he shot a record-tying 30 on the back nine in the Masters.

Hogan's best year must be reckoned as 1953, when he entered only five tournaments but won them all. First he won the Masters with 274, beating the old record by five strokes. After winning scores of 286 and 282 in the Pan American Open and Colonial National, he broke the Oakmont course record and finished six shots clear of Sam Snead to win his fourth American Open. After being criticized for never entering the British Open, he adjusted brilliantly to the smaller ball and alien conditions at Carnoustie to break the course record and win by four strokes.

Asked to single out the best shot he ever played, Hogan replied that he only remembered the bad ones. With his dour concentration he was rarely a favourite of the crowd. The papers thought otherwise: *Sports Magazine* awarded him the trophy for 'Sportsman of the Decade, 1946–56', and in 1965 he was named as the greatest professional golfer of all time in a poll of American experts. It would be difficult to dispute this.

Ben Hogan, regarded by many experts as the greatest golfer of all time.

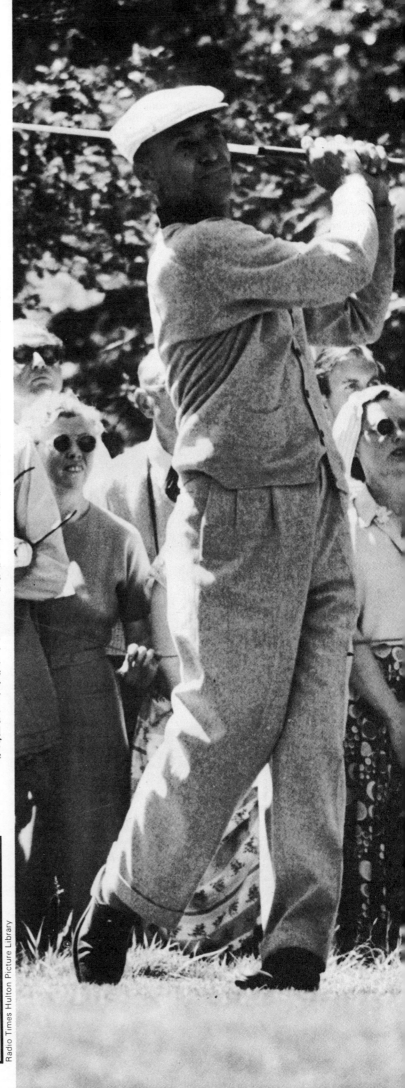

Radio Times Hulton Picture Library

Huggett

Brian (1936-   )

A stocky, determined Welshman, Brian Huggett is one of the finest fighters British golf has produced, and one of the leading British money winners of all time. In the 1960s, he twice finished in the top three in the British Open: in 1962 he was third behind Arnold Palmer and Kel Nagle, and in 1965 he tied with Christy O'Connor for second place behind Peter Thomson. The British press have dubbed him the 'Toy Bulldog', and nowhere are his bulldog qualities more evident than when he is playing in the Ryder Cup.

In 1969, millions of television viewers saw Huggett burst into tears after halving his match with American Billy Casper, for he thought he had won the Ryder Cup match for his country. But the match was actually halved, and Huggett had played his part fully in the 13–13 result. As in his previous two Ryder Cup matches, in 1963 and 1967, he had the task of giving the team a good start, and as usual made a brilliant job of it, winning the first foursome with Neil Coles. He reproduced this form again in 1973. Coming into the team for the afternoon foursomes on the first day, he played with Maurice Bembridge to sink the formidable team of Palmer and Nicklaus, a result that led to this famous partner-ship being split up for the first time for many years. The next day, he continued his winning ways and was one of the few Britons to win a singles match, ending the series with a total of three and a half points out of a possible four.

His gritty match-play qualities have also been evident in the *News of the World* Match Play Championship, which he won in 1968, and in which he was a semi-finalist in 1969, when he lost to Dai Rees. This match had a sensational finish: Huggett, one up on the 18th tee, lost the hole when Rees's wildly hooked tee shot hit a post and rebounded on to Huggett's bag. The law states that 'if a player's ball be stopped or deflected by his opponent, his caddie or equipment, *the opponent's side shall lose the hole*'. Rees then proceeded to win the 19th hole.

Huggett's golf is a triumph of determination and technique over physique. Barely 5 ft 9 in, he has adapted his swing to the big ball with conspicuously more success than many of his contemporaries, as he showed when he won the £2,000 first prize in the 1970 Carroll's international tournament.

Next only to Neil Coles, he has been the most consistently successful British golfer over the last decade. Scarcely a year passes without Huggett picking up at least one major tournament victory, and he is rarely far behind in the others. This consistency was rewarded in tangible form in 1973 when the courageous little Welshman won the American Express award donated to the golfer with the best aggregate of results on the European circuit.

HUGGETT Brian George Charles

Tournaments and awards

1961	Dutch Open
	Gleneagles Foursomes
1962	Dutch Open
	Singapore International
	German Open
1963	Cox-Moore Tournament
1965	Smart-Weston Tournament
1967	PGA Close Championship
	Martini International
1968	Shell Tournament
	Sumrie Tournament
	Martini International
	News of the World PGA match play
	Headed Order of Merit points table
	Harry Vardon Trophy
1969	Daks
	Bowmaker (tied with Tony Grubb)
1970	Algarve Open
	Dunlop Masters
	Carrolls International
1971	Daks Tournament
1973	Sumrie Better-Ball
1974	Portuguese Open

Representative appearances

Great Britain v USA (Ryder Cup): 1963, 1967, 1969, 1971, 1973, 1975
World Cup (Wales): 1963, 1965, 1968, 1969, 1971

Brian Huggett, tenacious British golfer with a fine tournament and match record over more than 15 years.

Jacklin

Tony (1944-   )

The first ten years of Tony Jacklin's career as a professional represented the most dazzling success story in the history of British golf. He reached the top when he won the United States Open in 1970 while still holding the British Open title he had won the previous year. Not that his career has been without setbacks. No modern golfer can win all the time, but Jacklin has shown his character by following each set-back with a step forward. More than any other golfer in Britain, he has star quality.

It is the ultimate virtue of a champion that he is not afraid of winning, and Jacklin has always known how to win with a flourish. When he won the Dunlop Masters in 1967, he holed in one at Royal St George's under the eye of the television cameras. In winning the British Open in 1969 he hammered his last drive straight down between the bunkers at the last hole, and later in the year he figured with Jack Nicklaus in the most dramatic Ryder Cup finish of all time. He squared at the 17th by holing a putt from the edge of the green, and then had a fine four to halve the 18th, and the match. And it was typical of Jacklin that he should hole an 18-ft putt for a birdie on the last hole of the 1970 United States Open when he had ample strokes to spare. This flourish, the skill, his good looks, and an engaging personality have brought a for-tune running into hundreds of thousands of pounds to the son of a Lincolnshire lorry driver.

As a youngster, Jacklin some-times used to caddy for his father at Scunthorpe Golf Club, and during school holidays he would be at the club all day, helping the greenkeeper, caddying, and practising. His first victories out-side local events were in the Lincolnshire Boys' and Lincoln-shire Open championships, and he turned professional in 1962 while still 17. The year before, he had been a member of the boys' international team. On moving to the Potters Bar club in Hert-fordshire, he came under the stern eye of Australian-born pro-fessional Bill Shankland, who once said of him: 'At that time he thought he was twice as good as he was, but he carried it modestly.'

In his first British Open, in 1963, he finished 30th on the same course, Royal Lytham, on which he was to win the title six years later. In between came the forma-tive years. He won the assistants' championship in 1964 and 1965, the second time immediately after his return from Canada where he won £1,000 in the Carling tourna-ment. It was his first taste of the big money to be made across the Atlantic.

His tour of South Africa in

Transworld

Britain's Tony Jacklin, who has been striving to recapture the brilliant form that won him the British Open in 1969 and the US Open in 1970.

1965–66 was not a great success, but in the northern winter of 1966–67 he really began to advance. He won two tournaments in New Zealand, including the PGA championship, and later in 1967 he showed up well in his first American Masters. Returning to England, he won the Pringle tournament, his first major victory in Britain, and then, after finishing fifth in the Open, he won the Dunlop Masters. By this time, he had already played for England in the World (Canada) Cup and had earned a place in his first Ryder Cup team. More significantly, perhaps, he had also been signed up by the American golf manager Mark McCormack.

On the American circuit in 1967, he won little except experience, learning the heartbreak of failing to make the cut (not qualifying for the final two rounds of a tournament) and having to pre-qualify the next time. But he took the rough with the smooth and in the early months of 1968 began to make his mark, finishing in the first 10 three times before becoming the first Briton to win a PGA-sponsored tournament in the United States. This was the Greater Jacksonville Open in Florida, and among all the many feats he has achieved since, it remains a landmark in his career.

It showed him that success was based on character and nerve to endure until his turn came round as much as on a first-class game. He was also appreciating just how important rhythm was. Technically correct and a brilliant bunker player, he did, however, have a tendency to swing too quickly, especially under pressure, to the detriment of his driving. He found it necessary to concentrate on his 'tempo' and not allow himself to be distracted by the galleries and interruptions that are a feature of modern tournament golf.

If British golf received a boost after Jacklin's Greater Jacksonville win, it had an even better one a year later when he won the British Open—the first Briton to do so for 18 years—against a field that included such greats as Nicklaus, Palmer, and Player. After rounds of 68, 70, and 70, he went out for the final round paired with Bob Charles, who had won at Royal Lytham in 1963. It was a man-to-man contest for the title, and Jacklin never faltered. He maintained his two-stroke lead, playing confident golf for a final round of 72 and an aggregate score of 280.

H. W. Neale

His personal success raised British morale, and when the Ryder Cup was played later that year, British golfers put up one of their best performances ever against the Americans. It was fitting that Jacklin should have taken part in the final act of the dramatic tie.

His progress in America was steady before his US Open success. In February 1970 he tied with the Los Angeles Negro professional Pete Brown in the San Diego Open but lost the 'sudden-death' play-off on the eve of flying back to Britain to receive the OBE. At Hazeltine in June, he jumped off in front of a star Open field bemused by bad weather and a course with a number of blind shots. Some moaned, others even pulled out of the tournament, but Jacklin concentrated on playing superb golf, retained his lead, and won by seven strokes—the most resounding victory in the event since 1921. He was only the second player to beat par in every round of the US Open (Lee Trevino did it in 1968). And in holding the US Open concurrently with the British one, he became just the

fourth player to do so, and the eleventh to win both at any time.

Returning to Britain loaded with honours and contracts, he made a gallant defence of his British title. In the still weather of the opening day, when there was a spate of low scoring, he played the first nine holes in 29 and was eight under par for 13 holes when the weather broke and ended play for the day. Inspiration died after that, but though showing signs of ragged-ness after three days play in the strong wind, he finished the leading Briton in fifth place. The following year, he proved con-clusively that he was not another British 10-day-wonder golfing prodigy when only the most exuberant flash of Trevino magic prevented him from regaining the title.

In the last couple of years, the pressure has begun to tell slightly on Tony Jacklin. He has come to appreciate the difficulties of rais-ing a family in England while at the same time attempting to endure the rigours of the Ameri-can tour. His repeat victory in the Greater Jacksonville Open in 1972 was to be his last by 1974,

the year in which he forfeited his American tournament players card.

With the runaway success of his first years affecting his life, Jacklin came to realize that it was more important to stabilize his career for the long-term future. But the indecision as to the years ahead affected his golf, and 1973 and 1974 were erratic years by his standards, years in which Peter Oosterhuis emerged as the first serious challenger to his supremacy in British golf.

But just as the sceptics mass to attack Jacklin, he brings out his best. In a face-to-face confron-tation with Oosterhuis in the 1974 Piccadilly World Match-Play, he proved himself with a shattering 7 and 6 victory. And the same year he went to Sweden to win the Scandinavian Enterprise Open in appalling conditions by a monstrous 11 strokes.

Joking about it afterwards, Jacklin made a telling remark which illustrated the pressures to which he is exposed as Britain's premier of golf. The highest-ever winning margin in any major tournament is 12 strokes, and having failed to equal that by one

Tony Jacklin displays the British Open trophy at Royal Lytham in 1969 while his wife looks on proudly.

shot, Tony Jacklin commented wryly: 'I can just see the headlines now. Tony Jacklin fails in record bid.'

JACKLIN Tony
Major tournament victories
1965 NZ Forest Products (tied)
1966 NZ PGA
Kimberley Tournament
1967 Pringle Tournament
Dunlop Masters
1968 Greater Jacksonville Open
1969 British Open
1970 US Open
1971 Benson & Hedges Tournament
1972 Dunlop International (Aus)
Vyella PGA
Greater Jacksonville Open
1973 Columbian Open
Italian Open
Bogota Open
Dunlop Masters
1974 Scandinavian Enterprises Open
Lagartos Tournament
Representative appearances
Great Britain v USA (Ryder Cup): 1967, 1969, 1971, 1973, 1975
World Cup (England): 1966, 1971, 1972

Jones

Bobby (1902-   )

To the question 'How great was golfer Bobby Jones?', the answer is usually given, 'Look at the record'. It is one that has never been seriously challenged. As an amateur he won, in the space of eight years from 1923, 13 of the world's major titles—the US Amateur five times, the US Open four times, the British Open three times, and the British Amateur once—all before he had reached his 30th year. His single victory in the British Amateur, in 1930, enabled him to win what was then the 'grand slam' of golf—the professional and amateur opens on both sides of the Atlantic—impossible in the changed conditions of modern golf.

As well as being a superb stylist, Jones was one of the most educated men who have ever played the game successfully. He held degrees in engineering, science, and law, graduating from the Georgia School of Technology in Atlanta, where he was born, and Harvard. He was responsible for the Augusta National course where, since 1934, the great American tournament, the Masters, has been played. His writings on golf are lucid and full of wisdom. He set the highest standards of sportsmanship, and this, together with his boyish good looks and drowsily rhythmic swing, attracted crowds to him wherever he played.

Jones showed early promise. He was just 9 when he won the junior championship at his club, East Lake, and 14 when he won his first Georgia State Championship. A year later, in 1917, he won the Southern Amateur and in 1919 he was runner-up in the Canadian Open and the US Amateur. He played in his first US Open at the age of 18, finishing in a tie for eighth place. In fact, so great was his promise that the public expected him to start winning everything at once, and his years of disappointment were made harder to bear by the interest his appearances aroused.

He first visited Britain in 1921, where he lost in the fourth round of the Amateur and made his first acquaintance with St Andrews in the Open. Though he later came to love the course above all others, he was so incensed by its intricacies that, in a fit of anger to which he was prone as a young man, he tore up his card. In 1958, when he attended the inaugural amateur world team championship (Eisenhower Trophy) at St Andrews in a wheelchair, he was made a freeman of the old burgh.

In 1923, having tied for second the previous year, he won the American Open after a play-off against Bobby Cruikshank, and this opened the floodgates to his unique record of successes.

He represented his country in

five early Walker Cup matches, and was undefeated in his singles, winning the last three against Britain's best by huge margins. In

American star Bobby Jones was so popular at St Andrews (*below*, in 1927) that he was awarded the town's freedom.

1930, after his unique grand slam, he made a series of instructional films, and in the belief that he had contravened the rules of amateurism, he retired, at 28, from competitive golf. In addition, he was beginning to find the strain too great. His fame drew large crowds to follow him and this, with the constant expectation that he would win, took its toll. He would sometimes lose as much as a stone in weight during championships, and often felt so sick he could not bear to wear a tie.

He retired to his law practice in Atlanta, loaded with honours and the respect of the golfing world. He continued to play at his beloved Augusta, and remained the inspiration behind the Masters tournament. But in the 1950s, he began to suffer from a muscular disease which eventually reduced him to a complete cripple.

JONES Robert Tyre, Jr	
Major tournament victories	
1916	Georgia State Amateur
1917	Southern Amateur
1920	Southern Amateur
1922	Southern Amateur
1923	US Open
1924	US Amateur
1925	US Amateur
1926	British Open
	US Open
1927	British Open
	US Amateur
	Southern Amateur
1928	US Amateur
1929	US Open
1930	British Open
	British Amateur
	US Open
	US Amateur
Representative Appearances	
USA v Great Britain (Walker Cup) 1921, 22, 24, 26, 28*, 30*	
*Captain	

Knudson

George (1937-   )

George Knudson, individual champion of the 1966 Canada Cup (World Cup) is probably the finest golfer Canada has produced.

Since he won the Canadian PGA championship in 1964, an air of mystery has grown up around this figure with long wavy hair and dark glasses, who flits on and off the rich United States tour, staying only long enough to satisfy his current financial needs (in 1968 he won the Phoenix and Tuscan Opens in successive weeks, then disappeared back across the border). He has won a reputation as a devoted, solitary drinker who can keep hours that would make Walter Hagen proud of him, yet has patterned himself after Ben Hogan in both swing technique and mental discipline. Hogan, in fact, has called Knudson the best swinger of the present generation.

Knudson has said that he aims for a 'flawless' swing, and the winning of championships and money seem secondary to his desire for perfection. Nevertheless, by 1970 he had won 10 United States tour events, and in 1969 shot a two-under-par 70 on the final day of the Masters Tournament and finished in second place behind George Archer. In 1968, his best money-winning year, he earned $71,360.

Despite his reputation for hard-drinking, Knudson was obsessed with physical conditioning programmes and gaining weight. Whenever possible he works out for two hours at a time in a gymnasium, lifting weights and doing calisthenics. In 1969 this programme gained him 20 lb and extra distance on his drives.

His last major victory was in the Kaiser International Open in 1972. Since then, Knudson's excursions to America have become increasingly less frequent, and today he has semi-retired from the full-time golf circuit.

Lacoste

Catherine (1945-   )

In the space of six years French golfer Catherine Lacoste built up a record of consistency unapproached in the amateur world since the days of Miss Joyce Wethered. Before her marriage in 1970, she announced her semi-retirement from the competitive game, having achieved the remarkable distinction of winning the American Open and Amateur championships, as well as the British and French titles, three of them in the same year.

Mlle Lacoste's disappearance from the international scene was almost as sudden as her first success. In 1964, the first world women's team championships were held in Paris, and Catherine

Ed Lacey

—aged 19—was instrumental in the French team's victory, while she tied for first place in the individual scoring. Four years later, in Sydney, she won the individual title outright.

Catherine's father was Rene Lacoste, the French tennis star, from whom she received the main guidance in perfecting her swing, and her mother was the former Simone Thion de la Chaume, who won the British Ladies golf championship in 1927. From them, Catherine inherited not only her skill, but her boundless energy and self-confidence. She also acquired an irresistible urge to reach the top and to shake off the tag of being the daughter of famous parents.

The year after her debut in the women's championship, Mlle Lacoste finished the second leading amateur in the United States women's Open championship, and in 1967 she returned to win the title against the best of the world's professional golfers. Also in 1967, she won the French Open for the first time, beating her chief rival in France Birgitte Varangot.

In stroke play, Catherine was supreme. Her long hitting—she made frequent use of the No. 1 iron—gave her a great advantage over her rivals. And in 1969 she won the British Hovis tournament with a score of 287—15 strokes better than her nearest challenger —at the 6,602-yards, par-74 Moor Park course. Three years earlier, in 1966, she had recorded a record 66 for the Prince's course at Sandwich on her way to victory in the Astor Trophy. But match play had often been her weak point. Twice she had led the qualifiers in the two rounds of stroke play that precede the match-play stage of the British women's championship. In 1969 she made special preparations for the champion-

Fox Photos

ship at Royal Portrush. Her powerful play was well suited to the windy conditions and she won the final 'one-up'. Inspired by this win and previous successes in the French Open and Spanish championships, she determined to try for the one victory she had yet to achieve—the US Amateur. Playing in Texas where the temperature rose above 100°F on occasions, she played par golf nearly all the time to complete a unique collection of golfing wins.

LACOSTE Catherine

Major tournament successes

1967	United States Open	
	French Open	
1968	US Western Amateur	
	French Closed	
1969	French Open	
	British Open	
	United States Amateur	
	Spanish Open	

World Amateur Team Championship (France)

1964	Team, 1st; Individual, equal 1st
1966	Team, 3rd; Individual, 3rd
1968	Team, 3rd; Individual, 1st

Legrange
Cobie (1942-   )

In 1964 a South African youngster called Cobie Legrange won six tournaments in Europe and Australasia, including the Dunlop Masters, and the world's golfing critics were convinced that another Bobby Locke or Gary Player had emerged from South Africa.

Several years later they were still waiting for proof from Legrange that he has the temperament to take his place in the international *elite*. Although he continued to win tournaments around the world, never less than two a year, he somehow missed out on the big occasions, and the most important win after his first Dunlop Masters in 1964 was his second, in 1969.

On the final day of that tournament he perhaps showed why he has so far missed the very top. He had led throughout and entered the final round with a six-shot lead over Peter Butler. But observers had noticed that a strange hesitancy had crept into Legrange's swing, causing him to 'stutter' on his backswing about a foot away from the ball. It had been noticeable in the earlier rounds, causing the newspapers to call him 'C-C-C-Cobie'. But in the final round he came to a full stop after 12 inches of the backswing and stuttered twice more before getting into full flow. It was nearly fatal, and if Butler had been able to exert any real pressure the result might have been very different.

1 George Knudson, probably the finest golfer to come out of Canada. 2 Catherine Lacoste (France) won just about every honour in the amateur game.

South Africa's Cobie Legrange never quite fulfilled the promise he showed as a youngster in 1964.

This apparent flaw in his temperament may well have prevented him consolidating the promise he showed 10 years ago, for Legrange's globe-trotting activities came to an end in the early 1970s when tournament success abroad deserted him. He has retired home to concentrate on the South African tour, where he remains a formidable force, though victories are slower in coming his way than they once were.

LEGRANGE Cobie

Tournaments won:

1964	Dunlop Masters
	Wills Masters (Australia)
	Western Australia TV Open
	*Wattis (NZ)
	St Moritz Open
1965	*Flame Lily (Rhodesia)
	Pringle
1966	Senior Service
	Gallacher Ulster Open
	Western Province Open
1967	General Motors Open (SA)
	Natal Open
	Pepsi-Cola Open (SA)
1968	General Motors Open (SA)
	Transvaal Open
	South African Dunlop
1969	Dunlop Masters
	Engadine Open
1971	Holiday Inns Invitation
1974	Schoeman Park Open

*Tied, no play-off

Lema
Tony (1934-1966)

One of the most tragic events in the history of golf occurred in 1966, when Tony Lema, the 32-year-old American who had won the British Open in 1964, died in a plane crash. Lema was only just beginning to find himself, both as an athlete and as a person. He was renowned for his extravagant and ostentatious life-style, and earned the nickname of 'Champagne Tony', though that came originally from his habit of celebrating success with presents of champagne to the Press. Ironically he

preferred whisky, but he made no attempt to water down his reputation as a high liver.

Born in Oakland, California, the son of a labourer, Lema had an early interest in golf and was a caddie at 12. After scratching around the tournament scene for several years, he and his brilliant putting suddenly came to the fore in 1964, when, following three major successes in the United States he captured the British Open title at St Andrews, finishing five strokes ahead of Jack Nicklaus.

The next year he amassed official earnings of over $100,000 to finish second to Nicklaus in the money race, and looked all set to challenge for the top position in world golf. In 1966 he won the Oklahoma City Open—by the widest margin in the US tour that year—and earned $48,200, before he was killed at mid-season. His private plane crashed—on a golf course—*en route* from the PGA Championship to a small pro-am tournament, and his second wife died with him.

Tony Lema—a plane crash in 1966 robbed the world of his brilliant golfing talents.

Littler
Gene (1930-   )

If one ignores the current big five of golf, one name keeps recurring as a constant winner and money winner on the American circuit. For over two decades, Gene Littler has swung along happily, enjoying every minute of his golf, unassailed by the whirlwinds that have overturned the game during his professional career.

Littler is the quiet man of the American tour. His modesty is as famed as Trevino's extroversion. 'I just don't crave attention', Littler has protested. 'My idea is to get the job done.'

He has done it with methodical efficiency. His first major victory was registered in 1954, when, as a 24-year-old amateur, he snatched the San Diego Open. The previous year he had won the US Amateur title. In 1955, and now in the paid ranks, he was acclaimed winner of four of the official PGA tournaments, including the prestigious Tournament of Champions, which he seized again the following two years.

Littler's greatest years as a tournament winner were in the late 1950s, culminating in 1961 when he returned one over par figures to pip Bob Goalby and Doug Sanders for the US Open. In terms of victories, the years that followed were lean ones, yet Littler remained consistently in the forefront of American golf, a constant threat in every tournament he entered. Throughout the 1960s, he was a regular member of the American Ryder Cup squad, getting involved in some never-to-be-forgotten duels. His match-play ability—alien to most Americans—was phenomenal, and by 1974 only Palmer and Casper had recorded more Ryder Cup victories.

Littler, for his fluent swing and effective though unspectacular golf, has been dubbed 'Gene the Machine'. It's not a soubriquet that upsets him, nor one that has made him complacent, for till the end his constant concern is to practise, practise, practise to improve his game. In 1969 he burst back as a winner in most untypical Littler fashion by knocking 21 strokes off par to take the Phoenix Open with a total of 265, the lowest score on the tour that year. Three more successes followed in the next two years, and Littler, one of the smallest golfers on the US tour, was again catapulted into the public eye.

Above, **Gene Littler at play in the 1970 US Masters. He was still winning in 1975 after a serious operation in 1972.**

Unfortunately, Littler's career received an unhappy setback in 1972, when a routine fitness test revealed cancer-infiltrated glands under his left arm. And though these were successfuly removed, his path back to tournament golf has been gradual and cautious.

LITTLER Gene	
Major victories	
1954	San Diego Open
1955	Los Angeles Open
	Phoenix Open
	Tournament of Champions
	Labatte Open
1956	Tournament of Champions
	Texas Open
	Palm Beach Round-Robin
1957	Tournament of Champions
1959	Phoenix Open
	Tucson Open
	Arlington Hotel Open
	Insurance City Open
	Miller Open
1960	Oklahoma City Open
	Eastern Open
1961	US Open
	Canadian Open
1966	World Series of Golf
1969	Phoenix Open
	Greensboro Open
1971	Monsanto Open
	Colonial National Invitation
1973	St Louis Childrens' Hospital Classic
1975	National Pro-Am Memphis Classic
	Westchester Classic

Representative appearances
USA v Great Britain (Walker Cup): 1953
USA v Great Britain (Ryder Cup): 1961,
1963, 1965, 1967, 1969, 1971, 1973

Ed Lacey

Above, **53-year-old Bobby Locke tees off the first in the 1970 British Open at St Andrews, where he won his fourth and last title in 1957 and later became an honorary member.** *Below,* **Locke, in familiar white cap, tie, and plus-fours, in action at Lytham in 1952.**

Fox Photos

Locke

Bobby (1917-   )

If Walter Hagen gave professional golf panache and Henry Cotton gave it professionalism, then Arthur D'Arcy Locke, known to millions of golfers the world over simply as Bobby, gave it an ingredient it needed to establish itself as a major world sport.

He gave it presence. With Bobby Locke in your tournament you not only had one of the greatest golfers the game has ever known but you also dignified the whole proceedings. Locke, who looked like an archetypal archbishop, could be depended upon to play superbly well, possibly win the tournament, charm every spectator with whom he came into contact—and do it all without a word or a hair out of place.

He was impressive in every sense of the word. Yet he had been an extremely volatile young man. Fortunately, for him and for golf, he realized sooner than most that the game is difficult enough without adding temperamental problems of your own making to it.

He saw the light in the first important final in which he played —the 1935 Transvaal Amateur Championship. He was then only 18, and when he found himself four holes down with six to play he was quietly certain that the match was lost. Then, as was to become typical in later years, he holed a long putt. His opponent, clearly not convinced that three up and five to play was a winning position, walked hurriedly off that green, hit a poor shot off the next tee and ultimately lost the match on the 19th. Locke had noticed the pointers and acted on them. He resolved there and then that he would never on the course betray any sort of emotion that could possibly give comfort to an opponent or interfere with his own highly distinctive play.

That year he went on to win the Natal and South African opens (the latter for the first of eight times) and the public began to realize that a new, if unconventional, star was upon them. The unconventionality lay in his method of hitting the ball—no golfer of his stature has hit the ball so crooked and won. Locke hit every shot way out to the right and hooked it back into the target, and on seeing it for the first time the spectator was strongly inclined to either disbelieve the evidence of his eyes or to dismiss the exponent as being not worth watching.

But Locke used that method the world over, won four British Open Championships with it, and confounded the Americans in their own nest in 1947 by becoming the second-highest money winner in the United States. The Americans, half in envy and half in respect, nicknamed him 'Old Muffin Face'.

Locke had one more important

asset going for him: he has been called the best putter the world has known—and it was he who established the sort of routine now followed by professionals the world over. The South African master believed that it did not matter which method you decided to use so long as you chose one, and stuck to it in all circumstances. This worked wonderfully for Locke. He went religiously through his routine with every putt, whether ten yards or ten inches.

Despite the apparent tranquility that surrounded everything underneath that famous and inevitable white cap, Locke was attended by incidents wherever he went, and two of them occurred when he was winning two of his British opens.

In his first win, at Sandwich in 1949, there occurred the 'Bradshaw Bottle' incident. The unfortunate Irishman Harry Bradshaw found his ball in the mouth of a broken bottle and decided to play it where it lay. He took a six, lost his composure,

and the round cost him a 77 and a tie on 283 with Locke. The South African won the 36-hole play-off by 12 shots.

In his last win, in 1957, he almost certainly infringed the rules of golf on the last green at, of all places, St Andrews. Watched by enormous crowds and all the rulemakers of golf, Locke had to mark his ball two putter lengths off the line of his putt. When the time came to replace it he put it back only one putter length away and thus technically infringed the rules. But only the worst kind of barrack-room lawyer could have insisted on disqualification, since Locke had won comfortably by three strokes.

That win was the last of Locke's important successes, although perhaps one of the ultimate honours was yet to come. In 1968, after a car accident had put an end to his serious playing career, he was invited, with Walter Hagen and Henry Cotton, to become an honorary member of the Royal and Ancient Club at St Andrews. It was an entirely fitting invitation to a man who, by simply being on a course, has added lustre to the game of golf.

Mann

Carol (1941-   )

Since she became a professional golfer in 1960, Carol Mann has given the United States Ladies PGA a welcome infusion of talent and personality. She has been a continual money winner on the ladies' professional tour, with her victories including the 1965 US PGA Women's Open, and was the first golfer to seriously challenge the authority Kathy Whitworth and Mickey Wright had stamped on women's professional golf.

Personality had been lacking in women's golf in America since the days of Babe Zaharias, but Miss Mann had that quality in plenty. A bubbling 6 ft 3 in blonde, Carol was the first women golfer to wear a mini-skirt in competition—a style that enhanced her long and attractive legs.

And when her partners in the pro-am events that precede tournaments score natural birdies, she rewards them with kisses. One of the few times she has been stumped for an answer was when an amateur made an eagle, and wondered what his reward would be if a birdie was worth a kiss. But all he got was two kisses.

Miss Mann's headline-grabbing career received another boost in 1970, when she played Doug Sanders in a stroke-play match.

LOCKE Arthur D'Arcy	
Tournaments and Awards	
1935—Transvaal Amateur	1950—British Open
Natal Open*	Dunlop Professional
South African Open*	Spalding
1936—Natal Open*	North British
1937—Transvaal Amateur	Yorkshire Evening News
South African Open*	Tam O'Shanter All-American Open
1938—South African Open	South African Open
South African Professional	South African Professional
Transvaal Open	Vardon Trophy
New Zealand Open	1951—South African Open
Irish Open	South African Professional
1939—South African Open	1952—British Open
South African Professional	French Open
1940—South African Open	Lotus
South African Professional	1953—French Open
1946—South African Open	1954—Egyptian Open
South African Professional	Egyptian Match-Play
Dunlop Masters†	German Open
Vardon Trophy	Swiss Open
1947—Canadian Open	Dunlop Masters
1949—British Open	Dunlop Professional
	Swallow
	Vardon Trophy
	1957—British Open
	Daks

*as an amateur †tied, no play-off

She lost by a whopping 12 strokes, but provided the press gallery with a week's supply of copy. 'There goes the women's liberation movement', she cracked after shooting her worst round in years.

In statistical terms, Carol's best year was 1969. She won $49,152 in official prize money (a record), won eight tournaments, and was second in the scoring averages. Since then, she has remained a challenging figure in golf, though she has devoted more and more of her time to administration and promoting women's professional golf. President of the US Ladies' PGA, Carol Mann has perhaps contributed more than any other woman, both in terms of golfing ability and in her untiring devotion to her beliefs, to elevating women's professional golf to its present status.

Carol Mann concentrates on her putt. Doug Sanders, who won their special match, concentrates on Carol Mann.

Miller
Johnny (1947-   )

Had Johnny Miller never achieved anything else, his record in 1974 would have assured him of a notable spot in the archives of golf. He won more money than any other golfer had ever won in a single year, and won more tournaments on an increasingly competitive tour than had fallen to any other individual since Palmer's heady days in 1962. Yet, almost incredibly, he began the 1975 tour in an even more sensational manner, winning the first two tournaments without going over 70 in any of his eight rounds.

Young, bland, good-looking, and flamboyant, Miller is the archetypal American golfing hero in appearance. Yet beneath the surface, he is a quiet, introspective man whose mentor is Billy Casper, and who, like Casper, is a devout Mormon. It was through his religion that his devotion to golf developed, for his talent was spotted and encouraged when he was a student at Salt Lake University. An outstanding amateur, he turned professional in 1969, finishing a nondescript 12th equal in the players' school, and his first two years on the circuit confirmed this pattern of hints of brilliance combined with more persistent mediocrity. The high points of Miller's golf sufficed to keep him in the public eye, tournament wins in 1971 and 1972 keeping him in a respectable position in the league of money winners, and he was repeatedly put forward as the primary potential challenger to the supremacy of Nicklaus et al.

Two events in 1973 justified the tributes Miller had continually received. In the US Open at Pebble Beach, he began the final round well down the list of challengers, confident of picking up a handsome prize but nothing more. A brilliant round dictated otherwise, and his historic record-breaking 63, which saw him charge past more than 20 competitors to win the championship, is one of the most dramatic and astonishing feats golf has ever known. Later in the year he made his first appearance for the United States in the World Cup, outshining his famous team-mate, Jack Nicklaus, to take the individual prize. Even this was little warning of what he was to achieve in 1974. When the opening tournament of the year, the Bing Crosby International, was abandoned after three rain-swept rounds, Miller, the leader at the time, was awarded the prize. Two weeks later, he added the Dean Martin-Tucson and the Phoenix opens to this victory, so becoming the first golfer in modern times to win the first three events of the tour.

Five more tournament wins in the year, and other high finishes, brought Johnny Miller a harvest of over $350,000. There are many who, on the evidence of this, promote Miller as the best player in the world today. Nevertheless, this opinion is somewhat premature, for there are a number of barriers Miller must pass before he can emulate Nicklaus and Gary Player. He must demonstrate over several seasons that he can maintain his form, win more major tournaments, and repeat his American victories abroad. If he can do this, then few will dispute that he is the most obvious heir-apparent to the mighty Nicklaus.

MILLER John		
Major victories		
1971	Southern Invitation Open	
1972	Heritage Classic	
	Otago Classic	
1973	US Open	
	Lancombe Trophy	
	World Cup (team* and individual)	
1974	Bing Crosby Invitation	
	Phoenix Open	
	Dean Martin-Tucson Open	
	Heritage Classic	
	Westchester Classic	
	World Open	
	Tournament of Champions	
	Kaiser International	
1975	Phoenix Open	
	Tucson Open	
	Desert Classic	
	Kaiser International	
Representative appearances		
World Cup: 1973		Ryder Cup: 1975
*With Jack Nicklaus		

Below, **Johnny Miller with wife and 1973 US Open trophy.**
Right, **About to drive.**

Morris

'Old Tom' (1821-1908)
and 'Young Tom'
(1850-1875)

The name of the Morrises is closely linked with the origins of the British Open golf championship. 'Old Tom' did not win the first championship in 1860—that honour fell to Willie Park—but in the seven years before his son took over, he won it four times. 'Young Tom's' first victory came in 1868 and, with his third consecutive victory in 1870, he won the Belt outright and the championship lapsed for a year. When it was revived in 1872, the trophy this time being a silver claret jug, he won again.

'Old Tom' was born at St Andrews and apprenticed to Allan Robertson in the ball-making trade. Robertson was, up to the time of the Morrises, the most famous of the St Andrews golfing personalities, and together the two took part in some famous challenge matches, notably against the Dunn brothers.

In 1851 'Old Tom' moved to Prestwick, the early home of the Open championship, but in 1865 he returned to St Andrews to act as greenkeeper to the Royal and Ancient golf club, a position he held until 1904. Much respected for his honest and sturdy quali-

1 'Young Tom' Morris wearing the British Open belt he won outright after his three consecutive victories from 1868 to 1870. 2 'Old Tom' Morris, his father, had won the Open four times prior to his son's hat-trick.

ties, and an unmistakable figure with his flowing beard, he took part in every Open until 1896.

His son was the more brilliant golfer, and although his career was tragically short, he is reckoned to have been one of the game's greats. He was 18 when he won his first Open, in 1868, and he won that and the next two championships with scores that were an average of nine strokes better than his nearest opponent.

He did not win in 1873 or 1874, but it is probable that the illness that caused his premature death was already beginning to affect him, and his demise was hastened by the death of his wife in childbirth in 1875.

The few photographs that exist of 'Young Tom'—one of them formed the basis for the monument of him that stands in St Andrews Cathedral—show him to be a forceful, dashing golfer. This is reinforced by the story that he used to break shafts simply by waggling the club.

MORRIS Tom Senior & Junior

Open Championship Wins
Tom Morris senior: 1861, 1862, 1864, 1867
Tom Morris junior: 1868, 1869, 1870, 1872

Nagle

Kel (1920-   )

A big-boned, burly golfer with a seemingly casual and uncomplicated swing, Australian Kel Nagle won one of the most coveted golf prizes of the 1960s—the Centenary British Open at St Andrews in 1960.

That win was one of the biggest shocks the golf world has known. Arnold Palmer was hot favourite for the event, having already won the American Masters and the American Open, whereas Nagle, aged 40, had won nothing bigger individually than the Australian Open. Bookmakers rated him no better than a 35-1 shot, but they had not reckoned on Peter Thomson, with whom Nagle had twice won the Canada Cup. Already four-times Open winner, including once at St Andrews, Thomson showed Nagle how to play the course, which lines to take and which to avoid. And then, realizing that his compatriot was putting better than anyone in the field, he went out to get some of that 35-1.

Nagle did not let him down. When he reached the treacherous 17th, the Road Hole, for the last time he was two strokes ahead of Palmer, who was playing the 18th. As he stepped up to a 10 ft putt for his par, a huge roar told him Palmer had holed for a birdie three and that it was vital to hole the putt facing him and get his four at the 18th to win. He stepped away from the putt, stepped back, readdressed the ball, and then calmly holed it. The worst was over and a straightforward four at the 18th gave him the title.

Perhaps the most surprising aspect of his win was the fact that Nagle had been playing world golf

for only four years. Until he was 36 he had largely stayed in Australia, to be with his wife and children, and it was not until his Canada Cup wins, coupled with some promptings from Thomson, that he decided to try his luck abroad.

In America he struggled for some time, but then, with the help of new clubs, he finished second in the Colonial Invitational. As well as the money, this placing gave him an awareness of his ability, and it was this new-found confidence that helped him at St Andrews.

Nagle confirmed his ability to a somewhat sceptical British public when, in 1962, he and Palmer again found themselves battling for the Open. But this time, at Troon, Palmer put together what he has described as the best four rounds of his life to finish six shots ahead of the Australian.

After that, Nagle again tried his luck in the United States, and in 1964 came nearest to winning a tournament on the American tour. He had played in nine events, finishing well in all of them, before going to Montreal for the Canadian Open, which he won. But although all the tournament stars play in this event, it is not officially rated by the US PGA. Nagle finished that year 22nd on the money list with $24,000, and the following year he won even more. Although he finished 26th in the list this time, he earned $34,000, a large part of which came from a tie with Gary Player for the US Open. It was the first time that two foreigners had tied for the championship, and though Player won the play-off with some ease, Kel Nagle, one of the most pleasant men in golf, had amply proved both to himself and to the world that he was one of the game's great players.

NAGLE Kelvin

Major Tournaments Won
1949	Australian PGA
1954	Canada Cup (with Peter Thomson)
	Australian PGA
1957	New Zealand Open
	New Zealand Professional
1958	Australian PGA
	New Zealand Open
	New Zealand Professional
1959	Canada Cup (with Peter Thomson)
	Australian Open
	Australian PGA
1960	British Open
	New Zealand Professional
1961	French Open
	Dunlop
1962	New Zealand Open
	Bowmaker
1963	Esso Golden
1964	Canadian Open
	New Zealand Open
1965	Australian PGA
	Bowmaker
1967	New Zealand Open
1968	New Zealand Open
1969	New Zealand Open
	Victoria Open
1973	NZ PGA
	British Seniors' Championship
1974	NZ PGA

Nelson

Byron (1912-)

American professional Byron Nelson set one of the most imposing records in golf—one that in the early 1970s looked like standing for all time. During the 1945 season, the 33-year-old Nelson won 11 consecutive PGA open tournaments, and in all that year won 17 titles. He shot 19 rounds in a row under 70 and compiled a stroke average of 68.33.

A few sceptics have contended that 1945 was a war year and that Nelson, exempt from military service because of haemophilia (caused by the inability of the white corpuscles to clot blood haemorrhages) faced competition that was less than trying. However, his unmatched stroke average was not much influenced, if at all, by the calibre of the fields—which were not all that bad anyway.

Nelson began his golfing career, as did Ben Hogan, as a caddy at Fort Worth, Texas. He turned professional in 1933, and just four years later won his first major title, the US Masters. In 1939 he enjoyed an extremely successful year, capturing the US Open (after a three-way play-off), the Western Open, the North and South Open, and the Vardon Trophy, and was runner-up in the PGA. It was considered the greatest achievement since Bobby Jones's grand slam in 1930. He won the PGA the following year, and in 1942 won his second Masters, beating his old rival Ben Hogan in a play-off.

His phenomenal 1945 season saw him win his second PGA title, and yet amazingly that was his only full year on the PGA tour. Before then he spent much of each season teaching in order to supplement his income, and in 1946 he went into semi-retirement while still at his peak. He was a nervous perfectionist, plagued by stomach disorders while competing, and the tour took a great toll on him physically.

1 Australia's Kel Nagle, aged 49, competing in the 1969 British Open. 2 Nagle putting in the 1960 Centenary Open, which he won. 3 Byron Nelson, US non-playing captain, at the 1965 Ryder Cup with British Premier Harold Wilson. 4 Nelson in the 1939 play-off for the US Open, which he won.

Colour Sport

Popperfoto

NELSON John Byron Jr

Major Tournaments Won

1937	US Masters
1939	US Open
	Western Open
	North and South Open
1940	US PGA
1942	US Masters
1945	US PGA
1951	Bing Crosby Invitational
1955	French Open

Representative Appearances
USA v Great Britain (Ryder Cup):
1937, 39*, 41*, 47

*Match not played

Nicklaus

Jack (1940-   )

In August 1973, Jack Nicklaus shot a steady but unspectacular round of 69 over the Canterbury course at Cleveland. He had played better golf in his life, he had gone round in less strokes. Nevertheless, it was an admirable round, for it enabled Nicklaus to build on the single-stroke lead he had held at the end of the previous round—the penultimate round—of the tournament, the US PGA. Any tournament leader who withstands the pressure of the chasing pack merits his applause. But for Nicklaus that day it was even more deserved, for he had just won his 14th major 'classic' title, beating the record that had stood in the name of Bobby Jones for more than 40 years.

Nicklaus's record is a phenomenal achievement moulded together since he turned professional in 1962. That year, 12 months after winning the US Amateur for the second time, he defeated Arnold Palmer for the US Open. Since then he has added the US Open twice more; has won the British Open twice; the US Masters four times; and the US PGA three times. His 271 in the 1965 Masters was 17 under par and three strokes under Ben Hogan's record, and his 275 at Baltusrol in 1967 equalled the US Open record. No event of any significance in golf has evaded his grasp, and the only possible target he can now have left is to complete the grand slam of all four events in one year. He has now won more from golf than any other player, and with well over 50 victories on the tour already to his credit, Sam Snead's tally from a more relaxed era cannot be dismissed as beyond his reach.

Ever since Nicklaus established himself almost immediately as a professional star, there has been speculation that he would possibly succumb to the lack of a challenge. Having done so much in such a short period of time, the pundits asked, could he sustain his interest and motivate himself to remain a great player? But though there have been periods of months at a time when even Nicklaus himself, floundering in what for him was mediocre play, had to wonder, they have always passed. In 1970, for example, he had done little to cause a great stir. But then, inspired by the Old Course at St Andrews, he came storming back to defeat Doug Sanders in a play-off and regain the British Open title.

Although more and more he plays a limited schedule and allocates more time to his family,

Jack Nicklaus has won more 'Big Four' titles than any other player and is always 'the man to beat'.

to fishing, and to making substantial additions to his income from off-the-course pursuits, Nicklaus nonetheless is driven by the urge to stay ahead, to continue to satisfy his urge for victory, although today a tournament win is no more than a bonus to his unsurpassable record. And if he is sometimes not at the top of his game in routine tournaments, he is always at short odds when playing for the four principal titles. At 30, he had, as Herbert Warren Wind (Nicklaus' collaborator on an autobiography) contends, arrived at a turning point in his illustrious career. He could easily go on to win many more important trophies and establish himself as possibly the

most successful player ever. Perhaps more important, though, was the fact that he was coming into his own as a personality.

In 1962, his first complete year on the United States tour, a pudgy, quiet Nicklaus upset national hero Arnold Palmer in the US Open, and millions of golf followers resented what they considered outlandish audacity. For some years afterwards, Nicklaus was often taunted by galleries, some of whom went so far as to kick his ball into the rough and jeer at his physique to his face. But by 1970, Palmer was no longer the leading force on the tour, and a more mature Nicklaus had done much to cultivate a large share of support for himself.

He had reduced from 210 lb to a dashing 190 lb, had styled his blond hair after the fashion of a modern film actor, and in general was enjoying a hard-earned new popularity. In additions, he no longer showed his emotions as much as he had earlier. The satisfaction of his golfing goals lent him a self-assuredness previously lacking, and he communicated it to the public. This, and his incomparable performances, at last established the popularity he deserved.

The Nicklaus personality may be phlegmatic, but his game is still spectacular. His controlled hitting is awesome, and 350-yard drives are not unusual. As the 10-year-old son of an Ohio drug-

gist, Nicklaus was taught by club professional Jack Grout to take a full swing and develop his power, worrying about accuracy later. Nicklaus swears by the approach, and a feature of his big, upright swing is the ferocious leg drive on the downswing.

When he was 12, he broke 80, and at 16 won the Ohio Open. He won the National Jaycee tournament at 17, and when he was 19 captured the US Amateur—a feat he repeated two years later. In 1960, when he helped the United States team win the Eisenhower Trophy at Merion, near Philadelphia, his 269 was 18 strokes better than Ben Hogan had managed in winning the 1950 US Open on the same course.

Nicklaus majored in business at Ohio State University, and the long Ohio State golf course further developed his powerful driving potential. But for all his strength and distance, Nicklaus possesses a subtle, finely effective short game, and can be a remarkably good putter. In fact, his superb blend of power and finesse have never been surpassed in golf. Bobby Jones, who was Nicklaus' first golfing hero, once said: 'I have seen many big fellows in my time, but they all had some weakness. Jack has no weakness. He should wind up shooting in the 50s'.

Jones does not even preclude the possibility of Nicklaus's emulating him by winning the modern grand slam – the four major tournaments in a year. By 1975 he had won two of them four times – the Masters and the PGA in 1963 and 1975; the Masters and the British Open in 1966; the Masters and the US Open in 1972. His dedication to achieving this feat appears immovable, the unique ingredient that drags the best out of Nicklaus in every major event. And, as Jones says, 'Jack is con-

siderably more powerful than I was, and has a good temperament. He has a tremendous, delicate touch on the greens. The "slam" is entirely within the realm of possibility for a player of Jack's capabilities.'

Jones calls Nicklaus's 1965 Masters record the greatest performance in golfing history, and few would contest this. Hogan's 274 in 1953 was figured to stand forever at Augusta, but Nicklaus shot a staggering 67, 71, 64, 69, hitting virtually every wood and iron shot precisely on line. It all too well illustrated something his fellow professionals already knew or were soon to learn: when Nicklaus is at his best he is, to phrase it quite basically, unbeatable.

NICKLAUS Jack William	
Major Victories	
1959	US Amateur
1960	Eisenhower Trophy (team & individual)
1961	US Amateur
1962	**US Open**
	World Series of Golf
	Seattle Open
	Portland Open
1963	**US PGA**
	US Masters
	Canada Cup (team* & individual)
	Tournament of Champions
	World Series of Golf
	Sahara Invitational
	Palm Springs Classic
1964	Phoenix Open
	Canada Cup (team* & individual)
	Tournament of Champions
	Whitemarsh Open
	Portland Open
	Australian Open
1965	**US Masters**
	Memphis Open
	Thunderbird Classic
	Portland Open
	Philadelphia Classic
1966	**US Masters**
	British Open
	Canada Cup (team*)
	PGA National*
1967	**US Open**
	World Cup (team*)
	Bing Crosby National
	Western Open
	Westchester Classic
	World Series of Golf
	Sahara Invitational
1968	Western Open
	American Golf Classic
	Australian Open
1969	Andy Williams San Diego Open
	Sahara Invitational
	Kaiser International Open
1970	**British Open**
	World Series of Golf
	PGA National*
	Byron Nelson Classic
	Piccadilly match play
1971	**US PGA**
	Australian Open
	Tournament of Champions
	Byron Nelson Classic
	Dunlop International (Aus)
	World Cup (team† and individual)
1972	**US Masters**
	US Open
	Westchester Classic
	US Match Play
	Walt Disney World Open
	Doral-Eastern Open
	Bing Crosby National†
1973	**US PGA**
	Bing Crosby National
	Greater New Orleans Open
	Tournament of Champions
	Atlanta Classic
	Walt Disney World Open
	Ohio Kings Island Open
	World Cup (team‡)
1974	Hawaiian Open
	Tournament Players' Championship
1975	**US Masters**
	US PGA
	Doral-Eastern Open
	Sea Pines Heritage Classic
	World Open
	Australian Open
Representative appearances	
Eisenhower Trophy: 1960	
USA v Great Britain (Walker Cup): 1961	
USA v Great Britain (Ryder Cup): 1969, 1971, 1973	
World Cup: 1963, 1964, 1965, 1966, 1967, 1972, 1973	

*With Arnold Palmer   †With Lee Trevino
‡With Johnny Miller

'When Nicklaus is at his best, he is unbeatable.'

O'Connor
Christy (1928-   )

Christy O'Connor was the first professional golfer in Great Britain to win a four-figure cheque, and, in the 1970 John Player Classic, the first to win a five-figure cheque (pounds sterling). Since 1955, when he first appeared in the Ryder Cup team, he has been one of the leading money winners in professional golf.

O'Connor's colleagues call him 'Wristy Christy' because he hits the ball with a pronounced flick of the wrists—a method that has served him well through the years. Occasionally his putting becomes a little too flexible and he has a lean spell, but any suggestion, as he plays through middle-age, that he is over the hill was strongly rebutted at Hollinwell in Nottinghamshire when he won the £25,000 first prize in the John Player event.

O'Connor has, at some time or other, won almost all that British professional golf has to offer, and his home town of Galway recognized this in 1970 when they made him their first Freeman. The one outstanding omission on his record is the lack of a win in the Open Championship, though he has the best and most consistent record in this event of any of the British professionals: between 1958 and 1969 he finished in the top six on seven occasions, and in 1965 came second, two shots behind Peter Thompson.

He has played in every Ryder Cup team from 1955 to 1969, and although his match-play record is not outstanding—he has won the British Match-Play Championship only once—he was one of the stars in the 1957 defeat of the Americans at Lindrick, defeating Dow Finsterwald 7 and 6. In the 1969 tied series at Royal Birkdale, O'Connor scored 22 points out of four appearances despite a troublesome back.

O'Connor derives considerable inspiration from playing in his own country. He won five Carrolls tournaments and the Gallaher event three times, all against the regular tournament field, and since 1958, when he first won the Irish Professional Championship, he has been considered the man to beat in that competition. In fact his most famous victory was for his country—in 1958, when, thousands of miles from his native soil, he and Harry Bradshaw fought their way around the rarefied conditions of Mexico City to win the Canada Cup (now the World Cup).

He has not looked back since that point, and he and his 'Black Pack'—a reference to the many priests always to be found in an O'Connor gallery—have seen many an inspired finish. The most notable was at his own club of Royal Dublin where, in order to win a Carrolls event, he finished eagle, birdie, eagle to the intense joy of the local crowd.

If there was to be any impediment to O'Connor's career, it would not be the will or the determination of the man himself. In the 1970s, rheumatism began to take hold of him and, having been forced to retire from several tournaments, he realized that his only solution was to systematically restrict, his appearances. But though his success has inevitably been limited recently, it is far too soon to even think about writing an epitaph for O'Connor's playing career.

O'CONNOR Christy	
Major tournament successes and awards:	
1956	Dunlop Masters
1957	British Match-Play Champion
1958	Irish Professional Champion
	Canada Cup (team*)
1959	Dunlop Masters
	Daks Tournament
1960	Irish Professional Champion
	Ballantine Tournament
	Irish Hospitals Tournament
1961	Irish Professional Champion
	Irish Hospitals Tournament
	Harry Vardon Trophy
1962	Irish Professional Champion
	Irish Hospitals Tournament
	Harry Vardon Trophy
1963	Irish Professional Champion
	Martini Tournament†
	Carrolls Sweet Afton
1964	Martini Tournament
	Carrolls Sweet Afton
1965	Irish Professional Champion
1966	Irish Professional Champion
	Carrolls Sweet Afton
	Gallagher Ulster
1967	Carrolls Sweet Afton
1968	Carrolls No. 1 Tournament
	Gallagher Ulster
	Alcan International†
1969	Gallagher Ulster
	Irish Southern PGA
1970	John Player Classic
1972	Carrolls International
Representative appearances	
Great Britain v USA (Ryder Cup): 1955, 1957, 1959, 1961, 1963, 1965, 1967, 1969, 1971, 1973	
Canada Cup (Ireland): 1958	

*With Harry Bradshaw †Joint winner

Left, **Irishman Christy O'Connor won more than twice as much money as anyone else on the British circuit in 1970, thanks mainly** *(below)* **to his success in the £25,000 first-prize John Player Classic at Hollinwell, Notts.**

Sport & General

Oosterhuis

Peter (1948-   )

Within a year of turning professional, Peter Oosterhuis was able to establish a domination of the British golf circuit which he maintained in the first half of the 1970s. A young giant of a man, Oosterhuis had made his mark on British golf while still a public schoolboy—beaten finalist in the 1967 British Amateur and a member of the 1967 Walker Cup team.

He turned professional at the end of 1968, while still a teenager, demonstrating the challenge he was to present to the established stars of the British tour by winning the Coca-Cola Young Professionals Tournament in inaugural season. Nevertheless, the transition from the tranquility of public school life to the hectic merry-go-round world of the professional tournament player could not have been without its initial difficulties, for, apart from this one success, 1970 was a lean year for Oosterhuis.

By another year, however, he had obviously adapted thoroughly. Touring South Africa as a prelude to the British season, he scooped three victories, an augury of his coming year in Britain. Returning home, he registered his first major triumph in Britain by winning the Piccadilly Medal, one of the most prestigious and rigorous tournaments on the circuit, and a succession of fine performances won him a place in the Ryder Cup team to play in America. By the end of the year he was topping the Order of Merit table, a position he was to hold continuously until 1974.

With Tony Jacklin still con-

127

centrating on the Amercan tour, Oosterhuis was undisputed champion of British golf. His avowed aim, however, was to not only emulate Jacklin but to surpass his compatriot's achievements overseas. Unlike other young British professionals, Oosterhuis was not deceived by instant success in the United Kingdom into rushing post-haste across the Atlantic to sacrifice his natural talent in the gruelling competitive world that exists there. A cool, assured, young golfer, he was well aware that temperament and control of his ability must first be developed before he committed himself to the final test, and his ventures to America were purely the token moves toward acclimatization and experience. Yet on one of these, in 1973, he almost pre-empted his own plans. A guest at Augusta in the Masters, the previously anonymous young Englishman was feted by the American enthusiasts as he led the tournament by three strokes

going into the final round. Ultimately he was to finish third equal with Jack Nicklaus behind Tommy Aaron, but his performance made his entrance to the tour an eagerly awaited event.

However, it was to be delayed a year, the only material setback Oosterhuis' career has encountered. He joined the players' school to compete for his tournament card in 1973, after an exhausting season and concurrent with the expected birth of his first child. Even for Oosterhuis, who has an apparently endless capacity to absorb the rigours of golf, it was too much, and he failed to qualify. The next year he redeemed himself, finishing fourth equal after a season that had seen him just fail to win his first American tournament, losing the Pensacola Open in a play-off to Lee Elder. Indeed, 1974 had been an outstanding year for him. He was the only golfer to seriously chase home Gary Player in the British Open, and his three major

European championships were supplemented by the runners-up position in another six.

Perhaps the most earnest and painstaking golfer in Britain today, Oosterhuis seems destined for international success. For all his height and power, his golfing strength lies in a desire to master all aspects of his game, and he is particularly respected for his dexterity on and around the greens. He complements his talent with an awareness of the importance of the mechanics of golf and golf courses, possessing one of the most complete sets of golfing statistics imaginable. By the end of 1974, Oosterhuis had played 62,301 games as a professional golfer, averaging 71.45 a round. The calculations are sure to be accurate, for the source is irrefutable—Oosterhuis himself.

Peter Oosterhuis established himself as Britain's leading tournament golfer in the 1970s ahead of Tony Jacklin.

OOSTERHUIS Peter

Major victories

1970 Coca-Cola Young Professionals Tournament
1971 Piccadilly Medal
Rhodesian Dunlop Masters
Leykor Transvaal Open
Park Open (SA)
Topped Order of Merit table
1972 Penfold Tournament
Clen Anil Golf Classic
Topped Order of Merit table
1973 French Open
Piccadilly Medal
Maracaibo Open
Rothmans International (SA)
Viyella PGA
Topped Order of Merit table
1974 French Open
Italian Open
El Paraiso Open
Raleigh Cup (Mex)
Topped Order of Merit table

Representative apearances
Great Britain v USA (Walker Cup): 1967
Great Britain v USA (Ryder Cup): 1971, 1973 1975

Ouimet
Francis (1893-1967)

The claim to fame of Francis Ouimet was his victory in the 1913 United States Open golf championship, which has been described as the most momentous of all time. Ouimet was a 20-year-old amateur, and unknown outside the state of Massachusetts, where he was born, when he forced the dominant British pair Vardon and Ray to a tie and then beat them decisively in a play-off. Up to that point, American golf had been dominated by British players or by Scottish immigrants, and Ouimet's victory put golf on the front page in the United States and opened the way for the rapid development of the game in the next decade.

Though quiet and unassuming off the course, he played with great confidence. The following year he won the American and French Amateur titles and finished fifth in the US Open. The fact that he had risen from caddy ranks inspired numerous other caddies, from whom some of the best players of the next decade were to spring.

Ouimet played in the first Walker Cup match ever held, in 1922, and took part in every subsequent one, as player or captain, until 1949. He served for many years on the councils of the United States Golf Association, and his popularity in Britain was recognized when in 1951-52 he was elected captain of the Royal and Ancient golf club, the first non-Briton to receive the honour.

Francis Ouimet plays himself out of a bunker in the 1911 British amateur championship.

Palmer
Arnold (1929-   )

By the end of the 1960s Arnold Palmer had won more money than any other professional golfer, won more major tournaments than anyone else, and for 15 years had dominated the courses of the world in a way unlikely to be surpassed. Yet if the many people who consider Palmer the greatest golfer in history were asked why, it would probably not be for these reasons. For, more than any other person, Palmer transformed golf from the second-rate pastime it was in the early 1950s into the

tremendous boom sport it became nearly a decade later. In America in the early 1970s courses were being laid out at a rate of two every day; in Europe golf was rapidly becoming a 'common denominator' sport; in Japan millions of players had to be content with driving-range golf—all because of the impetus given to the game by Palmer. He captured the imagination of the American public as few people in any walk of life have done. His election as American Athlete of the Decade in 1970 was almost a formality.

The reasons are not hard to find. America is a nation that worships the dollar, and Palmer has won more than anyone. It is a nation that insists its heroes are clean-cut, clear-eyed All American boys, and Palmer—5 ft 10½ in and 13 st 8 lb—is the epitome of that ideal. Among a brash, demanding people, Palmer, off the course, is humble, humorous, and honest. With his $800,000 private aeroplane and myriad business interests he is, in short, everybody's 'boy-next-door-made-good'.

On the golf course he becomes the archetypal hero figure. He hits the ball a mile, strides after it purposefully, belts it on to the green, and putts it at the hole as if there was nowhere else for it to go. If he finds his ball among trees, he is more likely to go for the shot between two branches only inches apart, and then emerge grinning and waving to the deafening cheers of his vast band of supporters—'Arnie's Army'—as the ball pitches on the green.

The son of a professional at the Latrobe Country Club, Pennsylvania, Palmer had an outstanding amateur career before turning

professional himself in 1954. He did not have to serve a long apprenticeship before winning his first major tournament, the 1955 Canadian Open, with four rounds of 64, 67, 64, and 70 for a total of 265, his best ever.

It was in 1958 that Palmer gave the word 'charge' to the golfing vocabulary. Although he had won nine tournaments in his first three years on the professional circuit, he had yet to win one of the 'big four' championships. In the week before the US Masters he tied for the Azalea Open with Howie Johnson, and although they were both still 'rookies' on the circuit, Palmer was considered the favourite. But he made the mistake of dismissing the play-off from his mind, and as a result lost it 78–77. From this defeat stems Palmer's philosophy of 'thinking big' about every round. He duly won the Masters, and two years later won the Masters again and the United States Open with the aid of his 'give it a go' policy.

In 1960 he had already won the Masters, but after three rounds of the Open was 7 shots behind the leader, Mike Souchak. It seemed unlikely that he would win, but he proceeded to birdie 6 of the first 7 holes, went round in 65, and took the title. This was the Palmer 'charge' at its best.

In 1961 he set British golf alight with his win in the Open at Royal Birkdale. In 1962 he took over completely. The Open was held at Troon, on baked fairways with an unpredictable bounce. American players were thought to be at a disadvantage, being used to lush, watered fairways and greens. But Palmer won by 6 strokes from Kel Nagle, with the best British player, Brian Huggett, third—13 strokes behind. For once Palmer abandoned his 'charge' technique and played very carefully, using a No. 3 wood or a No. 1 iron from the tee. Many consider that Palmer played the best golf ever seen in Scotland in that exhibition. He certainly put the British Open back on the golfing map in a big way. That year he also won the Masters, for a third time, and was beaten in the American Open only after a play-off against Jack Nicklaus which he lost 71–74, one of his rate play-off defeats.

By then, Palmer was a household name all over the world. He was a personal friend of President Eisenhower with whom he often played. And such was the magic of his name that he was able to endorse not only the usual golfing goods but a chain of dry cleaning stores and a brand of lawnmower. This outlet was masterminded by Mark McCormack, a young lawyer who became the first manager to exploit the potential of golf on a commercial scale. His shrewd management made Palmer a millionaire many times over.

At the beginning of the 1970s, only one honour had eluded Palmer in his long and illustrious

career—victory in the United States PGA championship. It was in the 1969 event that the critics thought they saw the first signs of the tremendous pace he had maintained beginning to tell on him. He had been suffering from bursitis in his hip, and this flared up in the first round. He took 40 to the turn, and came back in 42—his total was his worst in any major championship round, and he withdrew from the tournament.

While the critics began writing him off, Palmer took a three-month rest, played unobtrusively in a couple of tournaments, and then went to South Carolina for the Heritage Golf Classic. He won by three strokes after leading all the way, surviving a crisis in the last round when he typically saved a par at the short tenth after his initial tee shot had landed in water. He followed this with victory in the Danny Thomas Diplomat Classic, 'charging' the last 18 holes in 65 to demoralize Gay Brewer who had been putting like a demon. Palmer in fact picked up 9 shots in the last 17 holes from his rival, to win by 2 strokes. It was just like old times, and if the sportswriters ballotting for the American Athlete of the Decade needed any reminding, here it was. Palmer was duly elected.

In the 1970s Palmer ungrudgingly resigned his master's mantle to Jack Nicklaus, but then proceeded to attack the new maestro —as if he, Palmer, were a naive rookie challenging for glory. He knows better than any man that his best years are behind him, for if his skill has not diminished, his stamina has.

For all that, he remains a constant threat to the young aspirants on the American tour, recording three more victories in 1971 and two years later hitting the forefront once more by winning the gruelling Bob Hope Open. He has not won one of the classics since 1964, but year after year he has finished close to the leader in the US Masters and Open. There is a lot of golf left in the old man yet, the tour novices are forced to concede, even as Palmer grows closer to the day when he will be eligible to enter for the seniors' events. It is fitting that even today, Palmer, the man who has given more to golf than any other individual in his lifetime, should remain the leading focus of respect and admiration of spectator and fellow competitor alike.

The epitome of the 'boy who made good', Arnold Palmer is a hero to golfers and public alike. More than any other player in history, he helped take golf to the people and make it one of the greatest spectator sports in history.

Ed Lacey

131

Right **Palmer has always been popular with the crowds, and is a joy to watch in action.**

PALMER Arnold Daniel

Major Victories

1950 Western Pennsylvania Amateur
1954 US Amateur
1955 Canadian Open
1956 Panama Open
       Colombia Open
       Insurance City Open
       Eastern Open
1957 Houston Open
       Azalea Open
       Rubber City Open
       San Diego Open
1958 **US Masters**
       St Petersburg Open
       Pepsi Open
1959 Thunderbird Invitational
       Oklahoma City Open
       West Palm Beach Open
1960 **US Open**
       US Masters
       Canada Cup (team*)
       Palm Springs Desert Classic
       Texas Open
       Baton Rouge Open
       Pensacola Open
       Insurance City Open
       Mobile Open
1961 **British Open**
       Texas Open
       Phoenix Open
       Baton Rouge Open
       San Diego Open
       Western Open
1962 **US Masters**
       British Open
       Canada Cup (team*)
       Palm Springs Golf Classic
       Phoenix Open
       Texas Open
       Tournament of Champions
       Colonial National Invitation
       American Golf Classic
1963 Canada Cup (team†)
       Los Angeles Open
       Phoenix Open
       Pensacola Open
       Thunderbird Classic
       Cleveland Open
       Western Open
       Whitemarsh Open
       Wills Masters (Australia)
1964 **US Masters**
       Canada Cup (team†)
       Oklahoma City Open
       Piccadilly World Match Play
1965 Tournament of Champions
1966 Canada Cup (team†)
       Australian Open
       Los Angeles Open
       Tournament of Champions
       Houston Champions International
       PGA National†
1967 World Cup (individual and team†)
       Tucson Open
       Los Angeles Open
       American Golf Classic
       Thunderbird Classic.
       Piccadilly World Match Play
1968 Bob Hope Desert Classic
       Kemper Open
1969 Heritage Golf Classic
       Danny, Thomas Diplomat Classic
1971 Bob Hope Desert Classic
       Florida Citrus Open
       Westchester Classic
1973 Bob Hope Desert Classic
1975 Spanish Open
       Penfold PGA

Representative appearances
USA v Great Britain (Ryder Cup): 1961, 1963, 1965, 1967, 1971, 1973
World Cup: 1960, 1962, 1963, 1964, 1966, 1967

*With Sam Snead †With Jack Nicklaus

Panton

John (1916-   )

One of the most respected professionals on the British circuit, John Panton began his long golf career in 1934. A retiring nature and modest outlook have perhaps accounted for his not attaining the highest honours in the game, especially in later years when self-expression began to play an increasing part in the spectacle of professional golf.

But he has achieved several notable victories, his most successful year being 1951 when, after winning one tournament and finishing runner-up in a second, he carried off the Vardon Trophy for the best stroke average and made the first of three appearances in the Ryder Cup. His most important victory, however, was in the *News of the World* matchplay championship of 1956, when he defeated Harry Weetman in the final at Hoylake. In rough weather he showed, as he has shown on many occasions since, that he is a magnificent iron player. Some of his best golf has been played in wind, when his solid frame, sound swing, and compact style serve him well. In 1969, at the age of 53, he reached the final of the matchplay championship, losing at Walton Heath to Brian Huggett.

Panton turned to golf in preference to soccer, at which he was good enough to get a trial for Dundee. He was born at Pitlochry, and after serving through World

Scottish star John Panton graced the British golfing scene for more than 20 years.

War II went as professional to Glenbervie, where he has remained since. He won both the Scottish professional championship and the Northern Open seven times, and numerous other Scottish events more than once. His dominance in Scottish golf is shown by his having represented his country in the Canada Cup (now World Cup) 12 consecutive years from 1955. He was awarded the golf writers' trophy in 1967 after he had won the Teacher world senior championship, and in 1965 had shared the Frank Moran trophy with Eric Brown.

PANTON John

Championships and Awards
Scottish Professional Championship 1948, 49, 50, 51, 54, 55, 59
Northern Open Championship 1948, 51, 52, 56, 59, 60, 62
Daks Tournament 1951
News of the World Matchplay Championship 1956
Cutty Sark Tournament 1964, 65, 67
Teacher World Senior Championship 1967
Teacher British Senior Championship 1967, 69
Vardon Trophy 1951
Golf Writers' Trophy 1967
Representative Appearances
Great Britain v USA (Ryder Cup) 1951, 53, 61
World Cup (Scotland) 1955, 56, 57, 58, 59, 60, 61, 62, 63, 64, 65, 66

Phillips
Frank (1932-   )

One of the big hitters of Australian golf, Frank Phillips has had a checkered career. Often he has appeared likely to force his way into the big league of world golf. But on other occasions slumps in form have placed him well back in the placings in major golf tournaments.

The Sydney-born Phillips looked particularly promising in the late 1950s and early 1960s. In the space of five years he carried off two Australian Open titles from fields that included some of the world's best players. The first, in 1957, was won on the Kingston Heath course in Melbourne. More than 7,000 yards long, Kingston Heath suited Phillips' big-hitting style of play—and in winning the championship the Australian outstayed strong challenges from South African Gary Player and fellow-countryman Ossie Pickworth. In 1961, at the Victoria Club, he beat another world-class player, Kel Nagle, into second position. His four-round score of 272 had, at the beginning of the 1970s, been bettered only twice in the history of the Australian Open (by Gary Player and Jack Nicklaus).

It was after his first Open success that Phillips was chosen to partner Nagle in the Canada Cup (now the World Cup) series in Mexico City. However, it was not a really successful trip, with the Australians finishing only

fifth, 11 strokes behind the winners, Ireland.

Phillips regularly plays the Far East circuit and has tasted his share of success—including fine wins in the inaugural Malayan Open in 1962, and the Hong Kong Open four years later.

Phillips has always been plagued with poor eyesight. In his early career he played in spectacles, but later on switched successfully to contact lenses.

PHILLIPS Frank

Tournaments won
1957	Australian Open
1961	Australian Open
1962	New South Wales Open
	Malayan Open
1964	Victorian Open
1966	New South Wales Open
	Victorian Open
	Hong Kong Open
1971	Tasmanian Open
1973	Hong Kong Open

Pickworth
Ossie (1917-1969)

Unlike most champion Australian golfers, Ossie Pickworth rarely tried his luck on the tough overseas circuit. Instead he preferred to remain at home and pursue the less-exacting career of a club professional. But on the two occasions Pickworth did venture abroad, he had more than average success. In 1950 he went to Britain

Above, **Australian Frank Phillips, teeing off, enjoyed a fine domestic career.**

Below, **Ossie Pickworth stayed at home and won four Australian Opens.**

where he won the Irish Open and shared the *Daily Mail* tournament. Then in 1953 he and teammate Peter Thomson finished third in the inaugural Canada Cup (now World Cup) series in Montreal. After watching him in 1950, Henry Cotton described Pickworth as 'the greatest fairway wood player in the world'.

It was all-round play, though, that won Pickworth a record three consecutive Australian Open Championships between 1946 and 1948, as well as another one in 1954, three PGA titles, and many other major Australian championships.

Born opposite Manly Golf Course in Sydney, Pickworth started as a caddie there at the age of 15. At Manly he encountered Jim Ferrier, the first Australian golfer to succeed on the tough United States circuit. Pickworth picked up a lot of hints from Ferrier, many of which helped him down his tutor in a play-off for the 1948 Australian Open on the long Kingston Heath course in Melbourne. Ferrier tried vainly, then and later, to persuade Pickworth to try his hand in America. Ferrier was adamant that the young Pickworth would have caused a sensation there.

Pickworth rated 1950 as his best year. In addition to his British success, he downed South African Bobby Locke in one of the finest man-to-man matches seen in Australia. Locke shot a par 65 on the demanding par-73 Royal Melbourne course, but it was not good enough. Pickworth turned in a blistering 63.

Pickworth retired in 1957, only weeks after winning the Victorian Open and finishing second to Frank Phillips in the Australian Open.

PICKWORTH Henry Alfred	
Tournaments won	
1946	Australian Open
1947	Australian Open
	Australian PGA
	Ampol
1948	Australian Open
	Ampol
1949	Ampol
1950	Irish Open
1951	Ampol
1953	Australian PGA
	Ampol
1954	Australian Open
1955	Australian PGA

1 Dedication, hard work, practice, and above all the desire to win have made the little South African Gary Player one of the world's best and most successful golfers. **2** The all-black strip that Player regularly wears has made his figure easy to spot on even the most crowded golf courses. **3** With one of golf's most treasured prizes—the old claret jug trophy for the British Open—after winning the 1968 event. A happy smile shows that he loves to win.

Ed Lacey

Gerry Cranham

U.P.I.

Player

Gary (1935-   )

One thing, and one thing alone, has made Gary Player one of the best golfers the world has known: dedication. With the possible exception of Ben Hogan, whom Player worshipped, no one has worked harder at golf than the 5 ft 7 in tall South African. The rewards, however, have been immense. At 35, there was no need for him to hit another shot, but, because the competitive fires had not died out, he carried on. More than most, Player seems to have been driven by a need to win, and this has been accompanied by the dedication and desire to practise until his hands were raw.

Player tells the story of how, as a youngster, he would stand in the practice bunker at his club all day if necessary until he holed out five shots. That done, he would repair to the putting green where he would stay until darkness. All this hard work has repaid him a thousand times. He became the third man in history—and the first non-American—to win the four major tournaments—the US Open, US Masters, US PGA, and British Open. He has won numerous tournaments in all corners of the world, though not surprisingly he has grown somewhat weary of the continual travelling. After his second win in the British Open, at Carnoustie in 1968, his only thought was to get back to wife Vivienne and his children on their Transvaal farm.

When Player began his invasion of the world's circuits with a trip to Britain in 1956, at the age of 20, he had a very flat swing, a grip that featured a right hand far too much to the right, and a comparative lack of length. Yet despite these faults, he did well, giving intimations of golfing immortality when he won the Dunlop tournament and finished fourth in the Open.

But it was 1957 that made Gary Player. Although he did not win much he made his first trip to America, where he met his idol, Ben Hogan. Hogan told him he would have to alter both swing and grip if he wanted to sustain his golf in the face of the highest pressures, and so Player worked at this eight hours a day. That it paid off is self-evident, but few people could have made it pay off quite so quickly and spectacularly. The very next year he won his first American tour tournament, the Kentucky Open, and almost incredibly was runner up in the American Open. Then, in 1959, he proved he had really arrived when he became the youngest golfer ever to win the British Open.

He did it as he has always done —dramatically. On the last round he made an Arnold Palmer-type 'charge', and was six under par standing on the 18th tee. All he needed was a par four to equal the course record and become virtually sure of the title. Yet he hooked his tee shot into a bunker and took two more shots to reach the green. There, it seemed almost inevitable that he would three putt, and he did, missing the last one from about 20 inches. Player was in the depths of despair, comparing his plight with that of Sam Snead, who once lost the US Open by taking eight on the last hole. He need not have worried though, for none of the field was able to match his last round and catch him.

The first of his major American championships came two years later, at Augusta, and this time Player benefited from another golfer's collapse. Arnold Palmer arrived at the 18th needing only a four to win the Masters, but he finished with a six and Player won. And that was not Player's only piece of luck in the tournament. In the third round, always the most critical for a professional, he had hit a tee shot much too strongly and it seemed to be heading out of bounds when it hit a spectator and bounced back on to the green for Player to get his par. That year, 1961, he was leading money winner on the American circuit—another first for a non-American—and led the stroke average with 69.3.

Perhaps his finest year was 1965, when he won both the US Open and the US World Series as well as the Canada Cup individual title. He also took part in what has been called the finest golf match ever played when, in the Piccadilly World Match Play Championship at Wentworth, he beat Tony Lema after being seven down with 17 to play.

The match typified Player's approach to the game. He has called match play 'the raw blood and guts of golf', and indeed his game is all blood and guts. At Wentworth the crowds used to walk uncontrolled along the fairways, and Player, amongst the crowd, overheard two unsuspecting spectators chatting. One suggested that they go and watch another match as this one would soon be over. At the time, Player was four down with 12 to play, but he turned to the spectator and said: 'Sir, you are obviously not a golfer or you would know that this game is never won till it's lost. Stick around and you might see something'. He did see something. Player, five down with nine to play, squared the match on the 36th and won it on the 37th.

Because of his nationality, Player also became the first golfer to be involved in a racial demonstration on the golf course. This happened during the 1969 US PGA championship at Dayton, Ohio, when a local civil rights group threatened to wreck the tournament, run by the local chamber of commerce, unless more was done for the city's poor. Player was in the running through-

out and eventually finished second, but not before some ugly incidents.

In the last round he was playing with Jack Nicklaus when, on the way to the 10th, someone threw a cup of iced water in his face and called him a 'damned racist'. And on the green of that hole two demonstrators broke through the crowd and looked as though they were going to assault both Nicklaus and Player. But the police were ready and prevented blows being struck.

Had they but known, the demonstrators could hardly have picked a worse object for their attentions. Player has toned his concentration to such a pitch that he is capable of turning it on and off at will, and he is the last man in the world to be upset, on the course, by demonstrations.

As Player grows older, the spark does not fade from his golf. He continues to add victory upon victory in every continent of the world, remaining the most widely-travelled golfer around and undertaking demanding schedules that would exhaust a man 10 years his junior. It is not surprising that his self-discipline and mania for physical fitness have become legendary.

In the 1970s he had added the major championships of Australia and South Africa to victories in Europe, where, annually, appearances in only five or six leading events are sufficient to catapult him into the top half-dozen money winners on the circuit. And he continually expands his list of victories in the four classic events, the US PGA and Masters and the British Open again coming his way.

One of the major highlights in Player's career occurred in 1974. At Port Elizabeth course he won the otherwise insignificant South African Golf Classic, which became the 100th major 72-hole championship victory of his career, a unique feat in modern golf, and a personal triumph.

Player stands back as an official restrains an anti-*apartheid* demonstrator at the 1969 US PGA championship.

Gerry Cranham

Rees
Dai (1913-   )

One of the most popular men ever to grace British professional golf, Dai Rees has had a phenomenal career stretching from the time he won the *News of the World* Match Play in 1936 through to 1967, when, aged 54, he was runner-up in the same event. In that time he probably won more tournaments than any other British golfer except Henry Cotton.

For all Rees's personal material successes, however, his greatest hour occurred in a team event—when he captained the victorious Ryder Cup team at Lindrick in 1957. A Welshman, Rees is well endowed with the more volatile characteristics of that race, and they were seen to good effect on that memorable day. Even though he and Ken Bousfield had been the only foursomes victors, he was not disheartened. Going to each member of the team he told them that they personally had an outstanding chance of winning, an approach that obviously worked. The British team that day went 'mad' in a way without precedent. Rees himself beat Ed Furgol by 7 and 6, and the match was won 7½–4½.

That victory earned Rees almost every sporting accolade possible that year, and it also did much to start the golfing boom in Britain. But Rees has always been a fighter whose best is seen in match play. His eight appearances in the final of the *News of the World* event were still a record in 1970 and could well remain one, and he won the event four times.

If his career has one disappointment, though, it is that he has never won the British Open. Several times he has looked like doing so, but at the last moment victory has eluded him. In 1954 he lost to Peter Thomson by just one shot, after taking a five at the par-four last, and in 1961 he was only one stroke behind Arnold Palmer at Royal Birkdale.

Above, **Still playing well in his 50s and 60s, Dai Rees regularly earned a place in the Order of Merit table.**

Below, **Allan Robertson (third from right) with some of his contemporaries, including 'Old Tom' Morris (second left).**

Colour Sport

Popperfoto

REES David James
Tournaments and Awards Won
1936 *News of the World* Match Play
1938 *News of the World* Match Play
1946 Spalding
1948 Irish Open
1949 *News of the World* Match Play
1950 *News of the World* Match Play
1951 New South Wales Open
1953 Daks
1954 Belgian Open
Spalding
1955 Vardon Trophy
1956 Swiss Open
1959 Vardon Trophy
PGA Championship
Swiss Open
1962 Dunlop Masters
Representative Appearances
Great Britain v USA (Ryder Cup) 1937, 47, 49, 51, 53, 55*, 57*, 59*, 61*, 67†
World Cup (Wales) 1956, 57, 59, 60, 61, 62, 64
*Captain. †Non-playing captain

Robertson
Allan (1815-1859)

Allan Robertson was considered the greatest golfing figure in the first half of the 19th century. He died the year before the first Open championship, and so was unable to make his mark as a champion in the sense that the Morrises and the Parks were able to. But all accounts unite in describing him as the supreme golfer of his age, and in foursome challenge matches he was said never to have been beaten.

The Robertsons had been making 'feathery' golf balls in St Andrews for many years when Allan took over the family business in the shop overlooking the 18th green at St Andrews. 'Old Tom' Morris worked with him for a while, but a quarrel arising from his use of the new gutta percha ball caused a separation. On the links, however, they buried their differences and frequently partnered each other to notable victories.

The most famous of these was over the Dunn brothers from Musselburgh, the contest being decided over three courses each of 36 holes. North Berwick was the deciding venue, and Robertson and Morris won the last two holes and the match on the last green. Robertson was not at his best that day, but the victory still thrilled the large crowd of supporters who had crossed the Firth to cheer him on.

His robust, stocky figure was a familiar sight to all at St Andrews, and, though he was never club professional to the Royal and Ancient club, on his death the club recorded its appreciation of him both as a player and as one of a happy temper always anxious to 'promote the comfort of all who frequented the links.' He was buried in the graveyard of St Andrews cathedral, and a monument was erected to him in the town.

Saint Sauveur
Vicomtesse de (1921-   )

An outstanding golfer, the Vicomtesse de Saint Sauveur enjoyed a competitive career of nearly 30 years. Between 1937, when as Mme Lally Vagliano she won the British Girls Championship at Stoke Poges, and 1965, she represented France in every year except during World War II. Her connection with Britain was, in fact, very strong; she won the British Ladies Championship in 1950, the Avia foursomes in 1961 with her protegee Brigitte Varangot, and she played for Europe against the British Isles on four occasions, two of them as captain.

Petite, chic, and elegant, the Vicomtesse preserved her figure long after her children had grown up; and until the end of her playing career she hit the ball as far as almost any of her contemporaries. She owned a faultless

Ed Lacey

style with a wide arc and perfect grip, and she swung with all the force of her lissom figure. Her victory in the 1950 British Ladies came at Royal County Down, one of the longest and toughest of seaside courses. In addition to fine ball sense she had an attacking spirit which seldom left her shots short of the pin.

The Vicomtesse's record illustrates the enduring quality of her game. Although most of her successes came after the war, she won her first French Close title in 1939; she won it six times in all and reached the final as late as 1964, at the age of 43. Similarly she won the Swiss Championship in 1965, 16 years after her first title there. She also had triumphs in the Italian, Spanish and Benelux championships.

Her mother, Madame Vagliano, presented the Vagliano Trophy for competition between France and Great Britain in 1932, and in 1959 the event was extended to include the whole of the Con-

tinent. In this new version Britain won the first three and Europe the next three, and in all of them the Vicomtesse played a predictably prominent part. Thanks to her encouragement there grew up around her a small group of fine players—Brigitte Varangot, Claudine Cros-Rubin, and later Catherine Lacoste—who raised their country to the highest standard in women's golf.

Sarazen

Gene (1902-   )

Gene Sarazen has a secure place among the illustrious names of golfing history: he was the first man to win what has since become known as the 'Big Four'—the US and British Opens, the US PGA and the US Masters—an achievement emulated only by Ben Hogan, Gary Player, and Jack Nicklaus, and he was also the first to hold the British and American Open titles at the same time, in 1932, a distinction earned only by Bobby Jones (1930), Hogan (1953), Nicklaus (1966–67), and Tony Jacklin (1969–70).

Born in New York of Italian parents, Sarazen came up through the ranks of caddie and assistant and became a professional in 1921. A year later, at 20, he burst to prominence with a final round of 68, and victory, in the US Open, the third for which he had entered. It was no chance win: he followed

1 Elegant but strong, the Vicomtesse de Saint Sauveur attacked the courses of Europe for almost 30 years. 2 Thirty-five years after his US Masters victory, Gene Sarazen tees off in the 1970 event, looking remarkably fit in his 68th year, and ready for all comers.

it with a success in the PGA championship, and the next year he retained that title by beating Walter Hagen.

Sarazen visited Britain for the first time in 1923, but failed to qualify for the Open at Troon. He said he would return even if he had to swim and after finishing second in 1928 and third in 1931, he won at Sandwich in 1932 with a total of 283, which was to be the lowest for 18 years. In 1935 he overhauled Craig Wood—thanks to holing a full wooden second shot at the 15th for an albatross (3 under par)—to win the Masters.

In many ways Sarazen was quite un-American. He always wore

knickerbockers, he played quickly, his putting appeared almost nonchalant, and he swung fully and easily after the briefest of addresses. He was capable of dazzling streaks, one of which—completing the last 28 holes in 100 strokes—won him his second US Open in 1932. His game outlasted most rivals: 18 years after winning the first of his three PGA titles he tied with Lawson Little but lost the play-off, and when that event reverted to matchplay he reached the last eight in 1947. As late as 1958 his cheerful, stocky figure delighted crowds in the Open championship at Royal Lytham when, at 56, he finished in the first 20. He also made six consecutive appearances in the Ryder Cup between 1927 and 1937, losing only one singles.

SARAZEN Eugene	
Primary Championship Successes	
1922	US Open
	US PGA
1923	US PGA
1932	US Open
	British Open
1933	US PGA
1935	US Masters
Ryder Cup: 1927, 29, 31, 33, 35, 37	

Shade

Ronnie (1938-   )

Scotland's leading amateur golfer for nearly a decade, Ronnie Shade turned professional in 1968, far later than would seem necessary for a player of his ability and consistency. British stroke-play champion three times, in 1961, 1963, and 1967, he had played for Britain's amateur international teams every year between 1961 and 1967. And in his second season as a professional he won the £2,000 first prize in the Carroll International Tournament.

Though stroke-play was his forte, Shade was more than capable at match-play, and was Scottish champion for five successive years, from 1963 to 1967. He also reached the final of the British Amateur championship at Carnoustie in 1966, losing to the 18-year-old South African Bobby Cole. But the consistency necessary for stroke-play was his best quality, and to his three British amateur championships he added the Scottish in 1968, only the second time this event had been held. On the international scene, he helped Britain to her first win in the Eisenhower Trophy, the world amateur team championship, at Rome in 1964. And at the 1966 event in Mexico City he had the best individual score of 283 for 72 holes. It was an uncharacteristic lapse on his part in the 1968 championship to have a poor final round and contribute to the British team's dropping an eight-stroke lead to the eventual winners, Australia.

Shade's efficiency came from a

Above, **Ronnie Shade, outstanding for Scottish and British amateur teams in the 1960s.**

stiff, artificial swing, which earned him a reputation as a mechanical player. It was even irreverently suggested that his initials RDBM stood for 'right down the bloody middle'. Even so, when he turned professional he wondered whether he would suffer from a lack of length. But this doubt was dispelled by his first professional victory, and he looked set to add further honours to his impressive list which already included the MBE, given for his services to golf, in 1967.

Since that first victory, another of the same importance has eluded Shade in Britain, though he has never had any difficulty supporting himself on the circuit. In addition, he regularly supplements his income by winter visits to Africa, where he is a popular and successful guest, while he remains as consistent a winner on the Scottish professional circuit as he was on the amateur. His loyalty to his native land was repaid when he became one of the first Scots to represent his country at both levels, partnering Harry Bannerman in the 1971 World Cup.

SHADE Ronnie David Bell Mitchell
Carroll International tournament winner: 1969
Scottish amateur champion: 1963, 64, 65, 66, 67
Scottish amateur stroke-play champion: 1968
English Open amateur stroke-play champion: 1961, 63, 67
Great Britain teams:
v United States (Walker Cup): 1961, 63, 65, 67
in Eisenhower Trophy: 1962, 64, 66
Scottish international teams: 1957, 60, 61, 62, 63, 64, 65, 66
World Cup (Scotland): 1971

Snead

Jesse (1941-   )

One of the most determinedly able American golfers to burst on the scene in recent years has been a burly young man with the well known name of Snead. Jesse Snead, physically the antithesis of the legendary 'Slammin' Sam', is in fact his nephew.

Although there is no denying the influence of his famous uncle, it was no foregone conclusion that young Jesse would follow in his footsteps. On the contrary, anxious to assert himself in his own right, he made baseball his first-choice sport, but after three gloomily unfulfilled years, he turned his head to golf, though only as a club assistant.

Not until 1968 did he join the professional tour, to which he

Action Photos

took three years to adapt to any degree. When he did, however, the results were in the best traditions of his uncle: rocking the golfing establishment with a wholly unexpected victory in the Tucson Open, a triumph he repeated two weeks later in the Doral-Eastern Open. That year, 1971, Jesse Snead almost completed a unique hat-trick of wins, but was denied the Greater Hertford Open in a play-off. Also in 1971, and again in 1972, he tabled a succession of victories for the US Ryder Cup team against Britain. Since then, he has been a regular tournament winner and a powerful force in American golf. In 1973 he missed a sinkable putt on the last green to tie the Augusta Masters, but his inexhaustible form suggests it will not be long before he improves on that second place.

SNEAD Jesse
Major victories
1971 Doral-Eastern Open
Tucson Open
1972 Philadelphia Classic
1973 Australian Open
1975 San Diego Open
Representative appearances
USA v Great Britain (Ryder Cup): 1971, 1973

Snead
Sam (1912-   )

Known throughout his career by the nickname of 'Slammin' Sam', Sam Snead possessed one of the soundest and graceful golf techniques in the game. Only one victory is missing from his record —the United States Open—and it is only this omission which keeps him from the statistical company of Bobby Jones, Ben Hogan, and Jack Nicklaus.

Snead won practically everything else. He won over 80 tournaments on the United States circuit, but—sometimes cruelly—the Open always eluded him. The whole golf world winced in 1939 when, needing only a par 5 on the 558-yard 72nd hole at the Philadelphia Country Club to win, he somehow contrived to accumulate no fewer than 8 strokes. He hooked his second shot into a bunker, took 2 to get out, chipped short, and took 3 putts. Eight years later he reached the last green of a play-off against Lew Worsham—and missed a short putt to lose by one stroke. But nobody ever writes Snead off, least of all after his victory in the Greater Greensboro Open in 1965, when he was 52 years old.

Snead turned professional in 1934 and won his first tour event in 1937—the Oakland Open. At once people noticed his remarkably smooth swing, and he was selected to play in the Ryder Cup the same year. It was the start of a wonderful record in these matches —the best possessed by a player on either side. Of the six singles he played he lost only one, and that by one hole to Harry Weetman at Wentworth in 1953.

Snead's first visit to Great Britain was in 1946, and he celebrated it by winning the British Open by 4 strokes at St Andrews from Bobby Locke with rounds of 71, 70, 74, and 75. Henry Cotton (who was equal-fourth) was quick to point out that the overseas competitors had an advantage in strength because they had been eating better for the last year or two. Snead, for his part, did not endear himself to the British public by criticizing his accommodation, declaring memorably that 'when you leave the United States you're just camping out'.

Snead had a reputation for being a hillbilly, coming as he did from the mountainous part of Virginia. Although he cultivates this image with some care, he is a very astute businessman with seven corporations to his name and an annual income estimated in 1965 at between $150,000 and $200,000. As a golfer, he no doubt deserves it. He won seven major

Above, **Because Sam Snead failed to win the US Open, historians rarely place him among the giants of golf. Few of his contemporaries, however, would deny his greatness.** *Below,* **Non-playing captains Snead (left) and Eric Brown share the 1969 Ryder Cup at Royal Birkdale.**

U.P.I.

Syndication International

championships—three US Masters, three US PGA's, and one British Open. He also recorded the first sub-60 round in an American tournament. This was at his home course of White Sulphur Springs, and came in the process of winning the unofficial 'Sam Snead Festival' with a total of 259. The course measured 6,400 yards, and Snead did the last 9 holes in 28, with a birdie three at the last hole. He pitched to within 2 feet of the hole, and took a long time over the putt that was to make golf history.

World Seniors champion in 1964, 1965, and 1972, Snead made a diplomatic return to Britain as captain of the 1969 Ryder Cup team. His gracious gesture in allowing the Cup to stay in Britain for six months after the tied match in which the United States theoretically retained the trophy did much to obscure the animosities of the mid-1940s.

SNEAD Samuel Jackson

Major Victories
1937	Oakland Open
	Miami Open
	St Paul Open
	Nassau Open
	Bing Crosby Tournament
1938	Canadian Open
	Bing Crosby Tournament
1939	Miami Open
1940	Canadian Open
1941	Canadian Open
	North and South Open
	Bing Crosby Tournament
1942	**US PGA**
1946	**British Open**
	Miami Open
1948	Texas Open
1949	**US PGA**
	US Masters
	Wester Open
1950	North and South Open
	Miami Open
	Texas Open
	Western Open
1951	**US PGA**
	Miami Open
1952	**US Masters**
1954	**US Masters**
1956	Canada Cup (team*)
1960	Canada Cup (team†)
1961	Canada Cup (team‡ and individual)
	Tournament of Champions
1964	World Seniors
	US Seniors
1965	World Seniors
	US Seniors
1972	World Seniors
	US Seniors
1973	US Seniors

Representative Appearances
Ryder Cup (USA v Great Britain): 1937, 47, 49, 51, 53, 55, 59, 69 (non-playing captain)

* With Ben Hogan
† With Arnold Palmer
‡ With Jimmy Demaret

Dave Stockton, a leading money winner on the US circuit since winning the US PGA tournament—one of the 'Big Four'—in 1970.

Stockton
Dave (1941-   )

America's Dave Stockton takes a more cold-blooded view of tournament golf than many of his fellow professionals. A few years ago, he described as his golfing strategy the intention to play the tour as hard and as often as possible in order to amass enough money in four or five years to allow him to reduce his appearances to a minimum and so spend more time with his wife and family. The annual income target he set for himself was $100,000, and since 1968 he has only once fallen below it.

Stockton was born with golf in his blood, the son of a Californian golf professional. Yet in spite of this, it was not until he was

almost 17 that Stockton began seriously, but once started, the pleasure swiftly became a mania. Working in a lumber yard every summer gave him the strength and the extra cash he sought to develop his game, doing this with sufficient success to win a golf scholarship to the University of Southern California, from which he graduated with a degree in business management. In 1964 he joined the circuit, although his earnings that year crept only a few dollars over the thousand mark, but eventually his courageous decision paid off. Three years later he had elevated his position in the money earners list from 167th to 19th, pocketing more than $50,000. He also took home his first trophy, the prestigious Californian Invitation.

Two more victories in 1968 saw Stockton top the $100,000 mark for the first time, but, as so often happens, the next year was a lean one. His old weakness —erratic putting—haunted him again. Hole after hole he was hitting greens in regulation figures: hole after hole he would wreck his approach work by three-putting. The fewer putts dropped, the more timid Stockton became, and his game suffered. But in 1970 this affliction deserted him, and he reverted to his confident, fluent natural game, being duly rewarded in the autumn with victory in one of the 'big four' classics, the US PGA.

Since then, Stockton's game has gone from strength to strength and he has never faltered in the pursuit of his goal, a high spot in the money winners' league. Tournaments regularly fall his way, and the determination of his challenge in every event on the circuit has won him a place in the US Ryder Cup team. It now seems there is little that can prevent this attractive, personable golfer from quickly acquiring the earnings he seeks to support his family. One can only hope that he reverses his decision to limit his tournament appearances, for he would be a disappointing loss to American professional golf.

STOCKTON David

Major victories
1967	Colonial National Invitation
1968	Cleveland Open
	Milwaukee Open
1970	**US PGA**
1971	Massachusetts Golf Classic
1973	Milwaukee Open
1974	Glen Campbell-Los Angeles Open
	Sammy Davies Jnr-Greater Hartford Open
	Quad-Cities Open

Representative appearances
USA v Great Britain (Ryder Cup): 1971

1 The great James Taylor, five times Open champion. **2** Dave Thomas, consistently one of the best British golfers of the 50s and 60s.

Taylor
James Henry
(1871-1963)

The first of the golfing 'Triumvirate' to win the British Open championship, James Taylor outlived the other two, Harry Vardon and James Braid, and became the Grand Old Man of British golf. He spent his last years close to the Westward Ho! club, where he had started work as a boy, and of which he was made president in 1957. Taylor won the Open championship five times—in 1894, 1895, 1900, 1909, and 1913—and was second five times, a wonderful record of consistency.

When Taylor first won the Open, at Sandwich, it was said that the hazards he faced were the guideposts—and that typified the man's great accuracy. His game was seen at its best in windy conditions, the ball, hit from a firm stance and with a little grunt, flying low and straight, seeming to make a hole in the wind. The supreme example of Taylor's play in the wind came at Hoylake, where he won his fifth and last Open. Taylor went out in a gale which was blowing other men off their feet, his cap well down over his nose. His large boots appeared glued to the turf, and he played golf which has seldom been equalled.

Taylor's brother-professionals owe him much. In 1902 he founded and became president of the Professional Golfers' Association. He began as a caddy, and then as a green-keeper at Westward Ho!, moving from there at the age of 19 with a sovereign in his pocket. It was the start of one of the greatest careers in the history of golf.

TAYLOR James Henry

Major Victories
1894	British Open
1895	British Open
1900	British Open
1904	British Match-Play
1908	French Open
	British Match-Play
1909	British Open
	French Open
1912	German Open
1913	British Open

Thomas
Dave (1934-   )

One of the best post-war British professionals, Dave Thomas is a good golfer who very nearly became a great one. In 1958, at the age of 24, he tied with Peter Thomson in the British Open, and even though he lost the play-off it was generally conceded that in this big, burly Welshman Britain had her best prospect for world golfing honours in decades.

That he failed to fulfil these hopes and his own promise is one of the tragedies of the British game. He has always been considered one of the foremost long and consistently straight drivers in the world, and he has had as many good days on the greens as most professionals. Where his game falls apart is in his approach work—those little pitch shots to the pin from 50 or so yards out. In a poor round he would miss as many greens as he hit with the short irons. Thomas himself agrees that it has been this department of his game that has let him down. Others would go further and say that it has prevented him from taking a place among the greats of the game.

Yet in spite of his handicap, Dave Thomas has consistently won more than his share of prize money on the British circuit, and in the 1965 Open at Muirfield, he tied on 283 with Doug Sanders, one stroke behind the winner Jack Nicklaus. In the early 1970s, Thomas undertook a gradual retirement from tournament golf as eye-trouble became a growing problem, and today he concentrates on the golf architect business he runs with his ex-Ryder Cup colleague, Peter Alliss.

THOMAS David

Tournaments won
1955	Belgian Open
1958	Dutch Open
	Caltex (NZ)
1959	French Open
	Caltex (NZ)
1962	Esso Golden Round Robin
1963	News of the World Match Play
	Olgiata Trophy (Rome)
1965	Silent Night
1966	Swallow Penfold
	Jeyes
	Esso Golden Round Robin
1969	Graham Textiles
	Pains Wessex

Representative Appearances
Great Britain v USA (Ryder Cup) 1959, 63, 65, 67
Canada (World) Cup (Wales) 1957, 58, 59, 60, 61, 62, 63, 66, 67, 69

Radio Times Hulton Picture Library

Thomson

Peter (1929-   )

Because he has won the British Open championship five times—more than any other golfer except Harry Vardon, who won his sixth in 1914—Australia's Peter Thomson is regarded as the greatest small-ball player of his time. The small-ball qualification is important, for his appearances in the United States have been few, and he has shown a general dislike of playing conditions in that country. Yet Thomson's reputation rests on more than just his British Open successes. Representing Australia in the Canada Cup (now the World Cup), he partnered Kel Nagle to victory in 1954 and 1959, and was also involved as runner-up in 1955 and 1961.

After finishing leading amateur in the 1948 Australian Open, the Melbourne-born Thomson turned professional the following year at the age of 20. Successes followed in New Zealand and Australian tournaments, and in 1951 he began his long association with the British Open in which he was to establish such a unique record. At Royal Portrush, he finished on 293, 8 strokes behind Max Faulkner, and it was at once apparent that his intelligent game and philosophical attitude in taking the rough with the smooth suited him well for seaside championship golf.

In the next two years he finished second and second equal to Bobby Locke and Ben Hogan respectively, and then in 1954 he scored his first victory, at Royal Birkdale. The following two years saw him complete a hat-trick of British Opens, the second coming at St Andrews and the third at Hoylake. Two qualities made him

outstanding in this class of golf—his control of the ball in the wind and under hard, dry conditions, and his superb judgement of distance. His style was a model of orthodoxy, balance, and rhythm. In those days he was so accurate that he was often considered dull to watch, especially as for almost a decade he and Locke took charge of the Open. Thomson was runner-up to the South African again in 1957, and then picked up another championship at Royal Lytham in 1958, when he won the play-off against David Thomas.

Thomson made a few trips to America, but he did not play with much distinction, and he eventually gave up visiting there altogether. He found in Britain and the Far East an expanding and adequate market for his talents, and he was a regular visitor to Britain during the 1950s and 1960s. For a few months every season he would play in a select number of tournaments, and his victories and the money he won were out of all proportion to the number of events he played in when compared to the winnings of many other professionals.

But when the leading Americans began to take an active interest in the British Open in the early 1960s, it looked as if Thomson's reign in that event had ended. Then suddenly, out of the blue in 1965, he won his fifth championship against the strongest possible field. He found at Royal Birkdale conditions ideal for him—running fairways and a fair wind—and nobody could match his control or his accuracy in the short game, on which he was coming to rely more and more.

Though Peter Thomson was master of any seaside course, St Andrews was foremost in his affection. Winning the Martini tournament there in 1962, he set a new 72-hole record of 275 for the Old Course, improving on his own previous best of 278 in an Open on that course. When the Alcan tournament visited St Andrews in 1967, he failed to qualify for the main event, but he must have derived particular pleasure in winning the subsidiary event over the same course with a lower total than that which won Gay Brewer the Golfer of the Year title.

It was also at St Andrews that he won the first of four *News of the World* match-play championships, in 1954. Beneath the un-

THOMSON Peter William		
Major tournaments won		
1950	New Zealand Open	
1951	Australian Open	
	New Zealand Open	
1952	New Zealand Open	
1954	**British Open**	
	Canada Cup (with Kel Nagle)	
	News of the World Match Play	
1955	**British Open**	
1956	**British Open**	
1958	**British Open**	
1959	Canada Cup (with Kel Nagle)	
1960	Daks	
1961	Dunlop Masters	
	News of the World Match Play	
1962	Martini	
1965	**British Open**	
	Daks	
	Hong Kong Open	
1966	*News of the World* Match Play	
1967	Alcan International	
	Australian Open	
	News of the World Match Play	
1968	Dunlop Masters	
1971	New Zealand Open	
1972	Wills Open	
	Australian Open	
	Pepsi Yokohama Tournament	
	Chunichi Crown Tournament	
1973	Victoria Open	

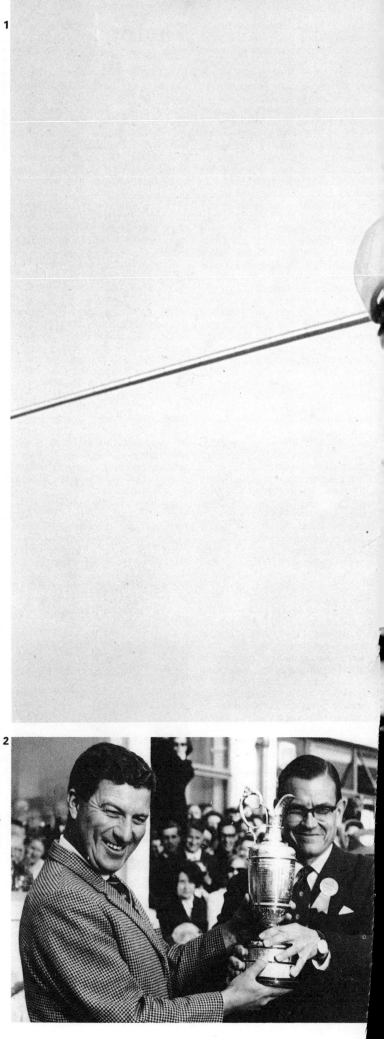

1 Peter Thomson's fame as a golfer rests largely on his five wins in the British Open Championship. But though he has rarely competed in the United States, Thomson was acknowledged as one of the all-time greats because of his successes in Europe and his native Australia. 2 Receiving the Open trophy for the fifth time after his 1965 victory. 3 Thomson on the green.

Tolley

Cyril James Hastings
(1896-   )

One of the leading names in British amateur golf between the world wars, Major Cyril Tolley won the British amateur championships twice, and was twice in the semi-finals—the last time in 1950—when he was 54. That his game lasted so long was due to a wonderful swing which enabled him to hit the ball great distances.

In 1919, after winning a Military Cross during World War I, Tolley went up to Oxford, where he won three Blues, and in 1920 he captured his first Amateur title. The next year, while still an undergraduate, he played in the first match against the United States—a predecessor of the Walker Cup series—and in the singles defeated a former US Open champion, Chick Evans. Another US champion he beat was the great Walter Hagen, in the French Open, which Tolley won in 1924 and again in 1928, each time against a strong professional field. His second victory in the Amateur championship came in 1929, bringing a highly successful decade to a most satisfactory close.

Tolley's style and manner on the course were often described as 'majestic', but like other great players he was highly strung, and though he nearly always rose to the big occasion he frequently went through agonies. He took part in seven matches against the United States in all, winning his singles against Jesse Sweetser in the 1923 Walker Cup and against Max Marston in 1924. In 1926, however, he came up against Bobby Jones and was beaten 12 and 11.

Perhaps the most satisfying Walker Cup series he was connected with, though, was that of 1938, when he was chairman of selectors and Britain gained their first-ever victory in the event. He was accorded the same honour in 1947, and for the year 1948–49 he was appointed captain of the Royal and Ancient golf club at St Andrews.

Ed Lacey

ruffled exterior, there is a hard **3** core that has made Thomson a formidable exponent of match play.

As he moved more and more away from the competitive tournament scene, Thomson, who owed much in his early days as a professional to the guidance of Norman von Nida, devoted more time to helping young golfers on their visits to Australia. And among his many business interests in his own country is a firm of golf course designers. Awarded an MBE in 1957, this most intelligent and articulate of professional golfers has done much to encourage interest in Britain for golf in Australia and the Far East, and it is not for want of trying that his idea of a world championship outside the United States has not been fulfilled.

Ray Green

Trevino
Lee (1939-)

Had Lee Trevino accomplished nothing more in 1971 than win his second US Open title, he would have done enough to rank among golf's leading players. Yet within weeks of that victory he was winning the Canadian Open and then crossing the Atlantic to annexe the British Open at Royal Birkdale—a title he retained the following year at Muirfield. Only three others—Bobby Jones, Gene Sarazen, and Ben Hogan—had won both the British and US titles in the same year. The El Paso-born American of Mexican parents had truly found golfing greatness.

Trevino first burst on to the tournament scene in 1967. That year he amazed everyone, first by qualifying for the Open after collecting only $600 in official winnings the previous year, and then by finishing fifth and winning ten times that amount. His style was unimpressive enough to move English golf writer Leonard Crawley to talk about his 'agricultural methods', but Trevino was so delighted with his success that he stayed on the tour and finished with $26,472 that year.

Nobody, however, considered him a serious challenger for any of golf's top prizes. The feeling was that he lacked discipline.

But the following year he was again to use the US Open to show just how good he really was. And his style in doing so soon made him one of the biggest crowd-pullers in golf and one of its most popular players. Trevino won the title after a four-round duel with Bert Yancey, and his score of 275 equalled Jack Nicklaus's Open record. He also became the first man ever to play four consecutive rounds in the Open below par figures—his rounds of 69, 68, 69, 69 over the par-70 East Course of the Oak Hill Country Club in Rochester, New York, gave him a four-shot winning margin.

Trevino is a good putter, a strong iron player, and is adept with his wedge. He jokes a lot with the gallery during a round, and seems to have the ability to switch his concentration off and on at will. He is mentally tough,

U.P.I.

Lee Trevino, one of the great characters of modern golf, combines an aggressive desire to win with an ability to switch himself on and off during a round. Fellow golfers have learned to treat him with the utmost respect.

Gerry Cranham

145

but also extremely generous. After leading the United States team to victory by winning the individual honours in the 1969 World Cup in Singapore, he used his winnings to establish a scholarship fund for Singapore caddies.

His only tour victory in 1969 was the Tucson Open, which he retained successfully in 1970, when he topped the money winners with $157,037. He missed the 'cut' only once in 34 tournaments and finished in the top five on nine occasions and in the top ten on another three that year. But 1971 was the year when Trevino consolidated his claim as one of the top three or four golfers in the world. And the tournament that established his class was the US Open, played at Merion, Pennsylvania.

Trevino shot 70, 72, 69, 69 to tie on 280 with Jack Nicklaus. The 'Golden Bear' was favoured to win the 18-hole play-off the next day, but Trevino, after falling a stroke behind at the first—where he amused the gallery by producing a realistic-looking toy snake from his bag—applied remorseless pressure. He turned one shot up, and though Nicklaus completed the final nine in par figures Trevino went another two strokes ahead to finish in a two under par 68 and become the leading money winner.

It was a popular victory, and one that recalled promoter Mark McCormack's remark after Trevino's successful defence of his Tucson Open title: 'Head-to-head, Lee will almost always win the money'. It was a statement that Art Wall, whom Trevino beat in the play-off for the Canadian Open, would not refute, and one that Trevino gave no one the chance to prove or disprove at Royal Birkdale.

Central Press

Van Donck
Flory (1912-)

A tall, slim, aggressive player, Flory van Donck was the finest golfer to emerge from Belgium and one of the best Europe has produced. A classical swinger of the club, he won 28 national Open championships in a career of almost 30 years, and in 1953, when he was at his peak, he beat the cream of British professionals to take the Harry Vardon Trophy.

But though he was a prolific money winner, van Donck fell just short of the highest peaks, and his greatest disappointments came in 1956 and 1959, when he finished runner-up in the British Open. Had he won, he would have been the first player from the Continent to take the title since the Frenchman Arnaud Massy won in 1907.

In 1956 he finished three shots behind a seemingly unbeatable Peter Thomson, but in 1959, at Muirfield, he was much closer. Had a desperately long putt gone in he would have earned a tie. In

Belgian Flory van Donck blasts onto the green in the 1956 Canada Cup, in which he represented his country 11 years running.

those days, the leaders did not go out last, and Gary Player had already returned, having taken 6 strokes at the last hole, while van Donck and Fred Bullock were still out. Player thought he had left the door open for these two, but unknown to him the Belgian had dropped two shots at earlier holes and he came to the 18th needing a birdie three to win. He hit a good drive, but his second, when it needed to be well up, finished on the front edge of the green. With that aggressive spirit that had served him so well in the minor tournaments, van Donck went boldly for the putt, but it slid past and he missed the next one as well. Player won his first Open, van Donck and Bullock tied for second place, and in later championships van Donck was never in a position to challenge for real honours again.

Vardon
Harry (1870-1937)

Harry Vardon won the British Open golf championship a record six times. James Braid and J. H. Taylor, the other members of the Great Triumvirate, each won it five times, as did the Australian Peter Thomson many years later. But Vardon is remembered for more than just his record. His genius for the game was unsurpassed and his influence upon it great.

Vardon did what only a great player can do. His play was such that he forced his nearest rivals to attempt a higher standard than they would have thought possible. He also had an enormous influence on method. His upright swing, rhythmic and graceful, surprised many who were used to a sweeping stroke with a wide arc, and he made popular the overlapping grip that, though it had

already been in use, is generally known by his name.

Vardon learnt to play as a caddy at Grouville in the Channel Islands where he was born, and it was on the advice of his brother Tom that he took a post at Ripon in Yorkshire. A year later he moved to Bury and then in 1896 to Ganton, where he beat reigning Open champion Taylor 8 and 6. In that Open year, Vardon and Taylor tied, and in the play-off Vardon again demonstrated his superiority, winning by 4 strokes over 36 holes. He beat Willie Park by one stroke in 1898, and then won easily at Sandwich in 1899. That same year he beat Taylor, in his prime, by 11 and 10 in the final of a tournament at Newcastle, County Down.

Though he was to win the last of his British Opens in 1914, Vardon was at his greatest in the years about the turn of the century, when he went up and down Britain breaking records. In 1900, he toured America, playing many matches and rousing enthusiasm in a country where the game was still young. He hardly lost a match, and won the American Open, with Taylor taking second place. The positions were reversed, however, when Vardon returned to Britain to defend his Open title. But the tour took its toll, and he was never so brilliant again.

Nevertheless, after being twice runner-up in the British Open, he won again at Prestwick in 1903 with a total of 300. This he regarded as the best of his achievements, for he was so unwell that he nearly fainted several times during play, and soon after he went to a sanatorium to recover.

In 1911 Vardon won his fifth Open, beating A. Massey so convincingly in a play-off that the Frenchman gave up at the 35th. He was involved in another tie in 1913, this time across the Atlantic, where he was defeated in the US Open by Francis Ouimet—a victory significant in American golf because it marked the end of British dominance. But Vardon still had one more title in his bag, and at Prestwick he beat Taylor by three strokes for his record sixth Open. There was almost another major title in 1920, by which time he was 50, when he returned to the United States and tied for second in the Open, one stroke behind the winner. He might have won had not a fierce wind got up as he was playing the last few holes and was tiring fast.

VARDON Harry	
Major tournament wins	
1896	British Open
1898	British Open
1899	British Open
1900	US Open
1903	British Open
1911	British Open
1912	*News of the World* Match Play
1914	British Open

Ed Lacey

Von Nida
Norman (1914-)

Norman Von Nida, in a remarkable career that spanned more than 30 years, achieved respect as one of Australia's finest ever golfers. He won almost every major tournament in Australia, including the Australian Open three times, four PGA titles, and 17 State Opens, as well as a number of overseas events. But at the same time he also managed to acquire a reputation as the 'bad boy of golf' following outbursts both on and off the course.

Golf was Von Nida's real love from an early age. He worked as a caddie at the Royal Queensland course in Brisbane, and soon after winning his first major tournament—the Queensland Amateur Championship—at 17 he turned professional. But a broken knee from a trick-shot golfer's mis-hit while trying to drive a ball from Von Nida's knee and a broken wrist kept him out of tournament play for almost three months.

In 1935, he was fit enough to try his hand in the big time, and was instantly successful, winning the Queensland Open, a title 'The Von' was to retain the following two years and win another four times on top of that. In 1936, Von Nida had his first real taste of international competition, beating the American Gene Sarazen two-up in a $100-a-side 18-hole challenge match. And the following year he added Walter Hagen's scalp to his belt when the two met in Brisbane.

Von Nida made his first overseas trip in 1938—to Manila, and

Norman Von Nida, three times Australian Open champion in the early 1950s.

Britain first saw him in 1946, when he won almost £1,300 after arriving with just £15 in his pocket. He returned the following year and won five tournaments and tied in two others to win what was then a record amount of prize money for one British season. His average of 71.23 for 50 rounds on the British circuit in 1948 won him the coveted Vardon Trophy.

On the American circuit, he rarely produced his top form, and he was best known there for incidents involving him, one of which was his brawl with the Illinois professional Henry Ransom. In Australia, he created a storm when he demanded an appearance fee for a charity match in Sydney. 'Singers and entertainers get paid for charity shows', he retorted. 'What's the difference. Golf's my living.'

He continued in active tournament play until 1963, and later was successful as a businessman and racehorse owner and breeder.

VON NIDA Norman	
Major successes and awards	
1938	Philippines Open
1939	Philippines Open
1946	Australian PGA
1948	Australian PGA
	Harry Vardon Trophy
1950	Australian Open
	Australian PGA
1951	Australian PGA
1952	Australian Open
1953	Australian Open

Press Association

Weiskopf

Tom (1940-   )

For many years Tom Weiskopf was the golfer with the ability to join the select team considered the leading golfers in the world—if only he could control his hair-trigger temper. And in 1973 he finally matured, gaining his first classic victory, a string of succes-ses on the US circuit, and making an impressive Ryder Cup debut.

In many ways, Weiskopf was like the errant son struggling to follow in the footsteps of a famous father. The idol who haunted him, however, was Jack Nicklaus. Like Nicklaus, Weiskopf was born in Columbus, Ohio: like Nicklaus he attended Ohio State University: and like Nicklaus, he bade fare-well to the campus before graduation day to commit him-self to professional golf. But by the time Weiskopf ventured forth on the circuit, Nicklaus was already hailed as the brilliant young challenger for Palmer's crown. Success did not come so quickly to Weiskopf, and after only three weeks on the tour he had to be disuaded by sympathetic friends from walking out of golf altogether. A couple of weeks later he picked up his first prize-money of over $1,000, enough to sharpen his enthusiasm all over again.

But for many years victory eluded Weiskopf as he allowed himself to be controlled by two facets—his inclination to cannon the ball as far as he could without regard to anything else, and his temper. A characteristic Weiskopf eruption came during the first

Peter Dazely

round of a tournament in Canada, when, standing on the 15th tee, he held a four-stroke lead on the field. But as he began his backswing, a camera clicked immediately behind. Weiskopf simultaneously continued his swing—shanking his drive wildly—and swelled with a rage that did not abate for the rest of his round. In four holes played with reckless fury, he dropped five strokes to par, at which point he withdrew from the tournament.

Throughout the 1960s, Weiskopf was more widely famed for his impatience than for his golfing skills, and not until 1968 did the latter begin to gain predominance, as a result of his first tournament win, the Andy Williams—San Diego Open. This victory was especially notable in that Weiskopf achieved it by allowing professional technique to suppress instinct. As he approached the final green tying for the lead, he rashly selected his four iron for the approach shot. This time, reason prevailed, and pausing to gauge the yardage to the green, he realized he had picked one club short. The final result was a perfect blow to the green and an eagle three for victory. Five months later he built on this triumph by pocketing the $25,000 winner's cheque in the Buick Open.

For the next few years, Weiskopf encountered only spasmodic

Tom Weiskopf demonstrates his fluent drive. After curbing his temper and his tendency to belt the ball regardless, he took his place among the world's top golfers.

Peter Dazely

149

success, but year by year he was mastering his temper while developing his golf. And in 1972, the golf world witnessed the occasion that allowed him to overthrow all the barriers which had previously restrained his success, creating in Weiskopf for the first time a self-confidence in his own skill which others had recognized for half a decade. Fighting for a mammoth $52,000 prize in the $260,000 Jackie Gleason—Inverarry Classic, Weiskopf had struggled for a share of the third round lead, and coming home in the final round, he found himself in a two-man battle with his old compatriot and rival from Ohio, Jack Nicklaus. Weiskopf sank a long putt on the 15th for an eagle to take a one-stroke lead, which he desperately retained with par figures as Nicklaus stood on the brink of birdies hole after hole. The importance of victory to Weiskopf became apparent when, walking ahead of his ball at the penultimate hole, he thoughtlessly walked through a bunker. Then, to the horror of the spectators, he rashly seized a rake to smooth his footsteps over. After much deliberation, it was ruled in his favour that his actions had not positively improved his position, and with clenched teeth, he matched par to gain what must have been the greatest psychological boost to his morale in his entire career.

A comparative fillip came his way the next year when he registered his first classic triumph, winning the British Open from the front. His self-assuredness as the pack chased him from the first round onwards drew much from the success he had already enjoyed that year. In fact, 1973 was a landmark in many ways in Weiskopf's history, for he finished third in the American money winner's table, earning over a quarter of a million dollars. He also added the Canadian Open and the South African PGA championship—on his first visit to that country—to his list of winnings. A creditable introduction to the Ryder Cup completed a year that was the final stage of Tom Weiskopf's growth into a golfer of stature.

Above, **Joyce Wethered with the Ladies' Open Championship cup, which she won four times.** *Below,* **Now Lady Heathcoat-Amery, she tees off at the Worplesdon foursomes in 1938. She won the event eight times altogether—with seven different partners.**

Central Press

Associated Press

Wethered
Joyce (1901-   )

Joyce Wethered burst on the golfing scene in 1920, when at the age of 18 she won the English Ladies' Championship. She had entered merely for fun, but her victory in the final over Cecilia Leitch—then an outstanding figure in women's golf—saw the beginning of an outstanding career. She won the English another four consecutive times and the Ladies' Open Championship four times, and in the opinion of golf writer Bernard Darwin, with whom she once won the Worplesdon mixed foursomes, she was 'the supreme woman golfer and one of the greatest golfers who ever lived'. She had learnt her golf at an early age, playing with her brother, Roger, at Dornoch, where her father had a holiday house.

Miss Leitch had a double revenge over Miss Wethered in 1921, winning the finals of both the Ladies' Open and the French Championship. But when they met again in the 1922 Open final Miss Wethered ran away by 9 and 7. They met again in 1925 in a great trial of strength, for Miss Leitch was then at her best and it was only on the 37th that Joyce Wethered won.

Four years later, in the 1929 Open final, she overcame the American Glenna Collett in one of the epic matches of the competition. On the Old Course at St Andrews Miss Collett started with fantastic golf, reaching the turn in 34 and having a putt to go six up. But Miss Wethered counter-attacked, was two down at lunch, and was four up at one stage in the afternoon round. Then it was Miss Collett's turn to counter-attack, and it was only at the 35th that the English girl won her fourth title.

That match was the climax of her competitive career, except for a successful trip to America in 1935 and a series of victories in the Worplesdon mixed foursomes, which she won eight times with seven different partners.

Tall and strong, she had an upright and rhythmic swing that produced long and accurate driving, and her iron play was remarkably firm, like that of the best men. But she also had other interests, and after her marriage in 1937—she became Lady Heathcoat-Amery—she played little golf.

Roger Wethered in 1921, when he tied with Jock Hutchison in the British Open, only to lose the play-off 150-159.

Wright
Mickey (1935-   )

Four times winner of the American Women's Open championship, Mickey Wright ranks among the few really great players of women's golf. She is considered to have greater length than her famous compatriot, Babe Zaharias, and her record in professional tournaments in America in the early 1960s set a completely new standard in women's golf. In the 10 years after turning professional, in 1956, she lowered the best women's scoring average from the 75–76 mark to the 72–73 mark.

Born in San Diego, the daughter of an attorney who had already decided the baby would be a boy and had chosen the name Michael, Mary Wright was most influenced by Patty Berg. She won the US Girls Junior Championship at 17, the year she entered Stanford University to study psychology, and in 1954 she was runner-up to Barbara Romack in the US Women's Amateur. That same year she turned professional, and two years later won her first tournament. She also made history by becoming the first player to be fined by the Ladies' Professional Golfers Association. The trouble arose when Miss Wright made her views plainly felt at the end of a round-robin tournament in which she had scored generally better than anyone else but, because of the scoring system determining the winner, had failed to win.

From then she went from success to success, her career reaching a climax in 1961 when she won 10 tournaments, 4 of them in a row. Her victory by six strokes in that year's Open, over a specially severe course at Baltusrol, included a 69 which, considering the length of the course—6,400 yards—must be one of the greatest ever played by a woman.

Mickey Wright's shy, retiring nature may not have permitted her to achieve the fame of other golfers, but her record and her game leave no doubt that she is among them. She once hit a drive in normal conditions more than 270 yards, and her usual length has reckoned at nearly 230 yards. Yet her driving was not her only forte, and it was in her long iron play that she was considered supreme.

WRIGHT Mary Kathryn 'Mickey'	
Major tournament victories and awards	
1956	Jacksonville Open
1957	Jacksonville Open
1958	US Open
	US LPGA
1959	US Open
	Jacksonville Open
1960	US LPGA
1961	US Open
	US LPGA
1963	US LPGA
	Woman Athlete of the Year
1964	US Open

Mickey Wright, leading woman professional of the early 1960s, blasts out of a bunker.

Wethered
Roger Henry (1899-   )

With Cyril Tolley, Roger Wethered was one of the leading figures in British amateur golf between the world wars. In 1921 he tied for the British Open, only to lose the play-off to Jock Hutchison, and in 1923 he won the British Amateur. But for his erratic driving, he might well have been among the outstanding golfers of his era, because his iron play was brilliant and he was a fine holer-out.

Wethered went up to Oxford after World War I, and he was still there when he tied for the play-off in the Open at St Andrews. He could have won because in the third round he had walked back on to his ball and was penalized one stroke—a costly error for he lost the play-off by nine strokes. His victory in the Amateur, however, showed just what he might have done had his driving been more consistent, for he drove magnificently in taking the title. He reached the final of the Amateur twice more, losing to T. P. Perkins in 1928 and to Bobby Jones two years later, but these appearances were due more to his great match-playing qualities rather than to flawless golf.

He played for Great Britain five times against America, appearing in the first Walker Cup matches, and he was nine times an England international. In 1946, he was made captain of the Royal and Ancient golf club, which he had served as a member of various committees.

Zaharias
Babe (1914-1956)

In 1950 an Associated Press poll produced the verdict that Babe Zaharias was the greatest woman athlete of the first half of the 20th century. The word 'athlete' was used in its American sense and it was in the widest context that Babe was being judged. Winner of two Olympic gold medals, she was twice selected for the all-American basketball team as a forward; in baseball she hit three home runs in a game and made a 313-foot throw from the centrefield to the plate. Diving, lacrosse, and billiards were other sports at which her immense natural skills found an outlet, and she is regarded as one of the greatest woman golfers of all time.

It was in track and field athletics that Mildred Didrikson, born in Port Arthur, Texas, of Norwegian parents, first illuminated the world of sport. In 1930 she set a world best performance for the javelin, with a throw of 133 ft 3¼ in. And two years later she amazed onlookers at the American women's championships by contesting eight events within the space of 2½ hours, claiming first place in five of them (one a tie) and amassing enough points (30) to defeat a 22-woman club from Illinois for the team title. Still in 1932, she dominated the Olympic stadium at

Los Angeles with characteristic *elan*. Few women's world records were official then, but in the 80 metres hurdles Mildred equalled the world best of 11.8 sec in the semi-final and then ran 11.7 sec to win the final the next day. The javelin gold medal went to her with a throw of 143 ft 4 in. The high jump was rightfully hers as well, and she did in fact clear the same height as the winner, which itself was a world record 5 ft 5¼ in. But the judges decided that the gold medal should go to Jean Shiley after ruling that Babe's dive-roll technique—which would certainly pass scrutiny today—was of dubious legality.

Banned from amateur athletics in December 1932 for lending her name to an automobile sales promotion campaign, Babe toured in a vaudeville act. 'I did the things I knew how to do', she explained, 'like putting the shot, acrobatics, and playing the mouth organ'. And in 1934 she entered on a

Mrs Zaharias (left) discusses an American putter with a British golfer in 1951. Probably the finest all-round sportswoman of all time, she followed a brilliant athletics career with an equally successful golfing one.

second chapter in her amazing sporting career—golf. By 1936 she was touring with Gene Sarazen and earning sizeable purses for a period in exhibitions. She then applied to be reinstated as an amateur within the statutory five-year period, and in 1940 she embarked on a serious golf career, taking lessons from Tommy Bolt for 5 or 6 hours a day. 'I'd hit golf balls until my hands were bloody and sore,' she once claimed. 'Then I'd have tape all over my hands and blood all over the tape.'

Meanwhile, she had married, in 1938, George Zaharias, a 285-lb wrestler known as the 'crying

Greek from Cripple Creek'. The genial George accompanied her on golf tournaments, blowing clouds of smoke from his cigar to indicate the wind direction.

The Babe's dedication and wiry strength—she had always been a tomboy type—paid off. She regularly drove 280 to 300 yards, and once reached 346 yards downwind on a hard fairway. Byron Nelson claimed that only eight male professionals could outdrive her. In 1940 she won her first major events, the Texas and Western Opens, and in 1946 she won the US Amateur title. In 1947 she won no fewer than 17 consecutive tournaments before conceding defeat and turning professional that August for a second time. In 1948 she won the first of three American Open titles, and her win in 1954 came after an operation for cancer in 1953. She had a one-year money record of $14,800 in 1950, when she won six major tournaments. In 1954 she won the Glenna Ware Trophy for the lowest stroke average—75.48 over 66 rounds.

But cancer was to cut Mrs Zaharias's golfing career short. In 1955 she was still making defiant statements about the disease, and set up a cancer fund. She was discharged from hospital after a third admission for cancer in January 1956, but finally succumbed to it on 27 September at Galveston, Texas.

ZAHARIAS Mildred (Didrikson)	
Golf—Tournament Victories and Awards	
Texas Open	1940, 45, 46
Western Open	1940, 44, 45, 50
US Amateur	1946
British Ladies Championship	1947
US Open	1948, 50, 54
World Championship	1948, 49, 50, 51
Athlete of the Year	1932, 45, 46, 47, 50
Female Athlete of the Half Century	1950